BCL-3d ed

BRITAIN —
A Future That Works

Books by Bernard D. Nossiter
The Mythmakers: An Essay on Power and Wealth
Soft State: A Newspaperman's Chronicle of India
Britain — A Future That Works

BRITAIN—

A Future That Works

Bernard D. Nossiter

Houghton Mifflin Company
Boston 1978

Library of Congress Cataloging in Publication Data

Nossiter, Bernard D
    Britain: a future that works.

    Includes bibliographical references and index.
    1. Great Britain — Economic conditions — 1945–
2. Great Britain — Politics and government — 1964–
I. Title.
HC256.6.N67   309.1'41'0857   78-16283
ISBN 0-395-27094-4

Printed in the United States of America

V 10 9 8 7 6 5 4 3 2 1

To my mother and father and Polly

Preface

Like my two earlier books, this one has emerged from reporting for *The Washington Post*. There is a natural rhythm that carries a reporter from his daily stint, perhaps the length of a newspaper column, to the more extended treatment of a magazine article and finally a book, an attempt to pull the pieces together, to make coherent the fragments of experience recorded on the run. Inevitably, daily journalism is what economists call an iterative process, much like the technique the army used to instruct soldiers in the mortar. You overshoot the target; you undershoot. Perhaps on the third round you get it right. A book, then, is a reporter's third round, his best shot at the target.

This one, like my others, says some things that will affront conventional opinion. But then I am always surprised at how soon conventional opinion absorbs yesterday's heresy. It is odd to think now that some were offended by the central themes of *The Mythmakers* — the conservative economics of the Kennedy administration, the existence and importance of corporate pricing power, the notion that American unions more often coalesce with rather than act as a countervailing force to the large corporations. All that is mostly taken for granted nowadays.

In the same way, *Soft State* reported that Mrs. Gandhi's democracy was considerably less than perfect, that India was more of a stagnant than a developing state (although cataclysmic famine was improbable), that caste, aggression and self-centered behavior were crucial characteristics of Indian life. None of this would strike any present observer as very remarkable. But unlike *Mythmakers, Soft State* was either ignored or roundly condemned by most journals. Quite right too. It appeared five years before Mrs. Gandhi's emergency made these things plain. Timing is essential.

Without invidious distinction, I can't name all the people who have tried to help me understand Britain — countless citizens who have invited a strange reporter into their homes and patiently offered tea and talk; scores of academics, officials, politicians and above all my colleagues in Fleet Street, radio and television. I have never understood why anybody bothers to answer the ignorant, sometimes impertinent, at best well-meaning questions of a stranger with a press card. But they do, almost everyone, everywhere, even for a paper they will never see. There is, I think, a rooted urge to get things straight, to have an accurate record in print. I hope I have responded more often than not with the care and attention shown to me.

I am grateful to my editors at *The Washington Post* who have indulged my whims at least as often as I have indulged theirs. Piers Burnett of Andre Deutsch and Austin Olney of Houghton Mifflin have both made useful editorial suggestions. Every writer should be endowed with a subscription to the London Library, whose patient staff and splendid collection relieve so much of the drudgery from research. Jane Russell helped hunt down some of the stray facts. Denis Van Mechelin prepared the endnotes.

My debt to my wife, Jackie, extends far beyond her chore of typing several versions of the manuscript. Without her love and support and that of my four sons, I am not sure I would ever sit very long at a typewriter.

Katounia, London, 1977–78

Contents

BRITAIN —
A Future That Works

I. Europe's Sick Man

The Voices of Doom

After Britain's voters in 1974 had twice rejected Edward Heath's claim that Tories alone could save the country from its unions, distinguished commentators pulled long faces. On both sides of the Atlantic, pundits agreed that the nation had fallen into a pathological state. Indeed, they vied with each other to catalogue the symptoms, to find the appropriate medical metaphor. Almost all declared that the illness would be terminal unless some drastic surgery was performed at once. It was usually the left lung that was identified as cancerous but sometimes the right.

Some thought the illness was spiritual. From the sanctuary of his office as editor of *The Times* of London, William Rees-Mogg wrote, "Britain certainly now suffers from this depression of lack of purpose, of lack of faith." Despite the tortured syntax, the gloomy message came through, and it mattered. *The Times* may have fallen far from its station a century earlier when its influence in Parliament earned it the title of "The Thunderer." Nevertheless, the paper still remained the authentic voice of, among others, senior civil servants, older academics and the rural clergy. They in turn are a vocal group who still set much of Britain's tone.

The Times' economics editor, Peter Jay, was, appropriately, more worldly than his chief. Jay foresaw a "remaining two or three years of phoney crisis, while our present Prime Minister continues to preside like a paper over the cracks, ably anaesthetising constructive political and economic thought and action." This "phoney crisis," Jay said, must "be endured before the breakdown of our present political economy becomes sufficiently manifest." However mixed the metaphors, Jay's message too filters through. After perhaps two more years under Harold Wilson and Labour, the breakdown of Britain's political and economic structure would become glaringly clear. When Jay delivered this warning in December 1975, he could not know that his father-in-law, James Callaghan, would succeed Wilson in four short months and would faithfully continue the Wilson policies that Jay had likened to papering over cracks. Nor could Jay know that he would soon be defending these very policies as Britain's ambassador to Washington. No doubt if he had foreseen all this, Jay might have postponed the moment of "manifest breakdown."

Eminent American commentators were just as gloomy and decidedly more blunt. Eric Sevareid startled a sizable CBS television audience in May 1975 by revealing that "Britain is drifting slowly towards a condition of ungovernability." He compared Wilson's regime to that of Salvador Allende in Chile on the eve of Admiral Pinochet's coup. "Not that the backlash in Britain need be militaristic," Sevareid hastened to assure his listeners, "but some kind of backlash is building up." Sevareid promised to report on its policy and leader as soon as he could find them.

His colleague Morley Safer was no less concerned and no less imaginative. Reporting just a few months later, Safer disclosed that Britain had endured "two decades of decline, or crisis . . . culminating this past year in a kind of anarchy." CBS billed this hour-long program as a documentary.

Cyrus L. Sulzberger, the retiring foreign columnist of *The New York Times*, delivered as a farewell piece of wisdom this solemn conclusion: after Churchill, "Britain's economy tumbled into the pit."

The consensus among eminent observers was so wide-spread that Vermont Royster, contributing editor of *The Wall Street Journal,* could write confidently: "Hardly anyone needs to be told now that Great Britain is the sick country of Europe. Everywhere you look the evidence abounds."

Indeed, the evidence was so abundant that the only serious question was whether Britain was simply *the* "Sick Man of Europe," as R. Emmett Tyrrell, Jr., asserted in his introduction to a remarkable book, *The Future That Doesn't Work.* * Or whether, as Irving Kristol wrote in the same volume, "Britain now vies with Italy for the title 'the sick man of Europe.'" The phrase had originally been applied to the backward and crumbling Turkish Empire in the nineteenth century. It summoned up an image of Britain that was truly alarming.

Academic contributors to Tyrrell's symposium were a shade more careful in accord with their scholarly tradition. Thus James Q. Wilson, the distinguished professor of government at Harvard, wrote of the *"apparent* political and economic decay of England . . . it is clear that the political economy of England has come *very near* to collapse." (The italics are mine, supplied to validate Wilson's mandarin caution.)

On the air, as distinguished from print, however, some professors were as colorful as their television interviewers. As late as November 1976, Milton Friedman cleared up for CBS audiences any lingering doubts over the Britain-Chile analogy. Friedman had won a Nobel Prize for reminding economists that money mattered, a point that some had overlooked.

The Nobel laureate said: "I think if you want an example

The Future's writers are strong on dubious historical parallels. The title of their book, *The Future That Doesn't Work: Social Democracy's Failure in Britain,* is a play on a phrase from Lincoln Steffens. After visiting the new Bolshevik state, Steffens returned to say, "I have been over into the future and it works."

for Britain that is highly relevant, the experience of Chile with first Allende and then the takeover by a military junta is an extremely pertinent experience. That's the road Britain is going down and that is the ultimate outcome." Friedman modestly added, "I don't know enough about Britain" to forecast whether its coup would be made by forces of the left or right. "But that's the only outcome that is conceivable."

Whatever the distinguished economist's lack of knowledge of Britain, his credentials to discuss Chile were unquestioned. He and a team of his epigoni had for some time served as advisers to the Pinochet junta.

Other notables also professed uncertainty over whether Britain's coming dictatorship, itself taken for granted, would fly a red or black flag. Lord Robens, chairman of Vickers, a maker of arms among other things, said: "We are almost at the stage of the Weimar Republic before Hitler. The political consequences of that are a dictatorship of right or left, I wouldn't care to say which."

Like Friedman, Robens enjoyed special credentials to talk of authoritarianism. According to the memoirs of Cecil King, Robens, while a minister in an earlier Wilson government, had fancied himself as premier in an emergency "businessmen's government." Elected politicians, of course, would be rigorously excluded.

Others were troubled by no doubt at all. Lord Chalfont, another former Labour minister and restless among the peers, told a television audience that Britain was precisely "halfway" down the road toward a Marxist state. In an article for *Commentary,* Robert Moss, a publicist for several of Britain's more extreme right-wing movements, endorsed and amplified Chalfont's political geography. Even Margaret Thatcher, leader of the Conservative party, embraced the Moss line, but she wrapped it in some ambiguous verbal cotton wool. Her adoption of the Moss view, however, should not have been surprising. He had written some of Mrs. Thatcher's speeches.

Whatever the precise differences over the country's immediate fate, all the commentators agreed with Tom Nairn that the British system was "near the end of its tether." Nairn happens to be a Marxist, an independent and provocative Marxist. But then, far left and right often find much in common.

One of the more restrained right-wing forecasts of democratic collapse came from Samuel Brittan in Tyrrell's *Future.* Brittan is the resident economist for the *Financial Times,* a splendid daily that is required reading for thoughtful businessmen, politicians and journalists throughout Western Europe. Brittan warned that the demands of voters in general and unions in particular "risk straining liberal democracy to the breaking point."

Jay adopted this notion of his friendly competitor, hesitated at its implications, then boldly plunged ahead. "Surely, it will be said," he wrote, that "Western democracy is not going to wreck itself on such absurd and obvious nonsense. Unfortunately, it probably will, at least on the eastern side of the Atlantic."

In fact, pundits have been forecasting the imminent destruction of the British system for a long time. Friedrich Engels, another economist-journalist, had written as early as 1844 that the Tory government of Robert Peel "has realized that the English constitution cannot be defended and is making concessions simply to maintain that tottering structure as long as possible." Jay, Brittan, Sevareid and the others could have adopted Engels' words almost without change one hundred and thirty years later.

Sometimes, of course, the gloomier commentators saw things that simply were not there. Chalfont was under the impression that Britain was about to lose "the kind of political democracy that we have known for a thousand years."

Absolute monarchs at least from William the Conqueror in the eleventh century to Charles I in the seventeenth would have been surprised to learn that they had reigned over a democratic system.

In the late winter of 1977, Moss flatly predicted the government would seek a new loan from the International Monetary Fund by the middle of that year. While he wrote, the government in fact was discussing the merits of paying off in advance the last loan it had taken. Britain's payments balance had changed drastically thanks to North Sea oil. Moss might have learned as much from the monthly figures issued on foreign exchange reserves. But like so many of the diagnosticians, he was not overburdened with fact.

Similarly, Sevareid paid another flying visit to London and found the place infested by "thousands" of "terribly poor Arabic-speaking immigrants." There were in fact hundreds of terribly rich Arabs descending on London for wine, women and real estate. What Sevareid had probably misread as Arabic were the Bengali, Urdu and Hindi signs of the shopkeepers in the city's Pakistani and Indian ghettos, places crowded with poor Asian immigrants. Even James Reston of *The New York Times,* the doyen of American commentators, told his readers at Silver Jubilee time, "The Queen has presided here during the hardest 25 years in this century . . ." In some ways, his was the most remarkable vision of all. During the century's first twenty-five years, Britain had endured the savage depression of 1908–9 and the carnage of World War I. The next quarter century was dominated by the Great Depression of 1929–39 and the exhausting struggle of World War II, bringing wholesale death and destruction to British homes for the first time since the Norman invasion. Whatever the Queen had presided over since 1952, there were no horrors to match these.

As Mr. Baldwin observed in Evelyn Waugh's *Scoop,* that classic comic documentary of the reporter's craft, there is usually a grit of hard fact embedded in even the flabbiest journalistic oyster. So too in the late and post-Wilson era. However fanciful and uninformed the comment on Britain's estate, the country was undeniably experiencing harder times. So, of course, was the rest of the industrialized West and Japan, and Britain's troubles were intimately linked with the global stresses. However, almost all the objective indicators of economic well-being or ill-being demonstrated that Britain's plight was more severe than that of her European neighbors, to say nothing of Japan and the United States.

Total production of goods and services at home, the gross domestic product, had reached a peak in the third quarter of 1974, then staggered up and down but always below this level for the next three years. Any industrial economy, no matter how sluggish, each year finds new ways of extracting more production from the same work force. So a stalled economy inevitably means fewer jobs. Thus unemployment was rising, more or less steadily, and this was a new and disturbing phenomenon. Since the end of World War II, Britons had been accustomed to full or nearly full employment. Its maintenance had been a pledge faithfully preserved by all governments, Tory or Labour. Normally, only one or two workers in a hundred would be jobless. But the total now rose to reach about six in one hundred by the end of 1977.

The welfare state with its relatively generous unemployment benefits protected many of the European jobless from the deprivation and misery of the 1930s. But unlike the Great Depression, the stagnation in output after 1973 was accompanied by a swift and bewildering rise in prices. In Britain, moreover, the inflation was nearly twice as bad as everywhere else in the industrial world. Prices in the shops, the level of retail prices, rose a fearsome 24 percent in 1975. Wilson's government then persuaded the unions to make comparatively modest wage demands, and the inflation rate obediently fell almost in half the next year. But a sickening slide in the foreign exchange value of the pound — it fell from $2.02 in March 1976 to as low as $1.57 in October — wiped out the benefits of a second consecutive year of union wage restraint.*

Britain imports half its food and most of its raw materials — apart from oil and coal. A falling pound meant more had to be paid out for copper, butter, aluminum and much else bought abroad. This pushed consumer prices back up again and they were rising at a 17 percent rate through the first eight months of 1977.

Worst of all, and as a direct result, the living standards of ordinary Britons, their command over goods and services, fell for the first time since the war's end. This was doubly disturbing. These standards had risen steadily since the war; material life for Britons had improved without a break. The country, like other industrial nations, took the improvements for granted. Elsewhere, the disturbing combination of inflation and sluggish output dealt some shock to these expectations. But Britain's Continental neighbors at least suffered only an arrest in the rate of increase or even enjoyed small gains. In Britain, there was actual decline. The real income after taxes of Britons — money income deflated to wipe out price increases — fell 4.3 percent in 1975, remained virtually frozen in 1976 and was falling another 2.4 percent in

---

*The pound's tumble has never been explained satisfactorily. The initial slide appears to have been triggered by the government's own financial authorities, who feared that a rising pound would damage Britain's exporters. Their action frightened the Arabs, multinational corporations and banks who kept large deposits of pounds in London. They pulled out their funds in a panic, swapping them for marks, dollars, yen and Swiss francs at any price. Any price became the price at which sterling exchanged and it was much, much lower. The whole exercise appeared to be a remarkable example of how markets can get things wrong. For much of 1977, the financial authorities — the Bank of England and its master, the Treasury — were once again selling pounds in a vain effort to keep the currency from rising, all in the name of protecting those exporters. There was wide agreement that the pound was undervalued, that it was too cheap. Several million tourists agreed, and poured into Britain to take advantage of the bargains. Indeed, when the authorities finally decided to stop holding the pound steady against the dollar, the currency promptly rose, and briskly.

1977. Over the three years, Britons' incomes had shrunk by about 6 percent. This meant fewer Sunday roasts, beers at the pub, dresses for housewives and suits for men, shorter holidays abroad, smaller outlays for cars and everything else everyone buys. At the bottom of the income ladder, some of this loss was made up by an increase in welfare benefits. But the overwhelming majority of Britons experienced some modest belt-tightening after a generation of ever-rising living standards. That is what really marked off Britain from the rest of Europe, North America and Japan. They too had all endured higher unemployment, worrisome price rises and sluggish production. But their living standards had not fallen, even the relatively modest amount endured in Britain.

The scribes and prophets of disaster, however, were not talking about this limited and recent slide in standards. They were bewailing "two decades of decline" or, as *Time* magazine put it in September 1974, "ten years of steady national decline." Indeed, many of them were writing before any drop took place. A charitable critic might credit them with prescience except for this annoying fact: they were describing Britain's entire postwar experience or at least the decade since Wilson first returned Labour to office in 1964.

The verdict of the commentators on those years would have puzzled ordinary Britons. Since the war, their living standards had doubled. They were better housed, better fed, better clothed, better cared for, enjoyed longer and costlier vacations, were better protected against adversity, than they had ever been in British history.

The commentators were not willfully perverse. What they were talking about was *relative* income, of British gains compared to others. Never mind the improvement in British living standards, they were saying (or implying). Those in Germany, Japan, France, Sweden and the United States had gone further and faster. Professor Friedman on CBS put it this way: "The fact is that before World War II, the ordinary

Englishman had twice as high a level of living as the ordinary Frenchman or the ordinary German.* Today it's exactly the other way around. The truth of the matter is that the British work [sic] — ordinary British man today is at a much lower level of income, of well-being, of goods and services he commands, than would have been the case if you had had a freer economy and less government control."

The ordinary viewer might have been forgiven for misconstruing the professor's artful language and for concluding that Britons had suffered a drastic, absolute drop in standards. Friedman's expression — a "lower level . . . than would have been the case" — is straight from the soapmaker who claims his detergent washes clothes "twenty percent whiter."

But Friedman, an economist after all, has committed no literal falsehood. British standards improved steadily after the war, but those in France and Germany improved more rapidly. This is another way of saying that the British economy grew and the French and German economies grew faster.

The Hudson Institute is another slick packager of economic information that sometimes commits truth. So its famous report *The United Kingdom in 1980* asserts that Britain's crisis is a failure to grow at the same "rate" as its neighbors. The Hudson prophets even acknowledged that the postwar years have brought all manner of improvement to the well-being of Britons. This, however, is an admission that threatens Hudson's real pitch. So the report's authors hastily add: "But the truth of the matter is that things have not improved as much as they should have improved . . ."

---

*The facts, according to calculations of the National Institute of Economic and Social Research, do not support Friedman's "truth." In 1938, Britons' real product per head was 22 percent — not 100 percent — higher than the French and Germans'. By 1977, French incomes were 45 percent higher and the Germans' 33 percent above the British — again not 100 percent.

This open-ended comparison puts Hudson in the same class as Friedman and the soap manufacturers. It is usually wise to beware of publicists and politicians who begin sentences with "The truth of the matter is . . ."

The fact is that Britons, like everyone else, consume absolute and not relative levels of income. If my after-tax pay rises from $20,000 to $30,000 — after subtracting price increases — my living standard has risen 50 percent. The after-tax income of my German colleague may have risen from $15,000 to $37,500 in the same period. His gain is three times mine and he ends up with 25 percent more. No matter. My standard of living has gone up. I have only fallen behind in comparative terms. This does not diminish by one whit the extra pleasure I get from another $10,000 of income.*

Take a closer look at the British worker. His father drove a motorbike and took the family each summer for two weeks in Blackpool. His son runs a Leyland Allegro and takes his family on a three-week package holiday in Spain. Is his pleasure diminished when he sees a German family with a bigger Opel? Is it likely that such relative deprivation will drive him to the barricades in Leicester for the revolution that Lord Chalfont sees coming tomorrow or the day after? Will transnational auto envy inspire Britain's middle class to march for the Chilean-style junta Morley Safer and Milton Friedman envision just over the horizon?

---

*There are economists who argue that relative income levels do affect the pleasure or pain derived from gains and losses. The most striking example is the frustration experienced by skilled workers whose differentials shrink when both they and unskilled workers get the same flat increase in pay. But this applies largely to workers in one country and loses much of its force when it is taken across national borders. There is no reason to think that many Britons' delight in rising standards was diminished by the faster growth in Germany or France. To be sure, the very rich are always conscious of international income and tax levels, of the limited gains at home compared with those abroad. They can and do make the appropriate adjustments — tax havens in the Bahamas or Jersey, for example — and so need not concern us.

Diagnosing the Disease

Undeniably, the British economy has advanced less rapidly than those of other industrial states. But is this a problem, as *Time* magazine frequently puts it, that threatens to tear apart the "social and political fabric"? Whether it is or not, the popular seers offer a broad spectrum of causes for Britain's putative sickness.

Most of the doom-laden broadcasters are well-off men, conservative in attitude, style or party affiliation. Unsurprisingly, they agree that the chief culprit for Britain's plight is the trade union. The unions are destroying Britain's economy through frequent strikes, mostly inspired by envy or class hostility rather than bread-and-butter considerations. Or the unions are plunging Britain into an ever-ascending spiral of inflation by imposing outlandish demands for higher wages. Or, more sinister, the unions are led by militant Communists plotting to undermine or overthrow parliamentary democracy and the private property system. Eric Sevareid, the CBS pundit, detected an even subtler plot. "The powerful Communist influence in trade union leadership," he disclosed, doesn't seek a Communist Britain all at once. Instead, "much more likely," it wants "a chronically weakened, dispirited Britain able to play no effective role in the world or the [Western] alliance. That would suit very nicely the long-range strategies of the Soviet Union."

Most commentators closer to the scene failed to detect Sevareid's subtle conspiracy but agreed at bottom that unions were the engine of Britain's spiraling decline. An abstract version of this theory came from Jay and Brittan, the columnists for *The Times* and the *Financial Times*. Democracy, they explained in separate but parallel contributions to *The Future That Doesn't Work,* is incompatible with the proclaimed postwar objectives of full employment and stable prices. Politi-

cal parties and politicians vie with each other in a public
auction, promising more and more to win the maximum
number of votes. But the electorate does not vote for and the
politicians do not commit themselves to extracting the resources that will pay for these lavish programs. Free collective bargaining, the demands of union leaders for selfish
workers, insures that the outcome is disaster. Large wage
demands give governments a Hobson's choice: either curb
union power by imposing a high level of unemployment, or
print money to pay for the political promises and finance the
union wage demands. Democratic governments are too
weak or too timid to repudiate their pledge of full employment. So they choose the second route, printing money, de-
basing the currency, creating an ever-worsening inflation. As
the price spiral accelerates, the social order crumbles and democracy breaks down.

According to Brittan, the "two endemic threats to liberal
representative democracy are: 1. the generation of excessive
expectations; and 2. the disruptive effects of the pursuit of
group self-interest in the market place." The first, of course,
is generated by politicians; the second flows from unions. As
a result, Brittan wrote, "both class and political tensions
were greater in the early 1970's than at any time within living memory." Since Brittan was born in 1933 he has no living memory of the 1926 general strike and only the dimmest
of infant recollections of the great stresses in the deeply depressed thirties.

Jay was more careful. "The essence of democratic politics
is a gigantic celebration of the fact that you *can* [his em-
phasis] get something for nothing . . ." (those wicked politicians) and "the role of free collective bargaining may be
regarded as a second and separate reason why conventional
postwar full employment policies were incompatible with
price stability." (Those monopolistic unions.)

Both Jay and Brittan are troubled by the fact that voters

are irrational, that they just aren't as well informed as, say, Brittan and Jay. Brittan blames the "generation of excessive expectations" on "the irrationality of the individual elector's spending much time or trouble informing himself . . . there is little check either on dark urges . . ." Jay observes that the roots of the British malaise are "complex and abstract. Therefore they are little perceived . . ." Moreover, "the fully perceptive statesman and the fully intelligent voter" rarely "establish contact."

There is more than a hint here that things might be better if bright chaps like Brittan and Jay — who both did well in school — were somehow in charge, somehow possessed all the votes and all the power. Then, no doubt, Jay's "fully perceptive statesman" and "fully intelligent voter" would "establish contact" — in Jay's own person. Even though he has since become an ambassador in Washington, such a happening is still unlikely on a broad scale. A faint echo of Plato runs through this, a suggestion that philosopher-kings (who have done economics at Oxford or Cambridge) could better order society.

The Jay-Brittan thesis is comparatively bloodless. For a much more entertaining version of the unions-as-devil theory, Peregrine Worsthorne, associate editor and house philosopher of the *Sunday Telegraph,* is hard to beat. The two *Telegraphs,* both *Daily* and *Sunday,* are aimed at the hurried businessman who has no patience with the careful, restrained prose of the *Financial Times. Telegraph* readers like their meat raw, and here is how Worsthorne serves it up in that essential book, *The Future That Doesn't Work.*

Even the "most statesmanlike of trade union spokesmen . . . quite unashamedly . . . admit . . . to being brazenly and ruthlessly concerned about promoting a sectional interest, however this may 'hurt' anybody else . . . Alone among the leaders of contemporary Britain they are totally unencumbered by a sense of guilt, and this uniqueness enables them to display a truly aristocratic disregard for public disapproval — a disregard so spectacularly provocative as to be literally awe-inspiring."

But Worsthorne's awe soon wears off. The unions, he explains, get away with so much in Britain because of "the contemporary obsession with social justice." Somebody must simply tell "the workers to go and get stuffed."

In Britain today, a terrible thing has happened. Policemen and soldiers must use restraint to carry out their duties and apologize for rough action. "Trade union violence, on the other hand, enjoys a much wider degree of tolerance."

"Many trade unionists are now the nouveaux riches and take home wage packets that make them the envy of professional people." They have become the top dogs in British society.

"The trade unions, by ruthless use of the strike weapon for a few weeks, can reduce a country like Britain to chaos far more effectively than the Luftwaffe was ever able to do."

In a *cri de coeur* that recalls Marx's famous call to workers who have "nothing to lose but their chains," Worsthorne summons the bourgeoisie. Give up your "chivalrous tradition wholly unsuited to the new reality of class war created by trade union militancy." Rules laid down by the Marquis of Queensberry and taught on "the cricket fields of Eton" are an impossible burden. Abandon them. Remember that "Herr Hitler was not a gentleman. Nor are the Communists in the unions who are fighting to win."

Emulate the middle classes of the Continent, Worsthorne urges. Happily, they are "no less prone to take to the streets — yes, and to the barricades too, if necessary — than are the workers . . .

"Resist . . . ruthless trade union power," Worsthorne pleads. "Fight . . . for bourgeois values against overwhelming odds."

Despite Worsthorne's stirring appeal, no bowler-hatted brigade has yet been spotted digging up paving stones in Threadneedle Street to defend the Bank of England from another "brazen . . . ruthless" union assault. But if Worsthorne's prose is freighted more heavily with metaphor than fact, it reflects the feelings of many commentators.

Tyrrell, the American editor of the *Future* book, asserts that "in England, the most grasping interest group has for years been the trade union movement." Irving Kristol, another American and a certified conservative, thinks trade unions should receive only some of the blame. "There has been more nationalization of industry in Britain, the trade unions are far more belligerent, and the 'left' socialists . . . are more influential. The consequences for the British economy have been disastrous . . ."

Sometimes events overtake the hot gospelers of union villainy, often enough to make less self-assured prophets more circumspect. A memorable exchange on a CBS program pitted Morley Safer against Jimmy Reid, the Communist leader of the Glasgow shipyard workers. It went like this:

SAFER. It's fair to say that trade union leaders, particularly Communist militants like yourself, have an extraordinary amount of power.

REID. To some extent, the British trade union movement is like a sleeping giant . . . that power has never been used.

Not long after the broadcast, the omnipotent Reid failed twice in bids for union office and returned to working-class obscurity. The votes were conducted under Marquis of Queensberry rules, if not the cricket code at Eton, which Worsthorne had thought should be scrapped.

In much the same way, events tripped up Robert Moss, the *Commentary* contributor who wrote that "the most powerful man in Britain is not an elected member of Parliament, not even the prime minister. It is Jack Jones, the leader of Britain's biggest labor union, the Transport and General Workers' Union."

Just five months after this appeared, Jones delivered an impassioned plea to his own union's convention — not for revolution but on behalf of a third consecutive year of wage restraint. Britain's "most powerful man" was voted down by his followers, and Jones, as planned, soon retired.

Whether the scenario breathes blood and fire or, as with Jay and Brittan, borrows the chaste terminology of Joseph Schumpeter's *Capitalism, Socialism, and Democracy,* the message is clear. Unions and their leaders are far too strong, far too selfish and are pulling down Britain's social edifice.

After the unions, the most frequently cited cause of Britain's plight is the welfare state — that great array of public outlays designed to sustain the jobless, protect the aged and the helpless from poverty, care for the sick and educate the young. Appropriately enough, an economical expression of welfare-as-disease is found in the *Wall Street Journal.* There, Vermont Royster wrote that Britain "offers a model study in how to bring to ruin a once vigorous nation.

"The formula is simple. You begin by putting upon a nation an economic burden it cannot bear. In Britain's case it was an all-encompassing welfare program . . . this must be paid for. This means either higher taxes or a resort to the government printing presses to create money, or both . . . Spend and spend, tax and tax, inflate and inflate."

A more sophisticated version of Royster's "simple formula" was advanced by a pair of Oxford lecturers, Robert Bacon and Walter Eltis, in their book, *Britain's Economic Problems: Too Few Producers. The Sunday Times,* Britain's most influential weekend newspaper, was so impressed with their argument it devoted no less than thirty-five columns of type on separate Sundays to its exposition.

There has been, Bacon and Eltis assert, a "collapse of Britain's economic performance . . .

"The explanation is that successive governments have allowed large numbers of workers to move out of industry and into various service occupations, where they still consume

and invest [sic] industrial products and produce none
themselves."

(The two scholars might but did not observe that the reverse is equally true: successive governments have tried to
retain workers in industry — through subsidies like those for
Concorde and state takeovers of collapsing firms like Rolls-
Royce — where they still consume and enjoy the fruits of investment in services although they produce none themselves.)

"Societies in this terrible position," the Oxford dons warn,
"must choose between very high unemployment or extra-
rapid inflation, which is now undoubtedly the case in Britain, as it is in much of Latin America."

Heavily buttressed by relevant statistics, Bacon and Eltis
demonstrate that there has been a rapid growth in Britain's
public sector, that part of the economy run and financed by
the government.

The people employed in this sector — civil servants, doctors, railwaymen, diplomats, highway engineers, teachers,
clerks and the rest of the vast army — sell little or nothing in
either domestic or foreign markets. The trading or private
sector of the economy must produce a surplus of goods to
sustain the growing ranks of government workers. The busy
bees of the private sector must produce a surplus not only at
home but also abroad to cover imported food and raw materials consumed by the governmental drones. Since 1961, the
drones have multiplied faster than the busy bees, imposing
an intolerable burden on the national hive.

After that fatal date, the ratio of jobs outside the industrial beehive compared to those within has grown far faster
in Britain than in Italy, the United States, West Germany or
France. The remarkable Japanese have actually increased
their share of industrial to nonindustrial jobs. (This was
probably accomplished by the large migration of less productive farm workers to more productive factories rather
than by a shrinkage in government jobs. The shift from

rural to urban life was, by 1961, more complete in Europe generally and Britain in particular than in Japan.)

Bacon and Eltis do notice that in Sweden the worrisome ratio was even higher than in Britain. Why this failed to destroy Sweden's society — an economic and political success by almost every indicator — Bacon and Eltis do not tell us. Somehow, they overlooked the fact that manufacturing jobs were an even smaller share of the U.S. labor force. By 1971, factory workers accounted for only 32 percent of all American jobs against 44 percent in Britain. A less committed theorist might conclude, given the Swedish and American examples, that the most modern economies are shrinking their industrial worker base.

At any rate, as Bacon and Eltis see it, Britain's "crisis" can be explained by the swollen "numbers in the public sector whose needs for capital equipment, imports and durable consumer goods had to be met largely from declining industry."

At first glance, it appears that the Oxford duet has committed an elementary error of those untaught in economics, the belief that only goods and not services have value, the Victorian businessman's notion that a steel I-beam has economic worth but a poem has none. In fact, Eltis, a Fellow of Exeter College, and Bacon, a Fellow of Lincoln College, do not fall into this trap. They know that the gross national product is made up of services as well as goods, that banking, insurance, travel agencies and even the writers of sellable books and popular songs contribute to the economy much like those who mine coal, smelt steel or assemble cars.

In a paragraph that deserves and will get closer examination, Bacon and Eltis write: "It is not only industry that exports. A British opera singer who stars at the New York Metropolitan Opera and brings dollars home is an exporter. So, more substantially, are the bankers, insurers, shippers and other specialists for whom Britain is famous. *Unlike most industrial production, Britain does these things better than a great many competitors"* (my emphasis). Premier Wilson, himself a former Oxford economist, recognized as much when he made the Beatles Members of (the order of) the British Empire in 1965 for swelling Britain's foreign reserves with concerts and records sold abroad.

The crucial distinction, Bacon and Eltis insist, is between marketable and nonmarketable goods and services, between the products and services that are sold for cash and those that are not. It is this last class that weighs Britain down.

A second look, however, suggests that Bacon and Eltis have indeed fallen for a more elaborate version of the I-beam and poem fallacy. According to their accounting, any resources spent on toll-free roads are a drain on those industrial bees. So too are the subsidized portions of their budgets spent to keep British Airways aloft and British Rail running. Any loss sustained by the Post Office is a drain; so too are losses in the nationalized ports. Several billion dollars have been invested to keep workers — and their bosses — employed building Concorde, the supersonic liner. Little of this will be recovered in the marketplace, nor will the sums spent to keep the production line going, even if more copies of the plane are sold. In the Bacon and Eltis accounting, here is another brigade of industrial drones.

Most economists would agree that these losses or subsidies must be paid by someone, taxpayers or the creation of inflationary pounds. But to class all workers in these enterprises as drones is obviously absurd. Loss-making postal, rail and air services are a subsidy to industrial producers. If they don't meet the full cost of sending messages and transporting goods, carrying salesmen to Germany or Nigeria, shipping widgets from Birmingham to Liverpool for sale in Brazil, these manufacturers do enjoy lower costs than their foreign competitors. They can, therefore, sell more abroad and swell the exports about which Bacon and Eltis worry. The toll-free roads are the extreme case. In the Bacon and Eltis accounting, the government planners, engineers and surveyors who design this utility and even the private construction firms who build it are all drones. But roads do not lose their economic value simply because they are built with funds from the state's nontrading sector rather than commercial loans paid off with toll receipts.

In the same way, doctors, nurses and teachers contribute to the national output even when they are employed by a state that does not charge consumers directly for their services. Indeed, the rapid growth of jobs in medical care and teaching, along with those in banking and insurance, account for the bulk of the expansion in nonmanufacturing employment which so troubles Bacon and Eltis. State-financed schools and medical care can even be viewed as another subsidy to industry. However dismal the performance of British workers, their productivity would be even lower if they were less healthy and less well trained. Medicine and teaching even contribute directly to Britain's foreign earnings (although not as much as they could if foreigners were charged an economic instead of a subsidized price for these services). The rich Arabs and others who seek British medical care — public and private — and the foreign students who fight for places in British universities all bring in foreign exchange.

Apart from North Sea oil and profits from banking and insurance, the fastest-growing contributor to Britain's foreign earnings is tourism. From £300 million in 1967, it has grown to an estimated £3 billion in 1977. The swelling army of tourists has been attracted by many things, among them the state-subsidized theaters, symphonies, opera, museums and many other services partly or entirely outside the trading sector. Joseph C. Harsch of the *Christian Science Monitor* has even argued that Britain would never have attracted its record number of tourists in 1977 if it had not been for the Queen. Whatever else may be said about that no doubt dutiful lady, she and her entourage are all financed by the state, are all in Bacon and Eltis' nontrading sector.

So too, of course, are the burgeoning ranks of civil servants. But every modern state is marked by a growing bureaucracy, whether for good or ill, and there is nothing unique about Britain. Robin Marris has calculated that local and national government account for 4.6 percent of all jobs outside the military in Britain; for the United States the share is slightly higher, 4.8 percent.

However unconvincing the Bacon-Eltis argument, at least the Oxford pair attempt to sustain their thesis with evidence rather than rhetoric. They rely on statistics that can be verified rather than on outraged, purple prose. This distinguishes them from most of the other diagnosticians.

Another notable exception is Leslie Lenkowsky, a Harvard graduate student and a contributor to *The Future*. He also examines the welfare burden. In *The Future*'s gallery of passionate Zolas, their accusing fingers pointed at unions, Communists and Labour politicians, Lenkowsky is a cool outsider. Other countries, he finds, have devoted as much or more of their resources as Britain to welfare programs and have not come to grief. Britain's welfare state has not even been an engine of equality, destroying incentive by leveling incomes and wealth. It "seemingly offers no great barrier to [the] accumulation [of wealth], at least for those likely to be skilled workers, managers and professionals." Except for the slump year of 1962, Lenkowsky observes, the living standard of the average Briton rose in every postwar year until 1974. "Since the end of the war the average Briton has not done that badly."

Lenkowsky asks: "Because of its early leadership among welfare states, might Britain have aspired to preserve a stature it could neither afford nor attain?" He answers: "The evidence suggests not." Quite simply, Lenkowsky appears to be saying that Britain could afford the welfare programs it undertook and they can't account for the country's economic plight, if any.

But this sort of thing does not sit well in *The Future*, so

Lenkowsky makes amends with some ex cathedra remarks. Britain's economic record in the 1970s, he tells us, was "calamitous." Despite what he has just concluded from the evidence, Lenkowsky insists that the welfare state and services like insurance and banking are all growing at the expense of industry. "If a nation is to remain prosperous, its industries must make good some of the loss," he contends. "The British attached great value to welfare programs . . . [If they] continue to do so, Britain will remain less prosperous . . ."

Here, of course, is a crude version of Bacon and Eltis, a simple expression of the I-beam and poem fallacy. Lenkowsky, like others untrained in economics, appears to believe that the growing number of service workers — the hallmark of an advanced economy — doctors, teachers, nurses, travel agents, bankers, planners and administrators, make no contribution to total output, will never earn any foreign exchange.

The burden-of-welfare writers sometimes offer a variant of their thesis. This holds that the state's outlays are depriving industry of the resources needed for investment in new plants and machinery. British industry, it is said, performs badly in the modern world because its plants are inadequate, backward, obsolete. The CBS program that catered to the popular American stereotype of Britain opens with a shot of a textile mill built in 1870. "It's still in use," a sardonic Morley Safer observes, while German, Japanese and American competitors "insist on updating and automating." It was a powerful image and even casual televiewers could get the point: British industry can't compete using the tools of a century ago.

The same theme is often played by quoting Charles Dickens' 1854 description of Coketown in *Hard Times* and suggesting it still holds for Britain today. The celebrated Hudson report approvingly quotes a passage: "It was a town of red brick, or brick that would have been red if the smoke and ashes had allowed it; but as matters stood it was a town

of unnatural red and black like the painted face of a savage
. . . it had a black canal in it, and a river that ran purple
with ill-smelling dye . . ."

Time magazine similarly revived the Coketown description
but wisely omitted the reference to black canals and purple
rivers. Its researchers, unlike Hudson, had apparently discovered that Britain has mounted a successful and expensive
campaign to clean up the Thames and some other water-
ways. This, of course, is another welfare burden, the squan-
dering of resources that might have produced fresh
investment in the mills that made Coketown infamous.

The less literary analysts like Bacon and Eltis put it this
way: the welfare state's "squeeze on industrial investment is
perhaps the most serious effect of all because it influences the
whole future development of the economy." Once again
they cite statistics, those for net industrial investment. As a
share of final industrial sales, investment ran about 8 or 9
percent in the 1960s, fell as low as 3 percent in 1972, and rose
to 6.3 percent in 1974. The numbers, however, tell little except that the 1960s were — comparatively speaking — boom
years when confident manufacturers enlarged their plants in
the expectation of greater sales. In contrast, 1972 and 1973
were recession years. Since 1974 was a year of recovery, investment rose again.

Sometimes — and notably by Hudson and the left — the
argument is made that Britain and its banks in the City invest far too much abroad, neglecting industry at home.
Hudson, however, also explains that much of the money that
City banks lend abroad comes, in fact, from foreigners. Arab
states with huge surpluses from their overseas earnings, multinational corporations, the international rich and others de-
posit their excess cash with City bankers to earn high rates of
interest or to take advantage of the City's supposed investing
skill. The bankers, in turn, put substantial sums into foreign
corporations, foreign real estate, foreign racetracks and other
likely sources of high yield. To the extent that the City is in-

vesting abroad the deposits of foreigners, it is hardly depriving British industry of British funds. Indeed, in Britain as in most modern nations, the bulk of any corporation's investment is financed from internal resources. The Lancashire maker of, say, widgets charges a high enough price for his product to cover three quarters of the outlays he will make for enlarging his plant and buying new widget-milling tools. Whether a City bank provides the widget-maker with the funds he seeks or puts its money into Paris real estate is not the major determinant of the widget-maker's level of investment.

The Hudson Doctors and Their School

The Hudson report on Britain in 1980 deserves a more extended look, partly because it has been so widely quoted by Britain's largely conservative press, partly because it is a fizzy cocktail of lurid prose and loaded numbers and partly because it sheds light on the methods of so-called futurologists, those who claim to foretell the social and economic fates.

The report is ultimately a product of Herman Kahn, whose Hudson Institute in New York peers profitably into the future for the Pentagon and other clients. The British study was prepared by Hudson in Paris, formerly a division of the master's U.S. shop. Paris Hudson now describes itself as independent, but Kahn still sits on the board. Its report begins with familiar, almost Orwellian, tones.

. . . the outlook for Britain is sombre . . . the economic crisis is linked to a severe deterioration in the country's social and political health . . . There is in Britain, in November 1974 [one month after the second Wilson-Labour victory], the dawning recognition that the nation is failing . . . Britain . . . is . . . [an] unstable and socially divided nation, economically depressed . . . the continental states . . . enjoy, overall, a rather more impressive political condition. Even Italy, supposedly the other sick man of Europe, suffers . . . rather less [and] gives better reason for optimism . . . talk of military dictatorship in London may be absurd; yet the anxieties and sense of frustration that inspire them, and also the revolutionary rhetoric that may be heard on the left, must not be underestimated . . . if the economic problems are not solved, there is serious reason to fear an eventual social and political upheaval in the country.*

The statistical evidence to buttress this case is, in Hudson's hands, massaged rather than cited. The futurologists look back and complain that British productivity — output per worker — has been severely damaged by excessive strikes.

"The trend from 1963 to 1972 shows employment disputes consistently on the increase," Hudson says gravely. But of course. Nineteen seventy-two was the year of a crippling coal strike. A trend line drawn from 1974, another coal strike year, through the first half of depressed 1977 would show an equally astonishing era of labor peace. Both "trends" are worthless and simply illustrate an old maxim about lies, damned lies and statistics. If Hudson wanted to endow Britain, for example, with a low or even negative growth rate, it could start with the output in the boom year of 1929 and draw a trend line to the depression trough of 1933. If Hudson wanted to bestow a high growth rate on Britain, it would begin with 1933 and draw the curve to, say, 1967.

Hudson, in fact, offers a chart of man-days lost through strikes in Britain and seven other countries in three carefully

---

* This spine-chilling scenario is unhappily marred by a naive error on the very first page. Hudson's seers describe the Labour left as "Selsdon men." In fact, "Selsdon man" is a term ascribed to the laissez-faire visions of Edward Heath and other Conservatives who developed them in a 1970 conference at Selsdon Park.

selected years, 1963, 1968 and that coal strike year of 1972.
To make Britain (and some others) look particularly prone
to disorder, Spain is included too. This is all the more remarkable since the text acknowledges that Spain outlawed
strikes in those Franco years. Comparing Britain only with
the more or less democratic nations chosen by Hudson for
the three years it selected, we find: Britain in 1963 lost
through strikes more than Holland and about the same
number of days per 100,000 workers as Germany and Japan;
however, France, Italy and the United States all lost many
more. In 1968, the British strike level was again surpassed
by France, Italy and the United States. Even in 1972, the
Italian level was higher.

Hudson's own carefully selected numbers, in sum, do not
add up to Hudson's predetermined conclusion.

Hudson's language is as slippery as its statistics: "British
per capita GNP is also dropping to a level that is one of the
lowest among the industrialized countries." Here again is
Milton Friedman's trick, a statement that is literally true
and substantively misleading. For the unwary, Hudson is
describing an absolute descent into ever-lower standards of
living. In fact, standards have been rising; they have simply
risen faster in Germany, Japan, France and others.

Britons, the report continues, pride themselves on something peculiar they call "quality of life." Indeed, this thing
is so odd that Hudson puts it in denigrating quotation
marks. The Paris seers concede they cannot measure the im-
measurable. Nevertheless, they take a crack at the task, pick
a handful of comparative social indicators from the Organization for Economic Cooperation and Development and
conclude that Britain has nothing to boast about. Its "quality of life" is "less than satisfactory." (What is "satisfactory"
Hudson does not say.)

In fact, of the five extremely peculiar indicators that Hudson picks to measure "quality of life" — cars, telephones,

doctors per thousand inhabitants, life expectancy and infant mortality — Britain emerges in the middle compared to other industrial nations.

Britain is second only to the United States in telephones and ahead of Japan, the Netherlands, Germany, Italy, France and Spain. Britain's auto population, a highly questionable indicator of life's quality, is larger than four countries and smaller than three. Britain is sixth of eight in doctors. Since Italy leads this list, the suspicion persists that Hudson has counted all those *dottori* who emerge from Italian universities with humanistic rather than medical degrees.

Spain is inexplicably omitted from the comparisons of life expectancy and infant mortality, so Britain's ranking here is probably lowered. (In Hudson's world, Spain seems to be included when its performance exceeds Britain's, excluded when it does not.) Even so, life expectancy for British females is put at seventy-four years, behind four European nations that range up to seventy-six and a few months, well ahead of the United States at seventy-one and a few months. Male life expectancy in Britain is recorded at sixty-eight years, behind four others and topped by the United States at seventy-one.

In the number of infant deaths per thousand live births, Britain trails three and leads three nations.

Even using Hudson figures and relying on Hudson's curious list of indicators, the British record displayed in Hudson charts and tables — as opposed to Hudson's ominous prose — is on a par with other rich, industrial countries.

The futurologists' crystal ball clouded over completely when it came to North Sea oil. "It is unlikely that Britain will be totally self-sufficient by 1980," Hudson asserts. By 1985, however, "there is little doubt" that North Sea oil "will all but eliminate the need for imports." Even this implies that at that late date a small fraction will still have to be imported to meet Britain's demand. ". . . By 1980 no appreciable difference will have been made to Britain's financial standing" as a consequence of the oil.

Three more inaccurate guesses could not have been made. Moreover, there was little excuse for these outlandish conclusions. The Hudson boys, by their own testimony, were writing at least as late as November 1974, when published figures on the probable flow were readily available and contradicted all Hudson's forecasts.

In fact, of course, the North Sea was supplying one half of Britain's domestic consumption by the end of 1977. Supply and demand were likely to meet in 1980, the year that Hudson said it could not be done and five years before the date by which Hudson insisted Britain would still be importing a trickle. What the futurologists could have said by consulting known data instead of their crystal ball is that Britain would likely be a net *exporter* of oil by 1980, selling a surplus abroad after meeting all the nation's domestic requirements.

The prize for fanciful analysis, however, goes to the claim that none of this would affect Britain's financial standing. Even if Hudson's underestimates of output had been correct, any barrel from the North Sea replaces an imported barrel of oil and saves foreign exchange. Britain's financial standing would fail to improve only if there was not a drop of oil in the British sector of the North Sea.

In fact, the flow is expected to provide Britain with comfortable surpluses in its balance of payments, starting in 1978. Financial markets belatedly discovered this early in 1977, two years after the futurologists' report. That is why, for much of 1977, Britain found itself deliberately holding the pound down against bidders who wanted the currency and were willing to pay more francs, dollars and marks for it. Since Britain was still suffering a much faster inflation

rate than its neighbors, there was only one cause for the strength of the pound: the present and future bounty from the North Sea.*

Why does Herman Kahn's Paris offshoot so abuse the evidence? Only the Kahn men can say for sure. But their report offers instructive clues. They tell us they have just completed a study paid for by the French government. It demonstrates that France has been the star postwar economic performer and will be richer than its feared German rival by 1995. (They do not tell us that their client ordered the report to appear on the eve of a national election for which it served as a useful piece of propaganda.)

They tell us too they approached the British for a similar commission but were turned down. Undeterred, they went ahead with their British study "in the public interest." Its conclusions are a remarkable fit between the "public interest" and Hudson's private, profit-making concerns. The report is a handsome piece of revenge on a niggardly British government which refused to follow the lead of President Valéry Giscard d'Estaing and hire Hudson's men. Its recommendations are neatly tailored to please the French patron and promote future jobs for Hudson. The study emphasizes Britain's supposed failure to set out "longer-term objec-

---

* Hudson can't even argue that the published data are suspect. Indeed they are. But anyone with experience of oil and governments knows that estimates of reserves and production levels are always understated — never overstated. Governments have no expertise of their own and rely on the seven great oil companies for the figures. The companies, in turn, minimize their findings in order to shrink government appetites for taxes and — above all — to support the fiction that oil is a scarce commodity entitled to an ever-ascending price. To tell the truth about North Sea reserves (or those anywhere else in the world) would invite governments to insist on their full exploitation. That could destroy the high prices so carefully and painfully arranged among Arabs, Persians and the seven. In 1969, the company-inspired government forecasts predicted Britain would draw at most one million barrels daily from its sector of the North Sea; three years later, the forecast was doubled. Most recently it has tripled, and the end is not yet in sight. Professor Peter Odell has estimated that the actual yield from a given field is typically eight times the initial estimate of its resources.

tives," precisely the sort of thing the Hudson men do so handily. The "principal recommendation," quite naturally, calls for a "six-year plan" drawn up *à la Française*. (This serves the double purpose of flattering the reliable French client and once again drawing attention to Hudson's supposed skill.) In fact, France's indicative planning is an increasingly irrelevant tool in Paris' economic policy-making. Giscard is suspicious of the technique and its influence has anyway been exaggerated.*

Other Hudson recommendations urge the creation of an elite school to train administrators — modeled of course after L'École Nationale d'Administration, whose eminent graduates include patrons Giscard and the premier of the time, Jacques Chirac; curbs on capital outflow or investment abroad, just as the French have; and the elimination of a hereditary peerage. The French, after all, do so well without one.

Of this last, Hudson did have the grace to say that the question of peers is "no doubt trivia [sic]." Nevertheless, "it seems to us weighed with symbolic importance."

The Hudson report in itself hardly deserves the detailed examination to which it has been subjected here. But it was and is symptomatic of a common attitude and a common approach. So many of Britain's diagnosticians have been equally loose in language, careless with fact and logic, preying on audiences who lack both time and incentive to challenge the blood-curdling descriptions and forecasts. The beauty of Hudson is that it embodies so many of the harsh judgments passed on Britain and employs such characteristically dubious techniques to support them.

In the United States, Hudson has frequently serviced the

---

*By me, among others. In *The Mythmakers* I suggested that indicative planning was one way of restraining the price increases of large corporations (as well as union wage demands) and could break through the seemingly irreconcilable conflict between price stability and high employment. Then I went to France and saw how little indicative planning had to do with anything.

Pentagon and its futurologist style has evidently traveled the few miles to the Central Intelligence Agency headquarters in Langley. An economist who is described as a "former" CIA analyst, Penelope Hartland-Thunberg, has surfaced a scenario as frightening as Kahn's team. But, in the best tradition of her agency, she comes up with a proposal to turn the sorry state of British affairs to Langley's benefit. In a paper delivered early in 1977, Hartland-Thunberg moans over the "sharp decline in British long-term economic growth, first observable at the end of the 19th century." She documents this nonfact by pointing to the *relative* decline in Britain's share of manufacturing exports between the 1850s and the turn of the century. Somebody outside Langley should have explained to her that this merely shows that Germany, France and the United States had started to industrialize, that it has nothing to do with Britain's growth rate.

The former CIA lady solemnly ticks off the standard causes for the nonexistent decline: "inadequate" investment, "anarchy [meaning strikes] at the shop level," an overlarge public sector. Britain, she says, must "reduce labor redundancies." Poor dear. The CIA's language experts have failed to teach her that "redundancies" in British jargon means layoffs and not, as she seems to think, unneeded workers or "overmanning."

But there is a silver lining for the CIA. Britain hasn't been giving U.S. policy the support to which Washington is accustomed. If we can convince the British to ignore the "hazard" of North Sea oil, they will run large deficits in their foreign accounts and come to Washington for big loans. Washington should "underwrite loans to Britain . . . contingent on a British commitment to NATO defense at or above some specified minimum . . . In fact, such 'strings' would solve a number of otherwise intractable international problems."

In sum, the Hartland-Thunberg thesis, a splendid piece of economic illiteracy, proposes a strategy for turning Britain into a perpetual debtor-client state for the greater glory of Washington, NATO and the CIA. This excellent nonsense is labeled "Economic/Strategic Watch Report," which presumably is the kind of packaging that insures the attention of the director himself.

There are still other thinkers with more ideas on why Britons have gone wrong. A frequent view holds that the nation has lost something precious, indefinable, intangible, but somehow important. For Rees-Mogg, *The Times* editor, it is nothing less than the loss of God. In his book, *An Humbler Heaven*, Rees-Mogg does acknowledge that God is also absent from the rest of Western Europe (which ought to mean that the British performance at least equals that of its neighbors); he is not sure about the United States. Anyway, "a loss of faith erodes respect for all the national institutions . .. [breeds] a steady increase in almost every form of notified crime . . . Those who stand out, who would be the nation's leaders, are resented and jealously pulled down . . . inflation . . . sectional demands . . ."

Rees-Mogg is something of a specialist on the jealous destruction of leaders. He fought passionately in his columns and speeches to preserve Richard Nixon, whom he saw as a victim of a vengeful press and political foes. Whatever this says of Rees-Mogg's judgment, it does show a fine Christian spirit. Nixon, after all, was close to Billy Graham if not to God and, at the hour of greatest travail, prayed on his knees for His intercession.

The supposed breakdown in law and order, attributed by Rees-Mogg to Britain's godlessness, is a frequent theme of more secular thinkers. James Wilson of Harvard is a specialist on U.S. crime, so the editors of *The Future* enlisted him to report on Britain. To the satisfaction of all, he disclosed that "England and Wales are in the grip of the most steeply rising crime rate of this century." If that wasn't enough to delight the shades of Jack the Ripper and other overpublicized villains of the crime-ridden Victorian era, Wilson discovered that criminality in contemporary Britain — allowing for population differences — was almost as great as in the United States. He arrived at this remarkable result by comparing "indictable offenses" per 100,000 in Britain during 1973 with the "index crimes" per 100,000 reported by the FBI. The U.S. edge was only about three to two, "not vastly more," Wilson concluded.

Even in a polemical essay, scholar Wilson must respect academic rites. He conceded that the FBI's "index crimes" and Britain's "indictable offenses" are "not exactly the same thing." As a result, he continued, "some may feel that any *gross* [my emphasis] comparison of English and American crime figures is misleading. To a degree, that is true." The degree, in fact, is very large indeed. The FBI's index, as its name suggests, is an indicator of trends in selected crimes. It is not a comprehensive figure. Britain's "indictable offenses" attempts to cover all felonies and a wide range of petty larcenies. It is much broader than the FBI measure and the two cannot be compared at all.

Moreover, as many police reporters and some statisticians know, any tabulation of crimes by the police measures police activity, not crime. If a used typewriter, worth perhaps £40, disappears from my London home, I call the Gerald Road police station. A policeman promptly calls to get the particulars and the incident is recorded as a crime, burglary. When I lived in New York, things were quite different. A thief could take $1500 worth of clothing and watches; if they were not insured, the 19th Precinct in Central Park would tell me, "Fa-get it, mista." So no crime took place.*

---

* This works the other way, too. If local police departments (whose reports make up the FBI index) are seeking big budget increases, a statistical crime wave is suddenly produced. Zealous police record every incident, no matter how trivial, and conscientiously upgrade its seriousness. Later on this will damage their percentage of cases closed or solved and thus reflect on their effectiveness. Never mind. By then the "crime wave" has produced the extra funds sought and a more relaxed approach to the recording of crimes will yield a better score of cases closed in the next year.

Wilson more wisely examines some specific crimes and calculates that burglaries are more frequent in the United States but auto thefts more common in England and Wales, a questionable contention. Then he gets down to some indisputable cases. No matter how police departments in New York, Detroit, Philadelphia and Chicago (to cite some of the more notoriously unreliable) manipulate numbers, they are less likely to misreport crimes of violence. In one brief paragraph, Wilson looks at two and they destroy his argument. For 1973, New York boasted 1680 murders; London, a city of roughly the same population, 110. New York counted 72,750 robberies — a lawless taking with threats or actual physical violence — while London reported 2680. In other words, your chances of getting murdered in New York are fifteen times greater than in London; your prospects of being robbed, mugged or threatened with violence are twenty-seven times greater. Comparisons between Detroit and Liverpool, Chicago and Manchester and any other pair of U.S. and British cities (Belfast, of course, is a special case) would yield equally marked differences. Wilson, however, still insisted that "Londoners may be only a little less dishonest than New Yorkers" but conceded that "they are vastly less violent."

A reasonable generalization would hold that serious crime has been rising everywhere in the West and Britain is no exception. But if violent crime is an index of social disorder, Britain is stable and the United States is not. Authorities, including Wilson, are perplexed by the reasons for the growth in crime in the industrial world. But crime scholars do agree that the increase is concentrated among the young. Since unemployment has also been rising in the West throughout the seventies, and since it too is heavily concentrated among the young, an observer could be excused for thinking there is some causal relationship between rising crime and growing joblessness.

Irving Kristol was given the task of summing up the sad

state of affairs depicted in *The Future.* He escalates Wilson's contribution and asserts that "all the objective indices of social pathology [in Britain] show steady increases." Kristol's list of "objective indices" is headed by "crime, juvenile delinquency." But as we have seen, using Wilson's figures alone, such measurements make the United States a far fitter subject for concern than Britain.

Scattered Shots from Left and Right

Despite the breadth of their diagnosis, *The Future*'s contributors somehow overlooked one frequently cited cause of Britain's decline, the disappearance of colonies. This, it is frequently said (especially in the United States), has robbed Britain of its traditional vigor. As Dean Acheson put it, "Britain has lost an empire and has not yet found a role." Similarly, Anthony Burgess, whose *Clockwork Orange* rivals any futurologist's nightmare, contended in an article for *New Society* that the end of empire has dissolved "the British ability to improvise new and interesting social structures . . ." Their need is evident, Burgess went on, for Britain is heading toward a "terribly dull" future, dominated by trade union louts.

The more or less peaceful postwar divorce from India, Kenya, Nigeria, Ghana and all those other possessions that once gave world maps a distinctly reddish hue has somehow devitalized the nation. Harsch of the *Christian Science Monitor,* for example, wrote regretfully of the "painful process of contraction of empire" in a gloomy piece on the occasion of the Queen's Silver Jubilee.

The classic statement of empire's importance is Lenin's *Imperialism, The Highest Stage of Capitalism.* Lenin and his followers argued that the colonial expansion of the late nineteenth century had prolonged the life of a dying capitalism by providing new sources of exploitation, new sectors of sur-

plus value to overcome the falling rate of profit. Indeed, in
Lenin's view this exploitation has dulled the sharp edges of
the class war, enabling the proletariat — or at least "a fairly
considerable minority" — in Britain, Germany, France, Belgium and Holland to enjoy something better than the increasing misery that Marx had foreseen as their lot.

In fact, of course, the proletariat or workers in all these
former imperial states have enjoyed sharp and unprecedented increases in living standards since they rid themselves
of their overseas possessions. But that is usually ignored by
those on the right, who bemoan Britain's lost empire. It is
explained away by the Marxist left, for whom the political
imperialism of the past has simply been replaced by "economic imperialism" imposed through trade.

Tom Nairn, the unorthodox Marxist sociologist, has written a widely applauded account of the link between imperialism and Britain's imminent demise. In *The Break-up of
Britain,* Nairn adds a fresh dimension to the classic Leninist
tradition. He argues that nationalism in Britain's ancient
kingdoms threatens the country with a fresh and destructive
wave of anticolonialism. Britain, he writes, "was quite unusually and structurally dependent upon external relations,
tied up with its empire . . . the loss of its critical overseas
wealth and connections was bound to promote internal
readjustments."

So, a ruling class that evidently did recognize its own interest turned to membership in the Common Market as an
"empire surrogate" or substitute. But the Common Market
merely provides "illusions of rejuvenescence." The loss of
colonies remains decisive. "No other nation was so dependent on imperialism or had got more out of it." Since the
early 1950s, when the colonies became independent, England has "fallen into ever more evident and irredeemable
decline — the United Kingdom of permanent economic crisis, falling standards, bankrupt governments, slavish depen-
dency on the United States, and myopic expedients."

Sometimes, Nairn suggests, Britain now enjoys a "new Imperialism . . . financial control of the world market." Why this has not provided a way out of the cul-de-sac is left unexplained.

Anyway, Nairn's principal innovation is a conclusion that flouts the founding fathers of Marxism. It will not be the class war that destroys British capitalism, he says; it is something else. It is "peripheral bourgeois nationalism [that] has today become the grave-digger rather than the intelligentsia or proletariat." It is "neo-nationalism [that] *has* [his emphasis] become the grave-digger of the old state in Britain, and as such the principal factor making for a political revolution of some sort — in England as well as the small countries." By "peripheral bourgeois nationalism" and "neo-nationalism," Nairn simply means the demands for regional autonomy and even independence, now voiced with increasing insistence, in Scotland, Wales and Ulster.

It is hard to determine from Nairn's lively book whether these ancient kingdoms are leaving England because of English rot or whether their departure will simply speed up the decay. Sometimes he seems to be saying one thing; sometimes the other. No matter. The result is clear. They go and bring down what is left of British capitalism in their wake.

Nairn concedes that the Scottish Nationalists are led by middle-class lawyers, teachers, businessmen, accountants and the like (hence his phrase "bourgeois" nationalism) and the movement has a "peaceable nature." He goes further. He allows that it is "defensible" to envision a peaceful rather than a revolutionary settlement, one in which the Scots negotiate a large measure of political and economic self-rule while remaining loosely affiliated to the Crown. But that prospect, he sternly insists, is probably not "real." Scotland is "more likely to be in the world's limbo of anomalies and stress-points." What is left of Britain's shrunken empire, the United Kingdom, is "in an almost terminal condition." The Scots are going and taking Britain's last asset with them, the oil that lies off Scotland's shores. The only question is "how many of them [Scots] would be prepared to fight for it."

This is a stirring picture that revives memories of "the '45," who two centuries ago battled to put a Scottish king back on his throne. It conjures up visions of Mrs. Margo Macdonald, a warm, witty and determined schoolteacher from the slums of Glasgow, the senior vice chairman of the Scottish Nationalist party, leading her battalions against Redcoats on the Tweed, a big, blond Joan of Arc freeing Scots of the British yoke.

A less dramatic but equally plausible scenario suggests that SNP victories at the polls will finally compel British governments to abandon halfhearted "devolution"* measures and offer Scotland genuine autonomy. The Scots would then control virtually everything in their domain — taxes, spending, education, environment, welfare, industry — leaving London in charge only of foreign affairs, defense and the currency. It is more than likely that this could be done without sending Margo into battle, except over a negotiating table in the Palace of Westminster. Electoral setbacks should concentrate the minds of traditional Labour and Tory politicians. In much the same way, it is reasonable to think that a fair division of the revenue from oil — only a portion of which actually lies off Scottish shores — could be fixed without a shot fired. But all this, of course, would weaken Nairn's revolutionary forecast.

The substantial wealth lying in the North Sea and now flowing ashore in ever-increasing quantities troubles prophets of doom on the right as well as the left. It all seems unfair somehow. Here is this fossilized stuff in the sea, pouring from oil rigs through pipelines — a modern deus ex machina, restoring Britain's balance of payments, giving

---

* A bureaucratic term meaning that the central government in London devolves or gives up some of its power over Scotland to a provincial legislature in Edinburgh.

strength to its ailing pound. Could God, after all, be an Englishman? Could the editor of *The Times* be wrong? Surely
not. Much better to do as the oil companies and deprecate
the stuff. Nairn, on the left, simply takes it all away from
Britain and gives it to a rebellious Scotland. Robert Moss,
on the right, denies its existence. The oil, he writes in *Commentary,* is an illusion created by "shamans of the British
cargo cult." This "miraculous 'cargo' can't save Britain
from a Communist doom." At the time Moss wrote, Britain
was already extracting 630,000 barrels a day, saving $65
million a week in foreign exchange. This level is expected to
increase four or five times before the peak is reached.

The futurologists at Hudson were a shade less anthropo-
logical but equally dismissive. Oil prices will fall, they predicted in 1974. There isn't enough oil to meet British
consumption entirely, even by 1985. Anyway, the Americans will be the chief beneficiaries. British governments
have given away the exploitation rights for a song to U.S.
companies.

So, for these and all the other reasons, it is clear that the
Britain most know — peaceful, comfortable, parliamentary,
more or less democratic — is hell-bent for destruction. Margaret Thatcher, the opposition leader, not unnaturally
thought she and her party could still save Britain. But if she
didn't come to power soon, she warned in mid-1977, the
country would march inexorably down the road to
communism.

Was she saying that the Labour government of James
Callaghan was "hell-bent on Marxism and the end of parliamentary democracy"? she was asked on the BBC.

Well, not quite, but almost. Callaghan, she coolly observed, depended on the votes of eighty left-wing MPs. A former chairman of this caucus, Mrs. Thatcher declared, had
said there was little difference between his views and those of
the Communist party. She didn't need to finish the equation, which would run: Callaghan needs leftists whose for-

mer leader is almost a Communist. Since equal terms are equal, that makes the avuncular, cautious Callaghan a, well, Communist. Her technique reminded American viewers of tactics successfully deployed by some Republicans twenty-five years earlier.

Mrs. Thatcher's BBC interlocutor came back to his question. Does a continued Labour government spell disaster?

"Each time you go on further along the Socialist road," Mrs. Thatcher replied sternly, "nearer and nearer to the Communist state, then the consequences of the Communist state will follow." This step-and-road imagery had been worked out with great precision by Lord Chalfont, the peer Labour created, who, in the House of Lords, soured on his party. It was reworked and inflated by Moss in his *Commentary* article. "Britain," Moss wrote, "has traveled more than two-thirds of the way toward becoming a fully communist society . . ."

This remarkable exercise in polimetrics (the quantification of the politically unquantifiable) was achieved this way: Chalfont and Moss examined Holy Writ, the ten points laid out in the *Communist Manifesto,* and tried to see how they fit the contemporary state of affairs. As Moss put it, "Six of the ten conditions for achieving Communism that were laid down by Marx and Engels thus appear to be in the bag for Britain." At least parts of the other four had also been realized. QED. Britain is — at a modest estimate — two thirds down that perdition road.

Less polemical analysts will recall that the *Manifesto* was written in 1848. Most of its ten points now appear to be quaintly reformist. They include free public education, the creation of a central bank, shifting rural citizens to cities, inheritance taxes, a progressive income tax, nationalized railroads and telegraph, increased nationalization of industry, and foreign exchange controls.

On the Chalfont-Moss scale, other countries well down the road toward communism are Germany, France, Norway,

Denmark, Sweden, Holland, Japan, the United States and more. Indeed, the whole world appears doomed. Which perhaps is what Chalfont and Moss believe.

All in all, the commentators had painted a pretty dismal picture. Britain in mid-1977 was torn by anarchy and law-lessness, dominated by strike-mad, Communist-led unions. The citizenry was sinking in an ever-descending spiral of im-miseration; living standards had been falling steadily since the end of the war (well, at least compared with some others). Successive grasshopper governments were squan-dering the nation's scarce resources in an orgy of welfare spending instead of investing in sensible things like steel mills and autos. The "internal condition" of Britain, wrote Moss, "poses perhaps the single most serious threat to the Atlantic Alliance." That judgment settled the argument over whether Britain or Italy was Europe's sickest nation.

It is now questionable whether Britain is America's "most reliable" ally, declared Eric Sevareid.

Oil was an illusion. Nothing could save the country.

But wait. Harsch of the *Christian Science Monitor,* the paper that speaks for those, among others, who believe in healing by faith, offered one faint gleam of hope. In a brilliant burst of innovative constitutional interpretation, he wrote: "What-ever goes wrong, she [Queen Elizabeth II, not I] is there to help sort things out, pick up the pieces, keep the system working."

This was an ingenious view of a monarch most Britons thought merely reigned and did not rule, was a passive polit-ical symbol rather than an active participant in the gov-erning process. Harsch's discovery, however, should not be dismissed lightly. His credentials were as good as most of those who despaired of Britain. He had, after all, gone to Corpus Christi College, Cambridge, and had served as NBC's correspondent in London for twelve years.

II. Examining the Symptoms

The Burden of Empire

One thing is conspicuously absent from the diagnoses of the pundits and professors: evidence. Almost to a man, they fastidiously eschew hard, verifiable fact to support their sweeping generalizations. They assert boldly; they employ colorful, even frightening imagery. They rarely stoop to statistics. This is particularly strange, moreover, since so many of Britain's gloomier analysts are economists or writers on economics by trade, men for whom every squiggle in a price, production or money supply index can be invested with the most profound meaning, sages for whom numeracy is as commonplace as literacy.

There are exceptions, of course. Lenkowsky, the Harvard doctoral student, and Wilson, the Harvard professor, both deploy statistics in their discussion of British welfare and crime. The fact that the numbers they cite buttress conclusions precisely opposite to those they state is a tribute to their scholarly willingness to admit unpalatable fact. The futurologists at Hudson also seed their study with numbers. But their use of statistics is better called creative salesmanship than scholarship. On the whole, however, few of Britain's despondent temperature-takers test their conclusions against the available evidence. This is an oversight that will now be corrected. Happily, even in a declining Britain, there is an

abundance of material with which to measure more carefully the patient's health.

Many of the writers and seers, conventional and otherwise, left and right, agree with Dean Acheson that loss of
empire has seriously undermined postwar Britain. The argument is rarely developed, but simply taken as a given on
which students of history must agree. Sometimes it is suggested that the loss has created a psychic trauma, depressed
will and morale, deprived Britons of a purpose in the world.
This is what Acheson seemed to be saying, that the independence of all those places in Africa, Asia and North America
has created an aching void. The emptiness, in turn, has
robbed Britons of energy, imagination and will. Unhappily,
this argument is unanswerable, or at least unmeasurable.
There is no known method for calibrating a national psyche,
of fixing the presence or absence of collective spiritual depression. But common sense can sometimes substitute for
statistics.

There is little doubt that the nabobs and lesser servants of
the East India Company suffered both pecuniary and psychological loss after the Mutiny of 1857, when control passed
from them to the British military and civil service. In the
same way, it is reasonable to think that families who traditionally sent promising sons to the incorruptible civil service
or the army in the ninety years following the mutiny felt
acute pain when Britain — more or less gracefully — gave
over independence to Nehru and Jinnah in 1947. These
Britons and their descendants lost something. But it is unclear that the millworker in Lancashire, the miner in Wales,
the shop assistant in London or the car worker in Coventry
felt any sense of depression when Kenya, Nigeria, Jamaica
and so many others followed India and Pakistan. It is quite
true that immediately after the war, Britain ruled over about
550 million of the world's population of 2225 million; today,
British rule is limited to about 55 million in a world nearly
twice as populous. Does the proverbial man on the Clap-

ham omnibus feel dispirited at the thought? Was his father or grandfather a happier, more energetic, more purposeful man because he was alive when much of the globe was colored red? Even if the evidence is lacking, experience suggests Acheson's proposition applies only to a limited group.

There is another aspect of the lost empire argument, however, that does lend itself to test. Baldly put, this is the contention that Britain's glorious epoch at the end of the nineteenth century was financed by exploiting colonies. We recall that the most striking expression of this theory is Lenin's *Imperialism.* Oddly enough, vulgarized versions of the great revolutionary's doctrine reappear in the most unlikely quarters, even among Americans who regard Marx and Lenin as works of the devil. A balance sheet version of imperial gain can be expressed as follows: the colonial center, London, draws from its colonies — India, the North American provinces, the Gold Coast — more goods and services than it puts in. This profit, this unrequited import, provides a surplus which is invested in the mills and machinery that gave Britain such a head start in the Industrial Revolution and maintains British economic and political supremacy through the Victorian era. This is an attractive idea, and the fertile Lenin used it to help explain why the British proletariat — workers who do not own the means of production — confounded Marx's forecast of increasing misery and refused to cast off their chains. A bit of the surplus extracted from empire was distributed to the proles and that kept them enthralled.

There is no doubt that empire profited a few and on an enormous scale. After the Battle of Plassey in 1757 established British rule over India, Clive, the commander, was given £234,000 as a "prize in solid money" — gold, jewels and cash. Multiplying this sum by at least thirty will give some notion of its present purchasing power.

In the years that followed, Clive's master, the East India Company, and its servants did very well indeed. According to one estimate, the company netted £2 million yearly in the ten years from 1783 to 1793. In modern terms, that might come to £60 million or $110 million a year, a handsome return on a trivial investment. By the end of the eighteenth century, colonels in the company's service were "legitimately" extracting £7000 a year each. This did not count what they could steal with very little effort indeed. Again, a multiplier of thirty will give some notion of how rich these enterprising souls became.

Elsewhere, the rewards of empire may not have been so staggering, although Cecil Rhodes and others could argue otherwise. But again we speak of enterprising individuals and their companies. The central question is whether British society as a whole profited or lost from the colonial venture. What do the national income accounts reveal? Was sixteenth-century Spain a historical sport, a nation made backward by war, extravagance and the inflationary import of bullion? Or does Spain's fate tell us something of the inevitable cost of empire, something Britain learned in time?

John Strachey, a Marxist writer of the 1930s who became a conventional Labour minister after the war, devised an ingenious test. If Britain as a whole gained from empire, then it did so through buying cheap and selling dear, extracting raw materials — jute, tea, cotton, coffee, gold, diamonds, copper and all the rest — at a low price and selling finished goods at a high price. In the language of economists, empire should have improved Britain's terms of trade. Moreover, British prosperity must go hand in hand with — even depend on — improving terms of trade. The prices of the things Britain exported or sold abroad must rise steadily compared to the prices Britain paid for the things imported or bought from overseas.

Strachey put some researchers from *The Economist* magazine to work on the question. Their findings seem to confound Leninists in Moscow as well as their vulgar descendants in Washington. Britain's terms of trade, the quantity of imports bought by a ton of exports, were at their worst in the heyday of Victorian imperialism; they improved markedly after World War II when the colonies were set free. If the pre–World War I year of 1913 is taken as 100, the ratio of export to import prices in the 1880s averaged 83. In other words, a given volume of exports at this high point of the Victorian era bought 17 percent less from the colonies than in 1913. But in the latest ten years covered by Strachey's table, the postwar decade of 1949–58, the terms of trade index reads 125. In other words, the loss of empire had improved the buying power of British exports by 50 percent compared to the late Victorian period. Prices for the goods Britain sold compared to prices of the raw materials Britain bought abroad rose sharply after the colonies went their independent ways. On this scale, the loss of empire enriched British society immeasurably.

Reliable statistics for terms of trade go back only to 1854, well after the Indian conquest but well before the African colonies were pouring out their riches, at least for the few. Comparing any other decade in the second half of the nineteenth century with the ten postwar years shows similar results: a huge gain in terms of trade once empire goes.

The table, moreover, discloses another peculiar fact. Britain's terms of trade were most favorable, the index reached its peak, in the 1930s. As helpful as the terms were in the postwar era, they were 11 percent more profitable in the depression decade. Depression decade? But favorable terms of trade are supposed to assure prosperity. Imperial exploitation rests on the notion that sweated black, yellow and brown labor is selling cheaply to the white master and buying dearly from him. Whatever may be said of the nation's postwar decline, surely the 1930s was the harshest period in modern times. The evidence suggests, therefore, that buying cheap and selling dear is not the high road to prosperity for society as a whole, no matter how much it may profit the few.*

All this is very perverse. Britain is better off without empire; even under empire, the highest rate of exploitation occurs in the period of greatest economic misery at home.

There is, moreover, another test we can apply to Strachey's conclusions. If his analysis is correct, the British economy should grow faster once the imperial burden is shed. Contrary to the prevailing view of left and right, empire in the Strachey model should have held Britain back. This happens to be the case. Whatever the commentators say, the fact is that the first thirty postwar years have seen the British economy grow faster than at any time in the hundred and twenty years for which reliable statistics on national income have been kept. From 1855 to 1945, the years of empire, Britain's production of steel, coal, textiles, banking services, transport, medical care, housing and all the other goods and services that make up a nation's total output multiplied four and a half times. In the next thirty years, this stream of goods and service doubled again. During ninety imperial years, the flow of goods and services grew each year on the average by 1.7 percent; in the thirty years without empire, British output grew 2.5 percent each year, a gain of nearly 50 percent.

Just why this is so is a complex story. One reason may well be that imperial markets were captive. African, Asian and Caribbean possessions were compelled to buy their goods from British mills and factories. This made life more comfortable — perhaps too comfortable — for the manufac-

---

* Strictly speaking, Strachey's ratio of export and import prices should have been confined to Britain's trade with the colonies rather than total trade to measure the "rate of exploitation." But this refinement would not have made much difference to his results. I have inverted his indices, expressing them as the ratio of export prices over import prices, for greater clarity. The Strachey technique produces a lower index number as terms of trade improve. Most people think that bigger is better, so inversion yields a larger index number as the terms improve.

turers of Sheffield, Manchester and Leeds; it also dulled the spirit of innovation and imposed a pattern of low productivity that prevails to this day. In any event, empire was a burden, not a spur, an Old Man of the Sea on the back of the British nation.*

Two tests — "exploitation" or the terms of trade and the relative gains in income — point to the same inescapable conclusion. Empire surely enriched some Britons — the nabobs, the plantation owners, the exploiters of diamonds, copper and gold. But Britain as a whole has prospered more by giving up empire and yielding gracefully to the postwar nationalist drive. For once, virtue not only was its own reward but brought tangible benefits in its wake. The colonies had been, as James Mill observed, "a vast system of outdoor relief for the upper classes." Lenin appears to have been wrong.

Indeed, our two tests ignore the burden that empire imposed on those who were not nabobs, soldiers or administrators. Their activities were a cost for the rest of society. When Lord Cromer collected debts for British bondholders in Egypt, that was a gain for the bondholders. But other sections of society paid for the soldiers and civil servants who made Cromer's mission a success. In much the same way, armies of men, in uniform and out, the brilliant Indian Civil Service, those splendid young district commissioners ruling over thousands of square miles of jungle and plain, all had to be transported, supplied and paid. To some extent, the costs were borne by the colonies themselves, from local taxes on salt, land and much more. But much of the cost was borne by Britons at home.

---

* Britain's growing population — one source of added output — does not explain away the conclusion. In the imperial era, income per head grew 20 percent from 1865 to 1885, another 25 percent in the next twenty years, only 9 percent in the next period marked by World War I and 39 percent from 1925 through the production-stimulating years of World War II. But in the first twenty post-imperial years, the growth per person was 44 percent, swifter than in any previous imperial generation.

None of this would convince the neo-Leninists, the New Left. In their view, the age of empire never ended. It has simply undergone a more rational, more efficient face-lift. Less ideological economists like Gunnar Myrdal have developed the notion with greater care. In this view, the rules of the global trading game, more or less free trade, consistently work to the disadvantage of the raw materials producers. The Third World may have political independence; in economic terms, it is still a colony of the industrial nations. The producers of copper, jute, tea and the rest sell their produce on free markets, competing with each other, pushing down their own prices. They buy back from the rich finished goods — autos, machine tools, airplanes, weapons systems and other no doubt useful implements — at prices that the rich, organized among themselves in a handful of collaborating producers, relentlessly push up. There is no mystery then about Britain's improved terms of trade after the colonies' departure. The rigged rules of the trading game insure that economic neocolonialism replaces old-fashioned and expensive political imperialism.

This thesis, of course, has been most attractive to Third World nations struggling with an endless host of domestic problems. Myrdal's notions had been inspired by a bright Argentine economist, Raul Prebisch, who spread them through Latin America. In 1964 the United Nations, a growing majority of raw materials producers in its ranks, gave the thesis an institutional form. This is the little-known and much-ignored UNCTAD, the United Nations Conference on Trade and Development. Prebisch was its first secretary-general.

But after the Arab, Persian and other oil-producing states created a cartel (sister to that maintained by the seven great Western companies who extract, transport, refine and sell their crude), the rest of the world began paying attention. The stilted dialogue between North and South, between producers of raw materials and makers of finished goods, was forced on a wider audience. There were demands for a "new economic order," changed rules of the trading game, an end to neo- or economic colonialism. All this was Prebisch and Myrdal amplified, the promotion of devices to reverse the forces that seemed to improve the terms of trade for the industrial world at the expense of the raw materials producers.

The trouble is that the evidence on which all this rests is very much in dispute. It is clear that the terms of trade for the Third World *improved* sharply during the Korean War. But since then the experts have been unable to agree on whose trade terms have been rising and falling, who is doing what to whom — even if the explosive price of oil imposed by the twin cartels of Arab states and oil companies is subtracted.

This dispute — and the digression that led to it — poses fresh problems for the fashionable commentators. If the theorists of neocolonialism are correct, if raw materials producers are increasingly disadvantaged in their dealings with the rich, then Britain never lost its empire. It simply gave up expensive political control of colonies for a new and much more profitable form of economic exploitation. Persia is simply Iran; the Gold Coast is a higher-yielding Ghana. Nothing has been lost and much added profit has been gained. In this case, of course, the chroniclers can not attribute Britain's "two decades of decline" or "hardest 25 years in this century" to the loss of empire. It never went away — at least in the eyes of the new Leninists in the Third World. If the neo-colonialists are wrong and the industrial nations win the trade game some years but lose it in others, the theorists of imperial loss are equally confounded. For as we have seen from Strachey and from the growth rates, there is no necessary link between British prosperity and the terms of trade. On the contrary, there is an inverse relationship between the era of fastest growth and colonial possession.

Welfare, Taxes and Equality

If empire — lost or refound — can't explain Britain's par-
lous condition, perhaps a debilitating welfare state can. The
nation, as many commentators have observed, squanders its
limited resources on the weak, the lazy, the old and the
young. A misplaced sense of compassion or vulgar political
pressure has turned Britain into an ill-fare state, robbing
people of incentives to work. A crushing burden of taxes
pays for this misplaced charity; a "politics of envy" (in the
words of a *Time* writer) is wiping out income differences between Britons. The place is one gray, homogenous mass, increasingly impoverished to support the bureaucrats and the
programs they administer. Britain's great wartime social invention, the report by Sir William Beveridge that called for
the creation of security from cradle to grave, has become an
iron collar, choking the life out of the place. As Royster of
The Wall Street Journal concluded, Britain is a model of what
not to do.

Again, however, cool evidence draws the heat from this
thesis. The dismaying fact is that Britain spends a smaller
share of its resources on welfare programs than the typical
modern state.

The Organization for Economic Cooperation and Development compared welfare outlays among its members —
twenty-four advanced nations in Western Europe, North
America, Japan and Australasia. Specifically, the OECD
determined how much of its total home-produced goods and
services each state spends on pensions for the aged, payments
to support children, outlays for the unemployed and cash for
the sick. Britain spends about one pound in fourteen for
such purposes, 7.7 percent of its gross domestic product. This
is indeed a large share. But it is considerably less than the
10.6 percent spent in the nine Common Market countries as
a whole. It is even a little bit less than the 8.0 percent re-

corded for the United States, conventionally regarded as among the least welfare-minded nations. The British devoted far less of their output to welfare than sturdy Belgium and thrifty Holland (14.1 percent), France and Germany (12.4 percent) or Italy (10.4 percent). The Scandinavian countries — Norway, Denmark and Sweden — are bywords for lavish welfare outlays. In fact, they too are below the European Economic Community (EEC) average but still ahead of Britain, devoting 9 to 10 percent of their resources to welfare. Only Japan, where a different tradition thrusts responsibility for cradle-to-grave protection on paternalistic and cartelized corporations, departs significantly from the pattern. Its share of government welfare outlays is a mere 2.8 percent.

But maybe there has been a sharp increase in Britain's share compared to others. Perhaps Britain does spend less than more "successful" states but the claims of welfare have mounted more rapidly than those of the rest. The OECD examined this question too, comparing the welfare slice in 1962 with that of 1972. Sure enough, Britain's spending had gone up smartly, from 5.7 to 7.7 percent. But this was about in line with the experience of all the others. For the Common Market nine, the welfare burden rose from 8.2 to 10.6 percent over the decade; in the United States, from 5.5 to 7.4;* and for all seventeen nations for which material was available, from 6.8 to 8.6 percent.

Lenkowsky, the Harvard researcher, was accurate. Britain devotes less of its income to welfare than its neighbors. The welfare burden simply won't explain the nation's "sickness."

Nevertheless, everybody knows that Britain is overwhelmed with government spending. If Britain is not frittering away resources on the helpless, it is still supporting an

---

* The 8.0 percent share for the United States cited earlier is for the latest year available to the OECD survey, 1974. The trend comparison runs only to 1972, when the U.S. welfare slice was 0.6 percentage points lower.

army of unproductive civil servants, robbing productive enterprise of needed men and materials. Again, however, what everybody knows has little basis in fact. It is hard to compare government budgets among countries because they are drawn up so differently. What one nation counts as a government expense another charges to industry. The Common Market has attempted to reconcile these differences, however, and provides one of the few meaningful comparisons. Its latest findings, for 1975, show that the government's outlays in Britain are a striking 46.3 percent of total domestic output. Nearly one pound in two that is produced is an expenditure of the state. But the average for the nine members of the EEC is almost exactly the same, 46.5 percent. The German state, supposedly devoted to free and private enterprise, actually swallowed more of its national output than Britain, 48.0 percent. France took less, 41 percent. But Holland at 55.3 percent took far more. Once again, the appetites of Britain's bureaucracy cannot explain the putative national decline. They are much like those elsewhere in Europe.

Again, the skeptical will ask, what of the trend? Do Britain's troubles flow from a sharply *rising* grab by the state? The evidence is otherwise. The EEC comparison discloses that for the period 1961–65, UK government outlays were 35.1 percent of the gross domestic product. This too was virtually the same as the 34.7 percent for the EEC as a whole. In other words, Britain's government spending in the early sixties was slightly higher than average; ten or so years later it was slightly lower.

Could *The Wall Street Journal* and all those other experts be so wrong? Surely they are right at least in asserting that British taxes drain the nation's energies. Once more, the OECD compares the burden among the industrial nations. Once again, there is nothing peculiar in the British performance. The OECD measured the total take of the tax collectors — everything including income taxes, corporate levies, sales taxes, social security payments — as a share of the gross domestic product for 1975. In Britain, the tax men collected 36.8 percent of everything produced, about one pound in three. The tax take in France (36.9) and Germany (35.2) was about the same. The tax men were much busier in Scandinavia, collecting 46.0 percent in Sweden, 44.7 percent in Norway and 43.1 percent in Denmark.

The U.S. tax take, 30.3 percent, was well below the British and European level. So was Japan's, at 20.2 percent. But if the tax burden is supposed to have broken Britain, why has it failed to crush her more prosperous neighbors in Northern Europe — France, Germany, Norway, Denmark and Sweden?

Perhaps the answer lies in the way taxes are collected. The British system, it is said, punishes the bright, the innovative, the entrepreneur. The "politics of envy" penalizes the most productive, destroying incentive and the will to work. At first glance, there is some evidence to support this conclusion. Britain does indeed collect a much bigger share of its taxes from progressively increasing levies on income and wealth than its chief Common Market allies. They rely much more heavily on sales taxes and social security payments, on the hidden and open taxes paid by consumers and workers. An income tax is "progressive." The more you earn, the bigger the share surrendered to the state. A sales tax is "regressive." A rich man and a poor man pay the same 8 or 10 percent levy when they buy tobacco, beer, cars, clothing or whatever. In the same way, all Common Market citizens are supposed to pay more or less the same price for food. This system to support farmers is achieved with a nest of identical hidden taxes imposed regardless of the income of each food-consuming family.*

---

* Recently, the system has been punctured by the floating exchange rates for national currencies. After the drastic fall in the pound, the British successfully resisted — at least for a time — the efforts of others to force higher, compen-

The Confederation of British Industry (CBI), an organization of Britain's leading corporations, has compared the tax structures in the four biggest EEC countries. It found that Britain's weighed most heavily on the best-off. In 1974, taxes on income and wealth provided 43.4 percent — nearly half — of all British taxes. But for West Germany, this "progressive" share was only 33.7 percent; in France, a derisory 20.4 percent; and in Italy, an equally painless 20.9 percent. In the three other countries, the tax burden falls more heavily on those with smaller incomes. The British might claim that theirs is a fairer, more just system, that it takes relatively more from those best able to pay. No matter. Here at last is a significant difference that might explain Britain's pathology.

As no less an authority than Prince Philip observed in a trade journal, the *Engineer*: "The successful technological innovators must become heroes again. They must be allowed to gain and keep their rewards for success . . . The Welfare State is a protection against failure and exploitation but a national recovery can take place only if innovators, and men of enterprise and hard work, can prosper."

Philip was expressing a widely held view, although it had an odd ring coming from him. For one thing, Royals are not supposed to make political pronouncements and his could be construed as a breach of this tradition. For another, some might regard him as Britain's premier welfare client, consort of the richest woman in the realm and uniquely free of the ordinary citizen's obligation to pay income taxes.

But if Philip's words have weight, then we must expect that differences in income and wealth in Britain are being wiped out. The comparatively heavier British reliance on wealth and income taxes must be destroying incentives to work, offering the same rewards for the lazy and the zealous,

---

sating food prices on Britons. So British consumers were not subsidizing Common Market farmers as heavily as the rules seem to demand. The later rise in the pound, however, is wiping out this advantage.

the little skilled and the highly skilled, the safe bureaucrat and the risk-taking entrepreneur.

Prime Minister Harold Wilson, eager to demonstrate that Britain under Labour had indeed become a more just nation, set up a Royal Commission in 1974 to examine how income and wealth are distributed. The results were so disturbing that Wilson and his successors buried Lord Diamond's report. It showed that incomes — earnings from pay, interest, dividends, profits, fees and the like — had indeed become more equal during World War II, when common sacrifice was crucial for national survival. But once the wartime controls were lifted, there was virtually no more movement toward leveling out incomes. The British result would not surprise any American expert; the U.S. experience has been much the same.

In the 1939 budget year (which ran to April 25) — the last before the war — Britain's highest-paid 1 percent of the population collected 11.7 percent of all personal incomes after deducting taxes. By 1949, their share had been sharply sliced to 5.8 percent. They gave up another percentage point in the next decade, but only 0.8 percentage points more by 1973. In other words, the share of the best-off 1 percent had been slashed by more than half from the prewar to the postwar period. But in the thirteen years after 1960, it fell only from 4.8 to 4.0 percent.

Going down the ladder of incomes, other brackets enjoyed much the same experience. Britain's best-paid 10 percent collected 34.6 percent of all after-tax incomes just before the war. By 1960, they were down to 23.1 percent. Thereafter, they more or less held their own, collecting 21.4 percent in 1973. Again, there was a big squeeze toward leveling incomes in the war and postwar period. Then it stopped.*

---

* Economists have worked out several measures of the degree of equality of incomes in a society. One of the most widely used is the Gini coefficient. The greater the equality of incomes, the smaller the Gini coefficient; the greater the

It can be argued that money incomes no longer reflect what is really happening to a family's command of goods and services, that welfare benefits are a far more powerful device than taxes to redistribute incomes. So the Royal Commission went through the exercise of computing the shares of different groups in a larger pie, one that included both incomes after taxes and welfare benefits, everything from cash handouts to housing subsidies. But once again, who gets what is little changed even with this refinement.

In the years 1961–63, the best-off 10 percent collected 23.5 percent of all after-tax incomes and welfare benefits. Ten years later their share was almost identical, 23.4 percent. Welfare benefits, which are supposed to flow largely to the worst-off, had not affected the pattern. At the bottom, the poorest 10 percent had indeed gained a larger slice, from 1.8 percent to 2.6 percent. But the share of the next poorest 10 percent did not change at all, and most of the other groups in between also showed little change. The pattern of postwar incomes, including welfare benefits, remains almost static in Britain. The leveling process stopped after the war.* The Labour government had good reason to treat the Diamond report with polite silence. Its findings destroyed some cherished beliefs about an increasingly more equal state. (Two years after the first study, Diamond issued a new volume that tried to sustain Labour's convictions. Unhappily, the statistics either refused to support claims of significantly increasing equality of incomes or led to bizarre results that puzzled the investigators themselves — e.g., an unbelievable finding that the richest 1 percent suffered a relative drop in wealth in 1975, a year of stock market boom.)

---

inequality, the bigger the coefficient. In 1939, Britain's Gini coefficient for income after taxes was calculated at 36.5. The wartime equalizer brought it down to 30.2 by 1950. It stayed within a percentage point or so of this level for the next twenty-two years, a remarkable statistical demonstration of the failure to make incomes more equal.

* The best-off, moreover, in Britain as in most industrial societies, enjoy a wide range of perquisites that never show up in the income and benefits sta-

The pattern for wealth — cash savings, stocks, bonds, land, yachts, homes, paintings, jewelry and the rest — is very different. Inheritance taxes are tending to make wealth — not income — more equal in Britain. But the maldistribution of wealth is so great, so much is owned by so few, that this change hardly supports an argument that taxes are stifling initiative. The biggest change, moreover, affects the wealthiest 20 percent and not the bottom 80. The share owned by the top 10 is slipping; that of the second wealthiest 10 percent is rising. In other words, managers, professionals and the most skilled workers are accumulating wealth while the richest inheritors lose ground. Reward after all does appear to survive for those strivers whose fate so concerns Philip.*

The evidence points to some heretical notions that Philip and other seers had missed. Britain's welfare "burden" is and has been less than that of most other industrial nations in Europe. The share of resources taken by the government is much like those elsewhere in the Common Market. The tax receipts to support these outlays weigh less heavily on the British economy than on those of its neighbors. To be sure, the British tax system goes much further than in other big EEC countries toward making incomes more equal. But even after welfare benefits are counted, there is great in-

---

tistics. Corporate executives enjoy company-paid cars, golf and club memberships, entertainment allowances, low-interest loans to buy houses and dozens of other opportunities for income in kind that the figures can't catch. To be sure, coal miners have traditionally received free coal for their dwellings, but most workers get only what the tax and welfare agencies report. In other words, British incomes are even more unequal than the Royal Commission reports.

* Britain's richest 1 percent owned 38.2 percent of all wealth in 1960. By 1973, their share had fallen substantially, to 27.6 percent. But those who ranked from 11 to 20 percent on the wealth ladder — the second wealthiest 10 percent — enjoyed a swift rise, from 13.1 percent to 19.2 percent. They were the big beneficiaries of the more equal distribution of wealth. Britain's poorest 80 percent owned only 10.2 percent of the nation's wealth in 1960; thirteen years later, their share had risen only to 13.6 percent.

equality in British incomes (and wealth); the movement toward equality of incomes stopped after the war. In sum, the welfare state and the taxes to pay for it cannot explain Britain's "sickness."

Indeed, the evidence points in a contrary direction. If Britain's tax system is far more "progressive" than those of Italy, France and Germany, why haven't incomes become more equal? The answer is supplied by the CBI. It noted that less than half of Britain's taxes are collected from levies on income and wealth; more than half fall on those least able to bear them. They pay taxes on the consumption of goods and deductions from their wages for social security. In other words, the distribution of incomes in Britain remains unequal and more or less unchanged because the "progressive" consequences of the income tax are wiped out by the "regressive" force of all the other levies.

As Wilson's Royal Commission rather sadly conceded: "The progressive effect of direct taxation is largely offset by the regressive effect of indirect taxation. Thus the tax system has little effect on the overall shape of the distribution." (The Diamond commission goes on to assert that welfare benefits have made total incomes more equal. But its own statistics show otherwise.)

What then does this tell us of Italy and France, where direct, income-equalizing taxes are less than half as important as in Britain, where the rich and the poor enjoy the same right to pay identical levies for food, clothing and other consumer goods? It must mean that the maldistribution of income in France and Italy is worsening, that more and more goes to fewer and fewer. This, of course, does not mean that incomes of French and Italian workers do not gain absolutely as their national economies grow. They do, but not as fast as those of their managers and employers. Indeed, another OECD study has found that France boasts the most unequal distribution of incomes among twelve leading industrial states; Italy runs a close second. Australia, Japan and Sweden emerge with the smallest disparities between rich and poor; British incomes are somewhat more equally distributed than the average.

It could be argued that the widening gap between the best-off and worst-off in France and Italy accounts for the faster pace at which their economies have grown since the war. But it may also account for the persistence of large Communist parties in both nations. Since the war, Communists in Britain have never received more than 0.4 percent of the vote in any national election; they have not won a seat in Parliament since 1945, when they took two. In contrast, the French and Italian Communist vote ranges from 19 to 34 percent; a major Communist role in the governments at Paris and Rome is regarded no longer as unthinkable but likely. Britain's tax welfare system may have inhibited economic growth (but then why have more burdensome systems not weighed on the Scandinavians and Dutch?); it has also prevented a further widening in the relative shares earned by the best- and worst-off. This could account for the fact that British political life — like that in Scandinavia and Holland — is more or less stable. The British and Scandinavian consensus is untroubled by an important revolutionary party. It is hard to conceive of a consensus in France and Italy.

The conventional commentators, most of whom yield to none in their anti-Communist passion, appear to have overlooked a rather simple point: no matter how fast an economy grows, a society is far more likely to be plagued by political instability if its fruits are distributed in an increasingly unequal fashion. This, of course, is not the only source of political disorder in a modern state. West Germany, for example, enjoys a tax system that is far less generous — compared to those of France and Italy — toward those least in need. Even so, Germany's democracy is thought to be a thin crust, a layer on top of a deep authoritarian base. History and culture, experience and myth, tradition and values, all shape

national political character. Nevertheless, a tax system that
freezes rather than widens the gap between best- and worst-
off is likelier than its opposite to promote a stable, democratic society in the West. Norway, Denmark, Sweden, Holland and Britain all bear testimony to this.

Unions, Militant and Otherwise

The idea that politics in Britain is stable conflicts with another favorite theme of the pathologists. A long line, mostly
on the right, have grimly concluded that Britain is controlled by all-powerful trade unions, that the unions in turn
are dominated by a handful of Communists and other wild-
eyed leftists, that this compound yields endless industrial
strife, to promote either ideological ends or, more sinister, the
secret subversive goals of the Soviet Union. In this view, the
Communist vote in elections is irrelevant. Britain may not
suffer from as many Communists as France or Italy, but
their strategic location gives them a disproportionate power.

The scenario is undoubtedly dramatic, even imaginative.
Whether it has much basis in fact is another question. Trade
unions do exercise power in Britain — as they do in the
United States, Scandinavia, Holland and other democracies. British trade unions, like their Continental counterparts (but unlike those in the United States), sometimes
count Communists or other leftists among their leaders. British trade unions do call strikes in an attempt to enforce demands for higher pay and the preservation of jobs. The
withdrawal of labor on an organized scale is the ultimate
weapon of any independent union.

The "Communist-dominated" image owes much of its
force to an analysis in *The Economist* of January 19, 1974.
This weekly is easily the most intelligent newsmagazine in
the English-speaking world, but, like any temporal commen-
tator, it can get things wrong. The article in question exa-

mined the executive boards of the twelve largest British unions, counted 335 members and declared that 41 were Communist. On the surface, that is indeed an impressive and possibly worrisome Red score. (Robert Moss, in his *Commentary* article, counts 50 "open Communist party supporters" among 345 executive board members in thirteen unions. His unsupported escalation of *The Economist*'s data is not uncharacteristic.) Even more frightening was the fact that Britain's two biggest unions, the Transport and General Workers and the Amalgamated Union of Engineering Workers, were both graded by *The Economist* as "Far Left" in political complexion. The next ten unions, with or without Communist board members, were ranked merely as "Left," "Right" or "Center." So the heart of the problem — if one exists — lies in the TGWU and the AUEW.

A closer look at the behavior of these "Far Left" unions and their leaders during the critical period since 1974, however, fogs the picture of revolutionaries bent on destruction. Britain's largest union, the TGWU, is a catchall of about 2 million or one sixth of all union members. It embraces truck drivers, dock workers, auto assembly workers and more. Its leaders invariably set the tone and pace for the union movement as a whole.

Until his retirement in 1977, Jack Jones was the general secretary and unquestioned leader of the TGWU. In his youth, Jones had been a man of the left — he fought with the International Brigades against the Franco rebellion in Spain — and all his life he has resisted any suggestion that his Socialist credentials were in doubt. The case for a left-led British trade union movement in the seventies rests heavily on the character of Jones. In his last years in office, he was frequently described as "Britain's most powerful man."

In fact, Jones' leadership was notably conservative. On the collective bargaining front, he helped design and carry out an extraordinary policy to curb wage increases, forcing workers to bear the burden of Britain's difficult battle against a dangerous inflation. The pinch was so effective that the real incomes of workers actually fell in the first two years of pay restraint while the nation's total output rose slightly. This strongly suggests that Jones and the union movement were redistributing income from their own members to other classes, hardly the activity of a Red revolutionary.*

Jones was most concerned not to promote class war but to restore the close traditional links between a reformist Labour party, of which he had been a lifelong member, and the union movement. They had been ruptured in 1969, when the earlier Wilson administration tentatively adopted a plan to inhibit union bargaining power. It was a faint echo of some U.S. legislation, the Taft-Hartley Act. Union opposition aborted the plan. But it left a bitter aftertaste. Both Jones and Wilson resolved that nothing like this should happen again, that voluntary agreement rather than legislative fiat must control state relations with unions.

When the Conservatives regained power in 1970, Prime Minister Edward Heath put Wilson's still-born idea into action, enacting an Industrial Relations Act to curb union strength. The unions, including and especially Jones' TGWU, fought back. They exercised an option offered by Heath's law and refused to register for the few benefits the act conferred. That also made most of the new law's penalties a dead letter. The episode illustrated that peacetime industrial relations and wage demands cannot, in a modern society, be determined by command. Just as the price, investment and output decisions of large corporations can be influenced but not ordered by government (except in war-

* The weekly pay of the average factory worker with a family — after squeezing out price inflation, subtracting his taxes and adding his welfare benefits — fell from £64.54 to £63.04 between June 1975 and June 1977. An almost stagnant gross domestic product still rose by 2.2 percent in the same period.

time), so too large unions in an open society can insist successfully on freedom of action over the two matters that most concern them — the shape of their demands and the right to strike.

To be sure, legislative rules determining how the game is played are acceptable — union recognition, boycotts, record-keeping, voting for union officials and the like. In the same way, corporations will accept rules governing their accounts, management-stockholder relations, recognition of a union as bargaining agent. But in a free society, both institutions strenuously resist any effort to inhibit by legislation their most crucial decisions. This rule may be bent on rare occasions. It is conceivable that in a time of high inflation and restless workers, union leaders might welcome wage controls. That would put the onus of a wage restraint they favor but fear on the government. In the same way, corporate executives might trade control over prices for control over wages in the same overheated circumstance. But this is a variant from rather than an exception to the typical behavior. It envisions leaders of both institutions welcoming the government's intervention.

When Labour came back to power under Wilson in 1974, Jones and the prime minister began drawing up a misnamed "social contract." It was not a contract because it bound no one. Moreover, it was clearly unequal, providing the government with large measurable advantages and the unions with little more than promises and hopes. But somehow this voluntary agreement worked. Heath's Industrial Relations Act, an empty shell, was repealed. The unions also gained new legislation dimly resembling the U.S. Wagner Act. It was supposed to stimulate union recognition. In fact, these provisions were so timidly drawn that determined employers could and did resist them; they never achieved their goal of enlarging union membership. Jones also won the promise of a special piece of law, making it easier for him to organize dock workers whose employers had moved to depots several miles from the waterfront. But Parliament refused to honor the government's pledge.

In return for this skimpy legislative fare, Jones persuaded his fellow unionists to limit their wage demands sharply. For the year beginning August 1, 1975, the unions agreed to seek no more than £6 a week per man, a wage increase of about 10 percent. This was an astonishing measure of restraint when prices were skyrocketing at more than 25 percent annually. The next year, the "social contract" was renewed. Inflation had been cut to about 14 percent, and the unions again agreed to limit their demands to something much less, a maximum of £4 a week, or 5 percent.

In the summer of 1977, Jones made his last appearance before a TGWU convention. He pleaded for a third year of wage restraint, a third successive year in which unions would agree voluntarily to slash the living standards of their workers. But "Britain's most powerful man" could not, as we have seen, prevail over the insistent demands of his own membership. He was voted down by a three-to-two margin. The workers had had enough.

Whatever the wisdom of Jones' behavior during this critical period, it clearly was not that of a Communist wrecker. He had exercised his influence on behalf of political and economic order, for stability against chaos. He may even have been the architect of a policy that had once again unwittingly redistributed British income — from the workers to every other class. In Marxist terms, Jones was a counterrevolutionary and an instrument of the capitalist order.

In much the same way, the leadership of the second biggest union, the AUEW, played a conservative, supporting role. The AUEW, with about 1.4 million members concentrated in auto and machine tool plants, was led by Hugh Scanlon. Like Jones — although with less enthusiasm — he accepted and enforced the wage restraint.

In 1977, on the eve of his retirement, Scanlon made one

last contribution to a conservative order. He persuaded the AUEW to support the last vestige of the government's policy to curb wages — an agreement that no union would seek more than one pay increase in a year. Scanlon's success swung the rest of the trade union movement into line and the principle of restraint was preserved for twelve more months.*

There is another important union, however, with a long history of stubborn opposition to the government of the day, and its actions have colored the stereotype of radical, irresponsible behavior. This is the organization of the 260,000 men who mine coal, set apart from the rest of society by dangerous, dirty and isolated work and fiercely independent. The union's right-wing leadership caused Britain's general strike in 1926. Its present leaders — a mixed bag of left and right — did bring down Heath's government in 1974. But was this a leftist plot?

During the 1970s, Communist mine leaders occupied key positions in Scotland and Wales. The big contingent of Yorkshire miners, about 64,000, was led by Arthur Scargill, a former Communist who had broken with the party but remains an open, militant Marxist. At the start of 1978, Communists and neo-Communists like Scargill filled 11 of the 27 places on the executive board of the National Union of Mineworkers. They were certainly influential; they were not all-powerful. The union's national leader during the turbulent 1970s was Joe Gormley, a shrewd and conservative man.

But as the TWGU demonstrated when they dismissed Jones' pleas, what matters in British unions (and most others in a democratic society) is not the ideological coloration or the commands of leaders. What counts is the sentiment, the feelings, the demands of the rank and file. The colorful

---

* The unions did reject the government's plea to hold gains to a specific figure, to 10 percent, the policy for which Jones fought his last and losing fight. But by the end of 1977, many were settling for amounts close to the government's target, preserving the practice as well as the principle of restraint.

Scargill, for example, was not elected leader in Yorkshire because he was a Marxist. He won his post because he had invented a successful tactic to help win a coal strike in 1972 and then staged a notable battle for mine safety.

In the fall of 1973, Heath had every reason to be concerned about Britain's raging inflation. His chancellor of the exchequer, Anthony Barber, had recklessly inflated the nation's money supply — by 28.3 percent in 1972 and by another 28.8 percent in 1973. The paper was spilling over to push up prices. Its full effect would not be felt for twelve to eighteen months, but the eventual consequences of Barber's action were clear. In addition, the commodities Britain bought abroad were climbing in price. The Arabs, Persians and the seven great oil companies were collaborating on a scheme that would multiply the price of oil alone by four times, a horrendous prospect for a nation that then imported all its crude.

Heath's response was to curb wages by fiat, to limit increases through law to £4.80 a week. The miners, who had once been among the best-paid industrial workers, had now fallen somewhere below the middle. They produced, moreover, an essential commodity, especially in a nation afraid of an oil boycott. The miners determined to ignore Heath's limit and knew they were in a position to exert their will. This is not the stuff of revolution but of collective bargaining. The miners began in a cautious fashion, pressing demands and simply refusing to work overtime. They feared Heath would order their nationalized industry to stockpile coal. This would enable the government to withstand any winter strike and then refuse to bend its wage curb in the warmer spring and summer. That, of course, was precisely what Heath had in mind. He was determined to preserve the wage limit he had legislated and to weaken the miners' will to resist.

There was still no strike, only an overtime ban, when Heath countered with a dramatic stroke: he ordered the nation's factories and offices to use electricity on only three working days in five. This was the famous three-day week, a Heath tactic to preserve fuel in the winter and break the miners' will in the warmer weather. Now the miners did leave the pits and a strike began in earnest.

Heath rashly decided to go to the country, to call an election on the simple issue: "Who rules — unions or Parliament?" It was this slogan that nourished the view of unions as radical wreckers. Heath's own advisers, notably William Whitelaw, the employment minister, pleaded for a settlement of the dispute with the miners before the voters went to the polls. Whitelaw even produced a formula that would save the government's face and give the miners more pay than the limit allowed.*

But Heath, more a gifted civil servant than a politician, stubbornly refused. With the country working only three days a week, Britons went to the polls in February 1974. The voters, of course, were not required to accept Heath's version of the issue — "Parliament or unions" — and many saw the referendum as a chance to express displeasure with an inflexible regime. In the end, what was surprising was not that Heath lost — the Conservatives got 38 percent of the vote — but that Wilson and Labour failed to win outright. Labour received only 37 percent but captured more seats. The big nationwide winner, for that one election, was the Liberal party, whose share rose from 7.5 to 19 percent. In effect, the voters refused to endorse Heath, but they were far from sure they wanted Labour.

Heath, an admirable man in many ways, had tried to enforce a revolutionary policy with revolutionary means —

---

* The formula recalled that employed by John L. Lewis, the United Mine Workers' president, in a notable wartime strike against President Roosevelt's wage control. Lewis proposed that the miners, who traveled long distances unpaid to and from the mine entrance to the mine face, receive compensation for this time. Lewis defied the no-strike law and won his "portal-to-portal" pay. Whitelaw proposed much the same solution to Heath, although it is not clear that the British miners would have accepted it.

largely to correct the reckless policies of his own finance minister. Unsurprisingly, a conservative British electorate turned him out of office.

Read superficially, the result was a triumph for the coal miners. The new government swiftly gave the union its demands in full and the three-day week was ended. But the whole affair, including Heath's election, need never have happened. Communist mine leaders did not defeat Heath; he destroyed himself. A year later the Conservative party agreed. After a second lost election, Tory MPs voted Heath out and replaced him as leader with Margaret Thatcher.

A more sensitive understanding of the need to win union (and corporate) assent to policies of restraint, a more flexible interpretation of a rigid formula, a less overt attempt to use state power to break the miners' bargaining tool, and even Scargill could not have led his men to give up their overtime let alone go out on strike. Three years later, Scargill tried to persuade miners they were better off striking than peacefully accepting a sure pay gain for a notional amount of extra work. Once they learned the facts, the miners would have none of it and even rebelled against Scargill in his Yorkshire stronghold.

Less than three years after *The Economist* had drawn up its disturbing box score of leftist influence in the unions, the weekly, scrupulous as ever, had a change of view. An editorial for July 30, 1977, said reassuringly, "As long as Labour is under the influence of the Liberals and a *largely-moderate TUC* [my emphasis] the parliamentary left will remain a largely irrelevent rump . . ." In *The Economist's* eyes, the TUC — Britain's AFL-CIO — was now a force for moderation, not radicalism. Since the Labour government depended on a union movement dominated by the moderates (as well as by Liberal MPs, whose thirteen votes at that time gave the new Prime Minister Callaghan a majority in Parliament), *Economist* readers need not have feared the left. The magazine, with its taste for numbers, then solemnly proceeded to quantify the TUC's good character. Of the 41 members on the General Council, the paper classed only 9 as "militant"; the rest were "moderates" or "floaters."

But even if the union leadership is less Red than conventionally painted, everyone knows that Britain's industrial relations are a nightmare, that the nation is plagued with endless strikes over trivial issues. Few remember that *I'm All Right, Jack* is a savage indictment of both union and management behavior; it is Peter Sellers' uproarious portrayal of a bloody-minded union official that remains fixed in the national consciousness.

By now it will come as no surprise that the popular view is again undone by facts. A study for the government's *Employment Gazette* compared the strike records of eighteen nations during the decade 1965–74. Unions in Britain, it turned out, were indeed far more strike-prone than their brothers in France, Germany and Japan. But they were markedly less strike-happy than those in the United States, Italy, Canada, India and Australia. Since French and German unions are weak — either because they lack organization and resources (France) or because of a collaborationist tradition (Germany, Japan) — a better comparison is with unions in similar political settings. On that basis, only the smaller countries of Scandinavia, Holland and New Zealand are less given to strikes.*

This conclusion seems patent nonsense to readers of the British press. Surely there is something wrong with the numbers. They must not count unauthorized or wildcat strikes. They must leave out the thousands sent home from a car plant when one key shop walks out. In fact, both groups

---

* The average number of days lost through strikes per thousand workers employed during the 1965–74 decade was: Italy, 1655; Canada, 1644; the United States, 1305; India, 1136; Ireland, 1018; Australia, 913; Finland, 810; *United Kingdom, 743*. Then came Denmark, 511; Belgium, 334; New Zealand, 322; Japan, 243; France, 274; the Netherlands, 65; Norway, 60; Germany, 50; Sweden, 46; Switzerland, 1.

of idled workers are included; the country is not especially strike-prone.

British strikes, moreover, are heavily concentrated in three industries — coal mining, dockyards and automobiles. The miners, as suggested already, are a special breed of workers, cut off from the rest of the work force, living in isolated communities and much less sensible to opinion at large. The dockers and the car workers frequently strike not over pay but to preserve their jobs. Both industries are declining; in the last generation, both have turned to new, labor-saving equipment. British workers, as we shall see, do cling to their jobs long after technological advance has made them unnecessary. Resistance to automation, to technological unemployment, does appear to be far stronger in Britain than in Germany, Japan or the United States. This is a powerful factor in the strike records of ports and car assembly plants.

But the central point lies in the overall record; British workers as a whole are far less ready to go out on strike than are those in the United States, Canada and Italy.

The *Employment Gazette*'s figures go only through 1974. Since then, British workers, caught between high unemployment and rising prices, have been even less ready to down their tools. Compared to the 743 days lost annually in the decade from 1965, the figures for the next two years of austerity were 540 in 1975 and 300 in 1976. Once again, British workers were far less strike-prone than their more or less equally hard-pressed brethren in other countries. Over those last two years, Canadians lost six strike days for every one in Britain, Italians four, Australians three and Americans two. Even the weak French unions walked out more frequently than the British.

These were some of the stubborn facts that impressed *The Economist* and produced its new label of "moderate" for union leaders.

One final test can be applied. If British unions are so

tough, why aren't their members getting richer, compared to other classes?

The Royal Commission estimated that the bottom 70 percent had collected only 43 percent of all after-tax incomes on the eve of the war. By 1960, their share had risen to 50 percent, the wartime equalizing process also seen in the United States. But thirteen years later, the lowest 70 percent had expanded their slice of all incomes by only two percentage points, to 52 percent. This slow gain hardly supports the claim of unbridled union power.*

Whatever the causes of Britain's "sickness," they do not lie in the conventional categories. Indeed, on examination, the popular images dissolve. British unions are, by and large, sober and moderate; they are not particularly militant or strike-happy nor do the handful of Communists appear to exert an unusual influence. Welfare payments and the tax structure have not succeeded in leveling incomes or wealth. Their "burden" is no more onerous than that in other industrial nations. The loss of empire has gone hand in hand with a growth in national product and well-being. The familiar symptoms of the British "disease" are imaginary. They appear to have been concocted to support a special interest or sustain a cherished set of stereotyped beliefs.

---

* To be sure, this a crude indicator. For one thing, British unionists within the bottom 70 percent could have made large gains at the expense of those unprotected by unions. Only half of the work force holds a union card. But that very fact, the failure to organize half the workers, is itself a reflection of the limited strength of British unions. Genuinely powerful unions exist in Scandinavia, where, as a rule, nearly 80 percent of the workers are organized. Paradoxically, there are few strikes in these nations. Unions are so strong and so secure that they can afford "responsible" behavior.

III. Leisure over Goods

A Glorious Reign

If professors and journalists have misled us about the causes of Britain's illness, is it possible that the whole episode is a case of hypochondria? Is it conceivable that the country has not been declining since the end of the war but, in fact, has been enjoying robust health — at least as far as social and economic indicators can measure such things? This, indeed, is so.

In the first thirty years after the war, as the discussion of empire suggested, Britain enjoyed the fastest rate of economic growth in its recorded history. This means that the yearly gain in the national production of goods and services — of autos and banking, clothes and travel, food and schools, steel and science — was more rapid than at the height of the Victorian era, when Britain's industrial supremacy was unchallenged; faster than in the golden Edwardian and early Georgian days before World War I, faster than in the interval between the two great wars, the last time Britain still pretended to be a world power. Since national income statistics for Britain go back only as far as 1855, it is possible that some earlier thirty-year period saw more rapid growth, although the slump-ridden decades after the Napoleonic wars are unlikely to have produced it. The evidence in any case is lacking. Rather than declining, Britain's postwar economy has enjoyed the most prosperous period in the nation's recorded history.

This unprecedented growth has transformed the living standards of ordinary people. When the Queen celebrated her Silver Jubilee in 1977, twenty-five years on the throne, each of her subjects on average enjoyed an income commanding four-fifths more in goods and services than his parents. Even allowing for the great rise in prices, "real" and not inflated incomes after taxes had grown 88 percent from 1952 through 1976.

At the start of her reign, the Queen's statisticians still counted 7 dwellings in every 100 without a toilet; by the Silver Jubilee, only 1 in 100 was so deprived. More than a third lacked a bath in 1952; twenty-five years later, 91 in 100 boasted their own bath.

Other gains were equally striking. Two secondary school graduates in 100 went on to university in 1952; twenty-five years later, the number had risen to 6. One home in 10 had a television set; by 1977, it was 9 in 10. One in 8 had a telephone; by 1977, more than 1 in 2.

People with higher incomes enjoyed better diets. Each Briton consumed 29 ounces of meat weekly at the start of the reign, 35 ounces at the Jubilee. Health improved dramatically, thanks in part to a 46 percent increase in the number of doctors for each thousand people. Men could expect to live to sixty-nine, three years more than their fathers; women to seventy-five, four years more than their mothers. In 1952, 276 babies of each 10,000 born died in their first year; a generation later, infant mortality had been cut in half, to 139.

The rising tide of prosperity had lifted the poor as well as the rich. The number living below the poverty line fell from one fifth of the population in 1953–54 to one fortieth in 1973, an eightfold gain. To be sure, the poverty line — as defined in an authoritative work, *Poverty and Progress in Britain, 1953–1973,* by G. C. Fiegehen, P. S. Lansley and A. D. Smith — is not an over-generous standard, a weekly income for a couple of less than £13.83, or about $26 at the exchange rate prevailing at the end of 1977. But the point is that 10.6 million Britons earned less than this sum at the start of the reign; in twenty years, the number so deprived had shrunk to 1.3 million. These gains, moreover, did not come at the expense of the rich. Briton's poorest tenth earned about three fifths of the median or middle income in 1953–54; by 1971, they were still earning the same three fifths of the median. This is further confirmation that all incomes in the time of Elizabeth had risen but they were no more equally distributed.

Britain had become a cleaner, sunnier, brighter place in which to live. Thanks to greater output, the nation could afford to spend resources cleaning up rivers, lakes and the air. It did so, and the famous pea soup fog that had once been a London hallmark disappeared. In 1952, the sun peered through London's winter smog only 70 minutes each day; twenty-five years later, Londoners enjoyed 107 minutes of sunshine daily between December and March.

The smoke and chemical fumes of the Industrial Revolution had all but wiped out the English oaks that were once a glory of London. Fewer than a dozen survive in Hyde Park. But as the first crocuses appeared in the spring of 1978, the Ministry of the Environment made an announcement that would have delighted Chaucer. Some fifteen oaks were to be planted overlooking the Serpentine; five birch trees, five limes and five alders could now be placed elsewhere in Hyde Park. Within a century, spreading branches, heavy with leaves, would once again cover a landscape denuded by Dutch elm disease.

Pollution had destroyed every fish in the Thames. It took £100 million and twenty years to revive a river that had been pronounced chemically dead, gave off fearsome odors and provided a fertile breeding ground for rats. Now, biologists count ninety-one species that have returned, even the choosy salmon. Pregnant prawns have been discovered in the cleaner waters, proof that they are breeding. Only 9 mute swans were left a generation ago; in 1976, some 600 were counted, floating majestically in the waters.

A wealthier Britain could afford to, and did, spend more on the arts and take longer holidays. When the reign began, subsidies for opera, theater, concerts and other forms of expression and creation were £887,213; by 1977 this figure had jumped to £41.7 million, or about $80 million. Only 3 in 100 Britons took more than two weeks' holiday in 1952. By 1977, two in three were enjoying holidays of three weeks or more each year.

It is true that the air had become more sulfurous (emissions of sulfur dioxide rose from 4.74 tons a year to 5.11). But this was another if costly sign of increased affluence; the emissions came from the exhausts of autos. Their numbers had swollen from 1 in every 6 households to 3 in every 4.

To be sure, this more or less uninterrupted spurt in postwar prosperity was rudely halted in the last three years of Elizabeth's quarter century. From 1974 to 1977, national output either was stagnant or fell a little. Starting with the fourth quarter of 1974 up to the fourth quarter of 1977, the average Briton's command over goods and services — after he paid his taxes and took account of big price increases — had fallen about 5.7 percent. Britons as a whole were forced to tighten their belts a bit, cut their buying of holidays, cars, meat, clothing and everything else by about one twentieth. It was the first marked fall in living standards since the end of the war and provided some color of substance to the gloomy diagnoses of the conventional interpreters.

But few of them had troubled to examine what had happened in the larger world; they simply assumed that Britain's plight was unique. Even stranger, they ascribed it to the very forces and institutions that had been at work during the preceding quarter century of record prosperity.

For most of the industrial West, the 1974–77 period marked a sharp break with the postwar experience of ever-rising incomes. Every Western nation suffered much higher price increases and unemployment than it had known for more than a generation; growth rates were sluggish. The phenomenon was called stagflation, an awkward mating of stagnation with inflation. Britain simply became a heavily publicized example.*

Britain's plight was undoubtedly worse than that of most of its neighbors. Although unemployment was at nearly the same level as elsewhere in the West, inflation was much higher. For the OECD countries as a whole, prices had risen at a yearly rate of 10.6 percent after 1973 through most of 1977; in Britain inflation was almost twice as bad, 17.7 percent.

But Britain's more intense inflation could not be blamed on excessive welfare spending, burdensome taxes, lost empire or Red unions. It had to do quite simply with that misguided effort by Heath and Barber to lift Britain's growth rate — already high by British standards — to even higher levels by those huge increases in the money supply. Now, Britons were indeed living beyond their means. Real incomes per head rose 15.4 percent from 1971 to 1974, but output or the production to pay for this gained only 8.0 percent.

The bills came due when Wilson returned to power. For all the Labour party's fitful rhetoric about socialism, the Wilson government turned to the most orthodox of devices to cope with inflation. It began reducing government spending, curbing the growth in the money supply, limit-

---

* Experts still disagree over the causes of stagflation. Some even argue that the period after 1974 was merely marked by a series of unhappy "coincidences." An OECD study by eight outside experts insisted that no great structural change had taken place, that sky-high oil prices, poor harvests and rising commodity prices, reckless spending and monetary policies by governments, had all come together at once. So bad luck and nothing fundamental was to blame. The OECD report, ordered by member governments at the urging of Henry Kissinger, the U.S. secretary of state, now passes for the received wisdom. It is safe to assume, therefore, that it will soon be shown wrong and that something more profound has created the great change.

ing — with union assent — wage gains, cutting back on living standards. Deliberate, conscious restraint sliced that 5.7 percent off British incomes. Without revolutionary changes in Britain's system of private property, reliance on market forces and its policy of open trading with the world, Wilson had no choice. The alternative would have been massive controls — over trade, prices, wages, output and everything else. Wilson's left MPs urged just such a course. But only Tory politicians at election time believe that the Labour party in power ever takes socialism seriously.

By the end of 1977, the OECD's experts were forecasting, along with others, that Britain's time of travail was over, that inflation was coming down and production was going up. A resumption of rising living standards, the familiar postwar experience, once again appeared likely. Continuing world stagflation, however, probably meant that the pace of Britain's revived prosperity would be held back.

The single most important cause of the change in Britain's fortunes was a geological accident. The oil in the North Sea, the "cargo cult" as it had been termed, was flowing ashore in ever-greater and more visible quantities. Instead of paying out £3 billion in foreign exchange to import oil — the cost in 1975 — Britain was moving rapidly toward self-sufficiency by 1979 or 1980. In the 1980s, the country will produce all the oil it burns and sell a surplus abroad, perhaps at the very inflated prices that have done so much damage to Britain and other Western nations.

A Treasury study in the summer of 1976 concluded that the oil would add £1.05 billion to Britain's balance of payments in 1977, £5.4 billion by 1980 and £15.9 billion in 1985 — more than $30 billion in that one year alone. (A more recent report trims the payment gains for the mid-eighties. But it probably reflected the strategically modest forecasts of oil companies, desperately trying to keep oil in the sea to prop up the wild prices they were imposing.) This would be more than enough to pay off the debts Britain had contracted during its hardest times, wipe out any deficit in the trade accounts with other nations and leave Britain with a handsome surplus in its balance of payments during the 1980s at least.*

For at least a decade, then, the nation's perennial concern with a balance of payments deficit — Britons buying and investing more abroad than they sell — is likely to vanish. Instead of Britons hunting for scarce marks, yen, francs and other currencies to pay for imports of raw materials and other goods, foreigners will have to find pounds to pay for the British oil they buy. Britons will not be forced to bid up the prices of foreign currencies because they will nòt need as many; home-produced oil is paid for in pounds. As early as 1977, other nations were already bidding up the price of pounds, anticipating their future demand.

The oil-created surplus in the payments balance will have then two happy consequences for a lucky Britain. Governments in London will no longer be bound by the balance of payments constraint, by fear that the pursuit of policies to mop up unused resources of men and plants will create an alarming deficit in the foreign accounts and thus come to an abrupt stop. Governments of all complexion will be much freer to adopt expansionary tax and spending programs to put Britain back on its postwar growth path. At the same time, the pound will tend to rise against other currencies. Instead of the sinking spells of 1976 that a year later threatened the program of wage curbs, the pound should climb.

This will be a powerful tool in the fight against inflation. A falling pound meant Britons paid more for foreign food,

---

* The oil companies and other scoffers with a vested economic or ideological interest frequently dismiss North Sea oil as a "mortgaged asset." If they mean anything, they mean that the earnings from oil will be eaten up by Britain's debt repayment. This is nonsense. In 1977, the government's total foreign debt was $22.2 billion. Oil earnings from 1980 to 1985 alone are put at £37 billion, more than enough to burn the mortgage.

holidays, television sets, cars, iron ore, copper and everything else brought in from abroad. That meant the prices in pounds of these goods and services were rising and further adding to home-grown inflation. With a climbing pound, precisely the opposite will take place. The cost of foreign coffee, copper, iron ore, package holidays and everything else will decline for Britons. The import sector of Britain's cost of living — about one fourth of all goods and services — should be falling throughout the 1980s.

Of course, there is nothing certain about any of this. The oil is secure (although its price is not), but a revival of reckless money supply policies, a wild explosion of domestic prices or wages, could undo oil's useful effects. A home-produced inflation could make exports of British goods and services so expensive that the surpluses generated by oil are wiped out. But there is no underlying cause, either in Britain's history, social structure or pattern of spending and taxes, to predict such a dismal outcome.

The central point is clear: Britain has, in terms of its own past, enjoyed unprecedented prosperity in the postwar era. As in the rest of the industrial world, good times were rudely shattered after the 1973 oil price increase. Indeed, due to some home-grown folly, Britain suffered more than most. But by the end of 1977, thanks largely to union wage restraint and geological chance, the prospects for resumed prosperity were better in Britain than in most other advanced countries.

What then have the pathologists been talking about? Are they writing in a world totally divorced from reality? If Britain is so well off, why do so many voices — in the United States, CBS, *Time* magazine, *The New York Times,* Harvard scholars, a Nobel laureate; in Britain, an ambassador to Washington, editors of *The Times* and *Sunday Telegraph,* certified intellectuals of the left, right and center — all sound like mourners at a wake? The answer is far from clear. But a

combination of herd instinct and ideological blinkers —
tinted red or blue — can lead the most distinguished flocks
astray.

If the Cassandras are talking about anything at all, it is
that slippery concept of *relative* growth and prosperity, not
absolute levels.

There is no doubt that compared to other nations Britain
is far less wealthy and powerful than it was fifty or a hundred years ago. Britain's wealth and income have risen;
those of others have risen faster. Britons are better off compared to their fathers, grandfathers and great-grandfathers.
Their neighbors and allies in Western Europe and the
United States are even better off. The National Institute of
Economic and Social Research — an organization enjoying
much the same esteem and some of the same links to government as the Brookings Institution in Washington — has prepared some instructive comparisons. At the turn of the
century, Germany's total output per head of population was
only 64 percent of Britain's. After the devastation of World
War II, the British lead was virtually unchanged. But by
1973, even after a generation of rising British incomes, German output had raced ahead by nearly 30 percent.* For
France, the comparison is almost as dramatic. In 1950,
French output per person was 17 percent behind Britain's.
By 1973, it was 32 percent ahead. Most startling of all was
the rise of Italy. A Briton produced three times as much as

---

* All these numbers are slippery since they must be equated through exchange
rates. So, when the purchasing power of the pound is undervalued more than
the mark, the differences between British and German living standards are
exaggerated. If the current rate is 4 marks equals 1 pound, then an income of
£5000 would seem to be the equivalent of 20,000 DM. In fact, German prices
for the same goods and services a householder buys in Britain are relatively
higher. Thus the £5000 will command more real income than 20,000 DM,
making the official comparisons of per capita income misleading. In April
1977, Robin Marris calculated that the prevailing exchange rates exaggerated
Germany's per capita income — compared to that of the United States — by
25 percent and understated Britain's by 20 percent.

an Italian in 1900. By 1973, and despite the great gains registered in Britain, the Italians had drawn even.

In those splendid twenty-five years of Elizabeth's reign, when Britain was expanding its output by 2.6 percent a year, the Italians were growing by 4.6 percent, the Germans by 4.8 percent and the French by 4.7 percent. Britons got richer; their neighbors got richer faster. That is the hard core of fact in the layers of gloom produced in the popular pulpits.

Growth and Its Sources

Why some nations grow faster than others — even when they are at roughly similar levels of culture and industrial development — is one of the most discussed and least understood questions in economics. Inevitably, economists seek answers in economic causes — these are the things they know about — but at best they produce partial and unsatisfactory replies. Perhaps the most careful attempt to measure the economic causes of economic growth was made by Edward Denison for the Brookings Institution in 1967. By then, it was apparent that Britain's postwar growth rate was lower than its neighbors' and Denison's work helped explain why. He attempted to determine just how much had been contributed to European economies by an array of separate factors — investment in new plants, increasing the number of workers, shifting inefficient peasants to more productive factories, transferring owners of inefficient one-man shops to large concerns.

"The distinctive feature of the growth experience of the United Kingdom," Denison wrote, "was the small size relative to other European countries, of gains from economies of scale." Translated into less formidable terms, Britain did not grow as fast as the others because it had fewer farmers to put into auto plants and its one-man shop owners were unwilling to trade the joy of being their own boss for the higher incomes of steel mills. Both these factors in turn meant that Britain's home markets did not grow as fast as those of its neighbors. The domestic demand for steel, autos, chemicals and the rest did not jump by leaps and bounds but at a more sedate pace. That meant Britain's steel, auto and chemical plants did not enjoy the same economies of scale, the same gains in efficiency and output, as those of the more rapidly expanding Germans, French and Italians.*

It now appears — at least according to Denison — that much of the postwar miracle in Germany, France, Italy (and also Japan) rested on a very simple historical fact. Britain had been undergoing a revolution in agriculture since the seventeenth century. Over the centuries, men and women had slowly drifted from countryside to urban areas, driven by enclosure acts that wiped out free grazing lands, drawn by the lure of higher factory wages. This adds to income and growth, at least as economists count it. A farmer who clings to his small plot may add only $1000 a year to the national product. By moving to a car plant, he could produce $3000 in added value, thereby enlarging the national product and speeding its growth.

Inefficient farmers have clung to the land (like shop-owners, some apparently prefer lower incomes and what they regard as a healthier life) more persistently on the Continent than in Britain. This is why the European Common

---

* Denison measured the contribution of each factor to the rise in national income from 1950 to 1964 and came up with these results: For Britain, the gain from farmers moving to factories added only 3 percent, the decline in one-man shops 2 percent and "economies of scale" from larger home markets, 15 percent. Altogether, these accounted for only 17 percent of the gains in British income. For Germany, however, the farm-to-factory shift created no less than 10 percent of the big gains in German income, the decline in the self-employed 2 percent and economics of scale a handsome 22 percent. Together, they made up 34 percent of Germany's large leap forward. In France, the force of these factors was even more startling: 14 percent for the flight from rural poverty, 5 percent from the shrinkage of small stores and 21 percent for economies of scale. Together, the three added up to 40 percent of the handsome French advance.

Market is such a lopsided affair. There are still enough farmers in Europe to compel consumers to provide large subsidies through rigged prices to bolster farm incomes.

Britain long ago used up the productive slack in its farm population; inefficient farmers had gone to the towns. But for most of the postwar period, and even today, France, Germany and Italy could and do tap a reservoir of underused resources, moving farm workers to city plants.

As Denison observed, from 1950 to 1962, the share of farm jobs in Britain's employment dropped a negligible 1.5 percent. This small shift could contribute little to Britain's slower rate of growth. But in Germany, farm jobs shrunk nearly eight times as rapidly, 11.6 percent; in France, the shift was 9.3 percent; in Italy, it was 14 percent. Even in the United States, which enjoyed higher growth rates than Britain's but lower than those on the Continent, farm jobs as a share of total employment declined by 4.7 percent.

But Denison was unsatisfied with the conclusions drawn from his own elaborate statistics. He suspected that even when the last possible Continental farmer and shopkeeper had moved into more "productive" factories, Britain would still grow more slowly. Somehow, its men and plants are less efficient.

Here his statistical inquiries ran into a dead end. He was reduced to explaining the slower British growth rate by "unaggressive management, labor resistance to change, and restrictive practices." All this, said Denison, "suggests that it must be a condition of long standing." If British growth rates are to match those on the Continent, "it requires a change of attitudes, practices and habits that is not readily made." Attitudes, practices and habits, in turn, suggest a work culture, a work ethic, something that can't be explained by tax or welfare legislation. It is also something that warrants more inquiry than Denison's statistical techniques will allow.

British industry, it is said, has been caught and overtaken

by the American, German, French and even Italian because British businessmen will not put enough money into new tools and factories. On the right, it is argued, British entrepreneurs and corporations are victimized by those familiar demons — lavish welfare spending, onerous taxes, radical and strike-mad unions. The executives lack both the cash and the incentive to build modern plants. On the left, the demonology is simpler: grasping capitalists salt away huge profits in yachts, girls, jewels and sunny seaside villas at exotic tax havens. They invest abroad but not at home.

Once again, however, the statistics puncture the popular wisdom. The fact is that Britain has enjoyed an investment boom in the postwar period. The funds spent in forming fixed capital have been rising steadily for a generation, both in absolute terms and as a share of total output. A table prepared by the National Institute of Economic and Social Research shows that the share of output devoted to fixed investment was an unimpressive 6 to 10 percent from the high Victorian period until the 1929 boom. During the Great Depression, investment was at a peak of 10 percent. By 1950, it had risen to 14.5 percent. Ten years later, it climbed to 18.3 percent, reached 20.5 percent in 1965, 21.5 percent in 1970 and 21.8 percent in 1975.*

In other words, present levels of investment are three times where they were in the late nineteenth and early twentieth centuries and twice those of the prewar period. Moreover, those levels are growing shares of an ever-expanding total output.

Lack of investment, then, will not explain why Britain has fallen behind the *pace* of others; the country has plowed back

---

* The NIESR table includes investment in housing as well as in plants and machinery. But the institute's experts say that if housing was subtracted, the trend of business investment over the past century would not be affected. The remaining NIESR calculations for fixed capital formation as a share of gross national product are: 1870, 5.0; 1875, 8.9; 1880, 7.4; 1885, 6.3; 1890, 6.1; 1895, 6.5; 1900, 10.3; 1905, 8.7; 1910, 6.1; 1914, 6.2; 1920, 8.2; 1925, 9.4; 1930, 9.8; 1935, 9.9; 1955, 16.7.

an ever-increasing share of its growing income into plants and machines.

A subtler and more plausible explanation may lie in the quality rather than in the quantity of investment. An executive who builds a badly designed plant for the wrong market and equips it with inefficient machines will certainly increase investment. But he won't do much to expand output. There is more than a strong suspicion that British businessmen are less skillful than their counterparts elsewhere, although neither the conventional right nor left has much interest in saying so. Just as it is difficult to describe with any precision what an executive does, so too it is extremely difficult to measure his performance.

One clue to the quality of British investment can be gleaned from what economists call the "incremental capital-output ratio." In plainer terms, this tells us how much extra production is generated from an extra slice of investment. If a widget manufacturer spends another $1000 on a tool to produce an extra $500 of goods a year, his capital-output ratio is 2. If he must spend $1500 to get that $500, his ratio is 3. The higher the ratio, the less efficient the capital, the less productive its quality.

Once again, the Confederation of British Industry has produced a useful comparison, this time of capital-output ratios in seven countries. The CBI looked at manufacturing for 1963–73 and found that any German or U.S. outlay yielded nearly 3 times as much production as the same British investment. Japanese and Italian investment was about 2.5 times more fruitful, the French 2 times as productive, the Swedes 1.6. This is a strong hint that British investment, however expansive, is mismanaged. The slower British pace of economic growth appears to have much more to do with the quality of Britain's corporate managers than with any lack of outlays.

The famous CBS image, a mill built in 1870, is entertaining but inaccurate. John Kenneth Galbraith's portrait in

The Age of Uncertainty, of a headless corporation making heedless decisions, is much nearer the mark.

Such a view is not widely held. The conventional wisdom — to use Galbraith's splendid Veblenesque phrase — holds that if personal characteristics account for Britain's slow growth, only those of workers matter. They cling to unneeded jobs, take long tea breaks, toil at a slow pace and — unlike Japanese, Germans or Americans — simply don't put their backs into it. All this may be true. But shrewd students of U.S. labor relations have long understood that every trade union takes its character and shape from the management with which it deals. In the United States, tough Henry Ford employing hoodlums to break unions forged the militant United Auto Workers in the 1930s. A more rational, unsentimental generation of executives followed, and the UAW turned into an equally rational, unsentimental union. In the jungle world of trucking, strong-arm businessmen employ tactics mistakenly associated with the "underworld." Unsurprisingly, the International Brotherhood of Teamsters is run by a hierarchy given to the same values. Firms in the steel industry accommodate each other on prices, foreign competition and much more; they enjoy accommodating relationships with a union that is troublesome only when the rank and file try to thrust forward an unsanctioned leader.

This insight applies to Britain. A British Leyland is plagued by walkouts, low productivity and defective workmanship; its top managers are so notoriously inept that they are regularly and frequently dismissed. One Leyland official complains anonymously in print, "The inertia at the top manifests itself in a lack of decision and a lack of direction." The press and composing rooms of Fleet Street provide another sterling example of obstinate labor relations and obsolete work performance; newspaper proprietors have typically been amateur businessmen, as much interested in power and prestige as in profits. Commercial television, on the other hand, while no more strike-free than any enterprise, shows another face of the model. Its employees are skilled, hard-working and mostly gain some satisfaction from what they do; the managers of the independent companies demonstrate they know what they are doing too. Regard the handsome profits they accumulate.

If British workers as a whole, then, are not very energetic, it is likely that British managers are not either. Here, one can only rely on impressions. The cold evidence is lacking, but the impressions are strong. The executive rush hour in London begins well after 9:30 A.M. It is then that Park Lane, Piccadilly and other important thoroughfares are choked with Daimlers, Jaguars, Bentleys and the like. (Of course not a minute is wasted; the executive in the rear of the car can almost always be seen leafing through his *Financial Times*.) The homeward flow westward to Belgravia, Surrey and other executive haunts begins building up at 4:30 P.M. An hour later, the only executive cars on the road are those bound for some social engagement (where of course "contacts" will be made, as the expense accounts and tax returns testify). Some managers no doubt extract the most from this not overly onerous day by eating a sandwich lunch at their desks. This, however, is much more a U.S. than a British practice. More likely, the executive takes a leisurely midday break, in his company's paneled executive dining room, in a well-appointed club or at a restaurant whose high prices would be insupportable if it were not for the generosity of tax collectors and expense accounts.

Happily, there does exist more objective evidence to suggest that, however intensely they may or may not work, British managers are drawn from society's less-equipped members. The best and the brightest British graduates rarely go into industry. They flock to the law, investment banking, the BBC and independent television, *The Sunday Times* and the *Financial Times*, the theater, book publishing, the Treasury and the Foreign Office. A 1977 study of the

Foreign Office by the prime minister's "think tank," the Central Policy Review Staff, actually complained that "the work is being done to an unjustifiably high standard" and "recommended that the Service should recruit a smaller proportion of the ablest candidates."

Peter Jay, described by *Time* and other authorities as one of the most promising men of his generation, is archetypal. After graduating from Oxford with an honors degree in economics, Jay took his talent first to the Treasury for six years, then divided his time between Fleet Street and commercial television. From there, it might be said that he has enjoyed a meteoric career in the Foreign Office, landing the post of ambassador to Washington as an entry position.

Only about one university graduate in eight chooses industry. For Oxford and Cambridge, the elite schools, the ratio is even smaller, one in eleven. At Cambridge in 1975, for every three who went into industry, one entered publishing, journalism, entertainment or some other cultural pursuit. At Oxford, industry claimed only four times as many graduates as commercial culture. For the universities as a whole, however, the ratio was eighteen to industry for one in culture. These figures do not count the large number who went into teaching. They simply illustrate that even business-minded Oxbridge graduates seek jobs outside industry and in the lively arts.

The reason for this is disputable. It is usually attributed to a snobbish disdain for grubby moneymaking. But the striking change in the class composition of British universities since the war, the rising share drawn especially from middle-class and to a lesser extent working-class homes, shakes this idea. Moreover, a substantial number of Oxbridge graduates do enter law and merchant or investment banking. This strongly suggests that even products of these ancient institutions are not immune to the lure of money.

A more refined version of the snob theory holds that educated Britons prefer making money to things, that merchant banking has status but engineers barely rank above plumbers. It is true that British university students traditionally flocked to the arts, the humanities and the social sciences while places in engineering and the natural sciences went vacant. (The stagflation that began in 1974, however, changed things; three years later, all the engineering and science places were filled by job-minded students.) But it is not clear that Brunel, the great builder, is valued less than Baring, the banker; that Sassoon, the financier, is esteemed more than Stephenson, the railway pioneer. Mathematics is difficult for many and this, as much as status, could have accounted for the unpopularity of engineering and science.

What is undeniable is that engineers rarely run large British corporations, that top executives come from law, accountancy, marketing and the like. Britain's management does not welcome high-powered university talent, neither the few engineers nor the more numerous generalists. Quite right too. The thrusting competition of trained young men might upset the executives' comfortable ways. The daily routine could become a lot harsher if new men capable of increasing incremental capital-output ratios invaded paneled boardrooms.

Just how this comfortable managerial life has been achieved is a question rarely discussed in Britain. The textbooks tell us that a comfortable and inefficient firm will either reform or go under because of pressure from its competitors. The unproductive will lose out to the more productive; the jungle world of competition will enable only the fittest to survive. Adam Smith's invisible hand, encouraging each to pursue his own interest, will create the maximum efficiency and wealth.

In Britain, however, industry lives by the adage that competition is the life of trade and the death of business, a sentiment nurtured by the captive colonial markets of the past. The plain and seldom-noticed fact is that British manufacturers and their executives are uniquely free from competi-

tive pressure and probably enjoy the most highly concentrated markets in the developed world. (The Common
Market, supposedly a free trading bloc, does not greatly affect the position. Firms in France, Germany and elsewhere
may be more energetic than Britain's but their competition
is sharply circumscribed. A network of formal and informal
devices bends the Market's free trade rules and saves British
concerns from the full rigor of foreign competition. This too
is worth a second look.)

Several commentators — serious ones like Denison and
self-interested ones like the Hudson Institute — have com-
mented on the lack of "aggressiveness" in British firms. But
if I am sheltered from competition, I am not compelled to be
aggressive. I rather like things as they are.

Nearly all large firms, of course, seek a quiet, monopolistic
life. A large firm is a bureaucracy and bureaucrats, government or private, prefer security to risk. Typically, throughout the West — in France, Germany, the United States
—any particular industry will be characterized by quasi-monopoly or "oligopoly," as the economists call it. Three or
four companies will control the bulk of the output. In the
United States autos are dominated by General Motors and
Ford; General Electric and Westinghouse divide up most
electrical machinery. Theirs is a genteel competition,
one that seldom involves price-cutting and aims at preserving market shares.

In the United States, of course, it is illegal for this handful
of "competitors" to sit down and fix prices or carve up markets — at least openly. Elsewhere in Europe and above all in
Japan, a more advanced view is taken of such behavior.
During much of 1977, for example, a major Common Market effort was directed at protecting the big steel companies
in the nine countries from engaging in anything so reckless
as price competition.

British industry appears to have carried this art further
than most, absorbing competitors to achieve an untroubled

life. It is difficult to compare concentration — the absence
of competition — among several countries, but a few scholars have tried. One pair, Leslie Hannah and J. A. Kay, calculates that at the start of the twentieth century, Britain's
hundred largest manufacturing firms accounted for 15 percent of all the value added by industry as a whole. Today,
the top hundred control nearly 50 percent and their share
has been rising steadily since the war. Thanks to "negligible
legal restrictions" inhibiting the merger or takeover of competing firms, Britain "has achieved increases in and levels of
concentration which are the highest among developed countries." So say Hannah and Kay.

S. J. Prais, another student of the phenomenon, comes up
with similar results. The top hundred manufacturers, he
calculates, claimed 16 percent of all manufacturing output
in 1909. By 1970, their share had grown to 41 percent. In
contrast, Prais puts the share of the top hundred U.S. manufacturers at only 33 percent and it appears to have stopped
rising, even during the big merger period of the 1960s. Prais
estimates the control of the industrial elite in Germany to be
just two-thirds that of Britain.

A Common Market survey limited to six major industries
concludes that only France is as monopolized as Britain. In
both countries, the four biggest concerns in each industry
account for no less than 79 percent of all the business. In
contrast, the top four Italian companies collect 66 percent
and the Germans 52 percent.

Prais, however, acknowledges that computing concentration for German and French industry is a somewhat misleading exercise. In both countries, a handful of banks hold
the controlling shares in many firms in many sectors. So
counting the output share of the big industrial corporations
alone understates the real degree of concentration. It is
quite possible that Germany, France and Japan are more
cartelized even than Britain.

Whether or not Britain is more or less cartelized than

others, the conclusion is clear. A relatively small number of firms control manufacturing. More and more industry falls into fewer and fewer hands. Whatever this does or does not do for the economy, it helps assure British managers an untroubled sleep.

Alfred Marshall, the father of modern economics, saw the process at work at the turn of the century. The wise Marshall said: "There are but few exceptions to the rule, that large private firms . . . are . . . inferior to private business of a moderate size in that energy and resource, that restlessness and inventive power, which leads to the striking out of new paths."

One of Marshall's lineal descendants, Sir John Hicks, caustically noted, "The best of all monopoly profits is a quiet life."

A highly concentrated economy, one with fewer and fewer firms producing more and more of total output, is, as Hannah and Kay observed, an open invitation to government intervention. Any government can let a small and inefficient firm go bust; the social damage is limited. But Edward Heath, the Conservative, had to eat his own words — he had promised to spurn "lame ducks" — and rescued both the collapsing Rolls-Royce engine company and the Upper Clyde shipyard in Glasgow. They were too big to go to the wall. Americans who recall their government's safety nets for Penn Central and Lockheed will appreciate Heath's dilemma. In much the same way (although with less ideological *Angst*), Labour preserved from its own folly the costly Chrysler car company, shipbuilders and much more. The economics may be dubious but the social and political consequences are compelling. The sudden, concentrated loss of employment in one area from the collapse of a big firm is too much to tolerate.

The effects on British managers of an increasingly protected life do not recommend themselves to anyone trained in classical economics. "Careerism and patronage" flourish;

"economic arteries harden . . . independent centers of initiative" disappear, say Hannah and Kay.

For executives, however, concentration offers a secure existence. It would be unfair, no doubt, to call it a well-paid and extended tea break. But it is reasonable to assume that this life will persuade the brighter, more ambitious graduates of Oxford and Cambridge to continue avoiding industry in large numbers; it is also reasonable to assume that industrial workers will seek some of the cozy security enjoyed by their protected bosses.

The Workers' Response

The notion that the work styles of Britain's blue-collar force are modeled on those of their bosses may bring outraged cries in London boardrooms. Men who according to their income tax returns think solely of business — even at company-paid outings to nightclubs, country clubs and restaurants — do not like any suggestion that these are perquisites of office rather than tools for work. It may even be true that British workers need no model. At any rate, the incontrovertible fact is that British factory workers are far less productive than those elsewhere in the industrial world.

It has long been an article of faith in the union movement and on the left that the low levels of British productivity flow exclusively from industrialists who refuse to equip the men with modern tools. The evidence, however, is otherwise.

Eltis and Bacon, the Oxford pair who worry about the rise in jobs outside plants, made a careful study of machine tools in Britain and the United States in 1974. They concluded that, on the average, these crucial tools to make tools were kept in service no longer in Britain than in the modernizing United States. They found, as our earlier look at investment in general would suggest, that Britain increased outlays for the most modern machines as rapidly as did the United

States. Even the U.S. lead in advanced, computerized, numerically controlled machine tools was only three years. Nevertheless, each American worker produced two to three times as much as his British counterpart. The U.S. machines were usually no newer or more numerous; the British simply employ more men to man them and run them fewer hours. (This should have led Bacon and Eltis to attribute Britain's lower growth to less intensive use of labor, not a declining plant force. The two scholars demonstrate how to get lost leaping from the particular to the general.)

Prime Minister Wilson's think tank reinforced this finding a year later with a long look at Britain's troubled car industry. "With the same power at his elbow and doing the same job as his continental counterpart," the Central Policy Review Staff wrote, "a British car assembly worker produces only half as much output per shift." Just as in machine tools, a Leyland auto worker may be as well equipped as his colleague at Fiat, Renault or Volkswagen. But the Leyland man will still turn out only one car for every two they make. In all, Britain actually produces 5 cars per worker each year. The U.S. level is 15, Germany and France, 7, and Japan, 12.

The single biggest reason, the think tank said, was "overmanning." On the British line, three men or more are at work for every two abroad. The British assembly line, moreover, moves at a slower pace. Men are not stretched as they are in Turin, Detroit or Wolfsburg. Poor maintenance, shortages of material and strikes also contribute. "Inadequate capital equipment is only a minor cause of low productivity," the report said. What really matters are the extra numbers working and their relatively relaxed pace.

The picture in these industries — machine tools and cars — is reflected in every other manufacturing sector. The National Institute examined how British industry was faring in 1970 compared to that in Common Market countries. Almost invariably, efficiency, or the value added by each plant worker, was lower in Britain than anywhere else. In food, drink and tobacco, for example, French workers produced 97 percent more than the British; Germans, 53 percent; Italians, 20 percent; the Dutch, 84 percent; and the Belgians, 63 percent. The Dutch were the most productive chemicals producers, 88 percent more than the British; Italy was at the bottom of the Continental list, still 33 percent ahead of Britain. Indeed, the British trailed all five Continental partners in all six industrial subsectors with only two exceptions. The British were more efficient than the Italians in textiles and in manufacturing a miscellany of building materials.

Britain's consistently low productivity — the physical volume of goods that a worker produces in a given period of time — is both measurable and indisputable. Perhaps the most dramatic illustration of the nation's easy work style came when Heath ordered industry on to a three-day week. To the surprise of some, this made barely a dent in total production. During the three months of reduced hours of work, output from factories fell only 6 percent. If these factories had been working at an efficient pace before Heath's order, production would have fallen two fifths, or 40 percent. It was nothing like that; rather, it was a remarkable demonstration that Britain's plants normally do three days' work in five.*

Why do British workers strain less than their counterparts in Europe and the United States? Why do they insist on tending a machine with three workers when two will do the job? Why do assembly lines move more slowly and machines run fewer hours?

---

* The difference between the expected drop of 40 percent and the actual drop of 6 percent somewhat exaggerates the slack. Many firms, particularly small ones, ignored Heath's order and worked with lights and power for a full five days. Others found that even in the bleak winter they could get some production on powerless days. All benefited from the well-known "Hawthorne" effect. The exciting change in working conditions, the sense of shared adventure, spurred an extra effort. But in general it can be said that workers determined to earn five days' pay in three days of work found they could do so.

Neither statistics nor economics will answer such questions. Like many interesting questions in economics — rapid development in China, stagnation in India, for example — a discipline that assumes material carrot and material stick are the sole motives moving men is far too simple-minded for practical use. But we have seen how businessmen enjoy the cozy, uncompetitive life — if they extract pecuniary monopoly profits, so much the better — because they find it more agreeable than hard work. There is no reason to think British workers are very different. They too enjoy a quiet life and do not want it disturbed. The lure of higher pay, a greater command over goods and services, is not irresistible to all people everywhere at all times. Particularly if it involves effort.

It is often said that British workers refuse to give up unneeded jobs because they have been scarred psychically by the drastic unemployment of the 1930s. This may contribute to their attitude but it does not explain the differences. Depression unemployment in Germany and the United States was much worse; German and American workers, however, are much more willing to give up an obsolete or overmanned job.

Another common explanation holds that Britain is a uniquely class-conscious society, that its workers and owners have more of a sense of separate and hostile identity than those of more democratic America — or of Germany, France and Italy. If this were so, then we might expect that British workers would get their own back at the hated bosses by shirking on the job. The trouble is that we should then also expect more strikes in Britain than in the United States and Italy. But the reverse is true. Similarly, the Communist vote should be higher in Britain than on the Continent. But it is in fact far lower.

In a thoughtful essay, "Britain at Work," *The Economist* tried to break down the elements of "class structure" that might account for part of the nation's low productivity. The paper observed that Britain's blue-collar workers punch a time clock; white-collar and executive types do not. Blue-collar workers whose skill does not improve must look forward to a more or less constant income over their lives; others expect promotion regardless of skill. Compared to managers, blue-collar workers get shorter holidays, eat in more Spartan company cafeterias, wash in separate lavatories and will never get a company-paid car.

All these things are undoubtedly true and may diminish a factory worker's appetite for work. But precisely the same differences are maintained in supposedly classless America, Germany, France, Italy and even Sweden.

At best, we can make a tentative guess, based on daily observation. Britons, to the dismay of the textbook writers, appear to be *satisficing* rather than *optimizing*. Workers and managers do not seek the greatest possible income; they seek instead an adequate or satisfactory level of income. They prefer tea breaks and long executive lunches, slower assembly lines and longer weekends, to strenuous effort for higher incomes.

This to be sure is a sweeping generalization that obviously does not apply to all Britons. It does not embrace stock market speculators like Jim Slater, who quickly made (and almost as quickly lost) a fortune through rigging share prices. It does not include Freddie Laker, a working-class boy who made a small fortune buying and selling war surplus materials, a larger fortune with one private airline and who is well on his way to a third with still another (which is giving fits to the international cartel because it competes with price cuts). It does not cover Britain's keen-eyed soccer and cricket stars, leaving the country for richer rewards elsewhere. It does not speak for the occasional worker disciplined by his union for trying to speed up the pace of work.

Above all, it does not describe countless craftsmen and artists, professionals and artisans, who enjoy their work. It cannot account for writers, makers of television or movie films, doctors, scholars, those who work in the theater, paint pictures, design buildings or jewelry, toil in laboratories, make cabinets or leather goods, attend the House of Commons after midnight, direct great departments or their own private enterprises — those for whom work is a joyful, creative form of expression, for whom pecuniary reward is a necessary but less than all-consuming motive. The preference for leisure over goods applies chiefly to those toiling in mines or on assembly lines, laboring at routine tasks in huge white-collar bureaucracies, public and private. Their work does not, cannot enlarge personality; quite the contrary. It diminishes it. They work because they must, to earn enough to support themselves and their families. It is these workers who have decided that there are limits to how long and hard they will labor for extra goods. This conclusion is supported by everyday experience as well as by the indirect statistical evidence.*

Britons, in short, appear to be the first citizens of the post-industrial age who are choosing leisure over goods on a large scale. Of course, almost everyone everywhere all the time would welcome extra income, command over more goods and services. Britons have not renounced material things. But many appear to have arrived at a level of income at which they regard the extra effort to obtain the extra income as not worthwhile. They prefer the slower pace, the under-worked style, to a more painful expenditure of energy that yields some extra income. In economic terms, many have reached that point where the marginal cost of extra effort just equals the marginal return in the form of more income.

---

* My favorite example came one Sunday when six busy Fleet Street editors and union executives plus one less-pressed foreign correspondent were taken three and a half hours by train to Manchester to record a television discussion shown nationally later that night. We were put to the long journey because no technical crews could be found in London willing to give up their Sunday joint or public house beers for the modest premium rates the BBC would have paid.

This, as every first-year student of economics knows, is a point of equlibrium.

British Leyland offers its car workers in Solihull an extra £13 or $25 a week, another 19 percent, to work a night shift. The workers flatly reject it because, as a spokesman said, "we feel we have a right to be at home with our families especially where marriages are under pressure."

A Cambridge study interviews managers who have worked in both Britain and the United States. These executives agree that American workers are far more likely to seek overtime to buy a second television set or to earn the down payment on a bigger house; the British worker, in a state-subsidized council flat or house, is satisfied with it and his lone color TV.

Now too we can assess the commentators more fully. Britain, of course, is not a sick but a more or less affluent society. It does grow more slowly than all other industrial countries and there is every reason to believe this trend will continue. It means that Britons will get richer, although not as rapidly as Americans, Dutch, Germans, French, Italians, Scandinavians and others.

This relatively slower growth is not the result of an excessive welfare or tax burden, not the dismal product of any equalizing of incomes, not the penalty imposed by militant, leftist unions or a bitter class struggle. It reflects an attitude, a life-style, a choice. It is a preference, at a historically high level of income, for leisure over goods.

Why this preference should appear in Britain before any other industrial country is not clear. It may prove as hard to answer as that perennial exam question, Why did the Industrial Revolution come to Britain first? Perhaps the two are related.

Most foreign observers are struck with (and sometimes irritated by) the generally relaxed manner of Britons. Ralf Dahrendorf, the German sociologist and director of the London School of Economics, who likes it, traces it first to "the fact that Britain is essentially at one with its history."

The country has never been torn apart by prolonged, bloody class revolution; its rulers have accommodated themselves to change and reform. It has never suffered the shame of invasion and betrayal (at least since 1066); after discrimination against Catholics ended early in the nineteenth century, neither the state nor society as a whole has openly persecuted a minority group. Britain has a conscious, quietly confident sense of identity. Most of its people seem to feel less need than others to demonstrate superiority in the production of cars, missiles, steel ingots, widgets.

This ease with one's own history lies behind a preference and respect for evolutionary change. Few Britons like abrupt changes, sharp breaks with the past. This attitude does not block change, does not make society immobile. But it surely favors gradual change. The Industrial Revolution, after all, took place over decades. Unlike most revolutions, it did not confront one set of armed citizens with another. It was British in character.

Few Britons would join the cult of zero growth; like others in the postwar Western world, most want and expect ever-higher levels of income, an increasing stream of goods and services. But Britons have also reached a collective, barely conscious decision on how much extra effort they will invest in the pursuit of more things.

Foreigners inevitably remark on British politeness. There is violence and crime in Britain as in every modern society. Race tension, another subject worth examining, breeds ugly clashes in London as well as in New York or Detroit. But on the whole Britons seem gentler, more relaxed, "unaggressive," as Denison put it. Whether this quality is a cause or an effect of the preference for leisure over goods, it exists. London, by some accounts, is the last livable great city. Productivity is higher in New York, Dusseldorf, Paris and Stockholm. There is a nervous intensity in these towns;

crowds hustle along city streets, heads down, businesslike. People in London streets tend to amble, look around, move more slowly. This hurts the growth rate but it may ease the psyche. "*Angst*" is a German, not a British, word. It is noteworthy that in the summer of 1977, the top ten sellers on the German nonfiction list all dealt with problems of health and one popular book was titled *How to Protect Yourself from Pressure to Perform.* It wouldn't find a market in Britain.

British justice can be as arbitrary and mean-spirited as anywhere else; judges are fallible and typically come from a class that better understands businessmen than workers. But British society, perhaps because it has been led so often by intelligent conservatives, values fair play and justice to a remarkable degree. It is a quality that in Western Europe is also visible in Holland, Norway, Denmark and Sweden, four Anglophile countries. The welfare state is one expression of a sense of justice. Unsurprisingly, it was given a strong and early definition in a British report. Britain is still a long way from equalizing either opportunity or income. But it has pioneered the belief that society has a responsibility for its more helpless members. This too retards productivity rates in manufacturing but appears to make life more tolerable.

Indeed, Britain is a very stable society. It has left and right fringes, but they play only insignificant roles. Britain is a society more or less at peace with itself, generally orderly, generally tolerant, more or less humane. If people worked harder, would these qualities be threatened?

The preference for leisure over goods can be measured in several ways. Cleaning the air and rivers imposes a cost on society, one that is borne either by manufacturers who must invest in new antipollution devices or by citizens who pay taxes to subsidize their introduction. No marketable goods are produced from this outlay. But the quality of leisure has been enhanced.

Similarly, the British have chosen to spend more and more on the arts. The results have been astonishing — a new Eliz-

abethan age at least in performance. Tom Stoppard and
Harold Pinter are not Shakespeare and Marlowe. Nevertheless, the heavily subsidized National Theatre, which frequently presents their work, is the envy of the Western
world. Along with the state-supported Royal Shakespeare
Company, it gives a lead to the to the commercial theater.
Taken as a whole, the London stage is the acknowledged
world capital for drama.

More of society's income has been drawn from electronics
and coal mines to encourage music. London alone boasts
five world-class symphony orchestras, all receiving state
funds (the BBC Symphony Orchestra, supported by license
fees on television sets; and the London Philharmonic, London Symphony, Philharmonia and Royal Philharmonic,
which gets Arts Council grants).*

There are two or more concerts in London on any given
night for each one in Vienna. The Covent Garden Opera
receives state funds; so too does the National Portrait Gallery, the Tate, the Victoria and Albert and other museums.
The money could have been invested to increase productivity in chemicals or shipbuilding; British society, through the
budgets adopted by elected governments, has chosen
otherwise.

Indeed, there may even be some indirect economic benefits from the collective decision for leisure over goods. Apart
from oil, as we have seen, the fastest growing component in
Britain's balance of payments is tourism. There were 8.8
million tourists in 1975, 10.1 million in 1976 and an estimated 11.4 million in 1977. They spent £2.2 billion in 1976,
enough to rank as Britain's sixth export industry; for 1977,

---

* Public generosity for the arts in Britain, however, is constrained by the preference for leisure over goods. The combined budgets of the four symphonies
aided by the Arts Council in 1975–76 just about equaled the sum spent by the
Berlin Philharmonic, whose musicians receive two and three times the pay of
their London colleagues. The Arts Council subsidy amounted to 15 percent of
the budget for the London four; Berlin got 72 percent of its funds from a
richer state.

their outlays probably reached £3 billion, or nearly $6 billion, a gain of more than a third. That pays for a lot of imported food and raw materials.

The tourists were drawn, of course, by many things, most notably by an undervalued pound that made British prices seem cheap to citizens of Copenhagen, Frankfurt, Paris and Des Moines. But it would be surprising if they were not also drawn, at least in part, by the British civility, sense of fair play, unhurried style, as well as the splendid music, theater and galleries. The choice of leisure over goods may yield rewards in that most competitive of markets, the struggle for tourist exchange. As other industrial nations rise to ever-higher levels of income, there is every reason to believe that at some point they too will devote more and more of their income to leisure. Tourism is a modern growth industry. Britain, for a variety of reasons, is well equipped to profit from it.*

By almost any indicator — statistical, political or the observation of unclouded eyes — Britain is a solid, healthy society, bursting with creative vigor. Its lackluster performance in what Blake called "these dark, Satanic mills" is less a symptom of sickness than of health. It is a country more at peace with itself than its own daily papers reflect. Even in a difficult year like 1974, a government census found that 84.8 percent of all men workers pronounced themselves as "satisfied" with their jobs; for women, the rate was 89.4 percent. This is not the response of a sullen, class-ridden, divided nation.

The press, both domestic and international, is vocationally compelled to take a short-term view of events and seize

---

* There is, however, a limiting point to this. Tourism is what Fred Hirsch called a "positional good." At some level, the sheer number makes life unpleasant both for tourists and hosts. Here the price mechanism is well adapted to control the inflow. As the demand from tourists for a fixed supply of Britain increases, prices charged to tourists should be increased and perhaps even an entry fee imposed.

on crisis, real or imagined. This craft compulsion accounts for much of the lopsided image broadcast by the media. With an inflation rate above its industrial homologues, an unemployment level close to the highest tides elsewhere in the West, with growing hostility between jobless whites and black and brown immigrants, Britain is hardly the New Jerusalem. Neither is it the sinking, chaotic, miserable swamp of the more imaginative journalists and professors. When and if stagflation is overcome throughout the West, Britain's preference for leisure over goods may yet serve as a model for others in the post-industrial age.

IV. One into Nine Makes Zero

The Great Debate

On the night of October 28, 1971, the cavernous, oak-paneled chamber of the House of Commons was packed. MPs squeezed together on the long, schoolboys' benches, governing Tories to the Speaker's right, directly confronting Labour members and minor parties. Government and opposition in the House are separated by little more than the width of the Speaker's big desk, a setting that heightens tension. There are not even enough seats for all 635 MPs. Churchill had deliberately retained this traditional design after the war to intensify the drama on big nights. So a score or so of the legislators stood in the rear to follow the debate. The steeply pitched galleries suspended below Gothic windows were jammed too. Diplomats, MPs' wives and Important Persons crowded out the general public. The press gallery behind and above the Speaker was filled. Even the rear rows were packed; they are reserved for but now rarely used by foreign correspondents since Britain's days of glory have ended. To be sure of a seat on this night, prudent correspondents had booked several weeks in advance.

It was, as Prime Minister Edward Heath was to repeat throughout the evening, a "Historic Decision," and those who thought they had played a part in bringing about such an occasion enjoy seeing history made. In fact, it was the climax to an unusually long six days' debate. It began when

Sir Alec Douglas-Home, Heath's foreign secretary, begged to move a banal-sounding resolution: "That this House approves Her Majesty's Government's decision of principle to join the European Communities on the basis of the arrangements which have been negotiated. "

The House was to answer a question that had fitfully engrossed the nation's leaders for ten years. Should Britain go into the Common Market? The argument had passionately absorbed some — but not all — on both sides of the House, and had crossed party lines.

For the yea-sayers, Market entry was nothing less than a wondrous instrument to redress Britain's postwar history, recapture the glories of an imperial past and restore Britain's industrial pride. It was a substitute for that red-colored globe and a chance to remake Britain as one of the world's great workshops. There was no place left for imperial adventure, but there were possibilities for a subtler form of leadership.

The European Economic Community, or EEC, to give the Market its more formal styling,* was then a grouping of important West European states, Germany, France, Italy, and three smaller countries, Belgium, Holland and Luxembourg. They had high ambitions to form a political and economic union, to exercise a collective weight in the world that none could exert individually. Britain, with its wise civil servants, its long tradition of stable democracy, was — so it was believed in London — a natural captain of this crew.

Once Britain joined, it could lead a rich and strong Western Europe, play a great-power role again, answer Dean Acheson's challenge, revive British influence and prestige. In the telling phrase of Tom Nairn (and Enoch Powell),

---

*More recently, the organization has changed its title to European Communities, a characteristic effort to suggest that it governs much grander things than economic relations. But the more familiar names are Common Market, Market, Community and EEC, and they all have the simple virtue of characterizing what the thing is really about.

the Common Market was to be an "empire surrogate."

There was, moreover, a second and closely related reason for entry in the eyes of the politicians and civil servants who promoted it. Power in the modern world, it was thought, rested on relative economic strength. This view was blessed by the prime minister's own official thinkers, the Central Policy Review Staff, who were to argue in another context, "In today's world a country's power and influence are basically determined by its economic performance." Britain's economy may have increased living standards for citizens, but those of France and Germany had increased faster and the gap was growing. Entry would change all that, or so it was said. French and German steel mills, car plants, chemical concerns and the rest would provide a tonic, a stimulus, for British industry. Productivity, modernization and the intensity of labor effort would all increase. The Market would be a breath of fresh air. British output and incomes would grow at the Continental level.

Thus, it was thought, entry would turn the British condition upside down. Wealth and power would flow. Britain would be reborn.

This remarkable notion, of course, was based on some profound misconceptions, about both the Common Market and the choices that ordinary Britons had already made. But on the night of October 28, the vast majority of those in the House, both on the floor and in the galleries, ardently believed or wanted to believe that these things were so. A large majority of the governing Tories and a substantial number of Labour MPs, led by Roy Jenkins, the party's deputy leader, contended that Britain's future depended on membership. Conversely, a modest platoon of Tories, commanded by Enoch Powell, a peculiarly brilliant if reckless nationalist, stood fast against membership, along with Labour's left and much of the Labour center. They regarded the whole venture as an entangling alliance that would diminish the very existence of Parliament. Some, like Powell, were not immune to the lure of grandeur but insisted that it resided in the British people and their legislature. Others, particularly among the Labour left, wanted to build socialism in one country, their country, and saw the Market's free trade rules as a threat to this dream. Like the Market's proponents, their beliefs rested on equally deep misconceptions about the EEC. But politicians are no more immune from fantasy than pundits.

For Heath, the disciplined, technocratic prime minister, the night had an especially intense personal meaning. The son of a carpenter, he had fought his way up the ladder, through a meritocratic state school for bright boys, an Oxford scholarship and tedious party service as a Conservative Whip, or organizer of votes. Ten years earlier, Heath had led a Tory team that first attempted to negotiate Britain's way into the Common Market. But at the very moment his labors appeared to succeed, General de Gaulle, the French president, said no. The old man was not convinced that Britain was ready to sever its close links with the United States. Moreover, since Germany was still a moral leper and was forbidden atomic arms, why should France admit the only other nation that could rival it for leadership in the Community of six.

A decade later, Heath got a second chance. He was on the verge of what he still regards as his greatest political achievement.

On the opposite bench, Harold Wilson had followed an almost identical route from the lower middle class to his party's leadership. During Wilson's first term as prime minister, he reopened the EEC negotiations killed in Paris, largely because he had run out of things to do at home. Wilson too had met with a de Gaulle rebuff, but Britain's application remained on the Community's table.

Heath had picked it up, convinced Georges Pompidou, successor to de Gaulle, that Britain had broken its dependence on Washington, and successfully concluded the bargaining begun so long ago. By this time, the Germans had become so strong economically that Pompidou feared that French dominance of the Common Market was in peril; he now saw that Paris needed London to establish an informal alliance that would hold Bonn and the others in check.

So on that October night in the crowded Commons, Heath looked forward to a historic triumph, the realization of his dream, the start of Britain's great leap forward. "I do not think that any Prime Minister has stood at this Despatch Box in time of peace and asked the House to take a positive decision of such importance. " So he began, in characteristically overripe tones, a carefully modulated accent that half-consciously hid his class origins.

In the press gallery, heads nodded in agreement; surely this was the most important peacetime decision ever taken. Virtually all leading newspapers, domestic and foreign, had solemnly insisted that it was crucial for Britain to join. Anyway, reporters like to be told they are recording great events. It feeds their sense of importance and assures their stories a more prominent display.

"Our decision tonight will vitally affect the balance of forces in the modern world for many years to come," Heath declared. There are forces in the United States, Heath warned, that may shrink Washington's commitment to Western Europe's defense, bring home the U.S. troops that embody it. "There can be no doubt of the growing pressures for Europe to consolidate its own defence position," Heath said.

This was a curious argument. Heath and many other pro-Marketeers were suggesting that EEC membership and defense were somehow linked. In fact, then and now, the Community is a commercial arrangement that has nothing to do with defense. (Indeed, Ireland, which is not even a NATO member, joined at the same time as Britain.) But Heath, like Pompidou and ambitious, federalist bureaucrats at the EEC headquarters in Brussels, dreamed of the day when the commercial arrangement would be transformed into a United State of Europe, a superpower with a single defense and foreign policy. It was this notion that gave substance to faith in the Market as a surrogate for empire.

As Heath came to the end of his address, the peroration was a little spoiled. Jeers, shouts and laughter from Labour left-wingers almost drowned him out.

"I have had the vision of a Britain in a united Europe," Heath cried (was he thinking of Martin Luther King's dream rhetoric?), "a Britain which would be united economically to Europe and which would be able to influence decisions affecting our own future, and which would enjoy a better standard of life and a fuller life . . . when this House endorses this Motion many millions of people right across the world will rejoice that we have taken our rightful place in a truly United Europe."

Others on both sides of the House enlarged on Heath's theme. Michael Stewart, a former Labour foreign minister, predicted that membership would increase Britain's "wealth-making power." He could not know that the first real decline in wealth since the war was to begin just two years after Britain joined. Robert Carr, Heath's employment secretary, insisted that the Community's "high priority" on full employment would spread its blessings to Britain while the EEC's large and tariff-free market would inspire the nation's laggard industry to adopt "the most refined and specialized methods of production." Christopher Tugendhat, a promising young Tory MP, foresaw employment rising because membership would draw Continental investors to build plants in Britain. Neither Carr nor Tugendhat could foresee that membership would be accompanied by — but not the cause of — rapidly lengthening jobless queues.

But above all it was the political theme, the vision of a Britain that once again would have world influence, if not world power, that inspired the enthusiasts for entry. A

Churchill son-in-law, Duncan Sandys, saw a yes vote ending "growing isolation and weakness and the beginning of a new period of partnership and growing strength." Young Dr. David Owen, only thirty-three and a future Labour foreign minister, pictured a Britain "better able to exercise an influence for good in international affairs and in East-West relations . . ."

The secret dream of the pro-Marketeers was best expressed by Heath on a later occasion, when he was free from office and able to speak more candidly. The Community, he said, has already proven its political strength, containing the "tremendous" economic potential and "drive" of Germany, binding it to France with chains of coal, steel and trade, making unthinkable another war like those that had torn Western Europe apart three times in a single lifetime. "Europe, peaceful, strong and free with *Britain giving it leadership and using its influence,* has been a major theme of my parliamentary and political life" [my emphasis].

The Community had undeniably served as a vehicle to bury the dangerous rivalry between France and Germany and this stands as its enduring political achievement. What possible difference British entry would make to this accomplished fact or why anyone should assume that Britain would automatically lead the Community was never explained, simply asserted.

The opponents of membership were overwhelmed in numbers and rhetoric. At the homeliest level they warned that the peculiar arrangements of the EEC would drive up Britain's food prices — 50 percent, claimed Douglas Jay, an economist who should have known better, a former Labour minister who had been driven from the party's front bench in part because of his overzealous opposition, and the father of Ambassador Peter, who inherited the family suspicion of the EEC. The balance of payments, cried the elder Jay, would plunge into the red by no less than £700 million. This would "cripple" the economy.

But again it was the political argument that brought together personalities as disparate as Michael Foot, a fiery ora-
tor and leader of Labour's left, with Enoch Powell, the Tory
ultranationalist. Foot, his shock of white hair waving with
each gesture, warned that the EEC would destroy Parliament's sovereign control over "taxation, coal, steel, the levels
of unemployment and regional policy."

Powell, dark-haired, pale white skin, intense, humorless
and rigorously logical (once his bizarre assumptions were accepted), was no less eloquent. A yes vote is "an irrevocable
decision to part with the sovereignty of this House and to
commit ourselves to the merger of this nation and its des-
tinies with the rest of the Community . . . [It is a] vote
against the vital principle by which this House exists."

If Powell's rhetoric now seems overblown, he can take
some wry comfort from the equally exaggerated claims made
by the Market's proponents. Both friends and foes were victimized by illusions of power that Brussels does not possess.

So the motion carried comfortably, 356 to 244, and Britain was in. Jeering Tories waved their agenda papers at the
glum Labour ranks. There were cheers for a glowing Heath.
Right-thinking journalists and statesmen applauded everywhere in the West. President Nixon thought the event "will
greatly strengthen the efforts of the President to create a co-
hesive transatlantic partnership for years to come." Willy
Brandt of Germany called it "a great day . . . historic
event for Europe." A French spokesman insisted, "Europe
has become stronger and more credible in the world." Paul-
Henri Spaak of Belgium, an EEC architect, declared simply,
"I have waited for this moment for thirty years."

Three months later, Heath and nine other European leaders* signed at Brussels a Treaty of Accession. Britain, for all

---

*The others came from the original six, Ireland, Denmark and Norway to
make a Community of ten. To the astonishment of all sober people, Norway's
citizens then rejected the pleas of its Labour and Conservative politicians,

practical purposes, was now a member of the enlarged Community and would remain so for as long as anyone could see. Even though membership was now more or less fixed, Britain staged a strange rerun of the debate in the spring of 1975. Its outcome, too, was a foregone conclusion. But it served three special purposes: It helped heal the bitter division inside the Labour party. It shed considerable light on the meaning of Britain's membership. Finally, it all but buried as a serious political question whether Britain would get out. From time to time, Labour leftists return to the attack, but these are ritual assaults. Barring some world economic catastrophe, it is hard to see how Britain can leave.

The second debate was promoted by Wilson. He had returned as prime minister in February 1974 after Heath's disastrous fight against the coal miners. Unsurprisingly, Britain's newly won membership in the Common Market figured only marginally in the election campaign.

Wilson had played a curious and ambiguous role in the great debate. As prime minister in the sixties, he had initiated the membership application that Heath successfully pursued. But as leader of the opposition, straddling a divided party in 1971, Wilson looked both ways at once. He wasn't against the EEC as such, pleasing right-wingers like Jenkins; Harold Lever, chief economic adviser in the cabinet; Shirley Williams, the prices and consumer minister; and others. But Wilson professed to object to the "terms" Heath had negotiated, arrangements for New Zealand's butter sales to the EEC, Britain's payments to the Community and other marginal matters. That pleased his left wing, Foot, and such other ministers as Peter Shore and Anthony Wedgwood Benn. Wilson's position made up in political re-

business leaders, trade union chiefs and an almost unanimous press. In a referendum, the Norwegians voted to stay out. This sturdy example of Viking independence was widely and popularly interpreted as a peculiar piece of backwood parochialism. Ever since, and partly thanks to its North Sea oil, Norway has flourished, and the Community was reduced to nine.

alism what it lacked in intellectual elegance. Evidently, he didn't think it mattered much whether Britain was in or out.

This made him an exception in the House but probably reflected the view of many ordinary citizens. In an unusually open speech, he was to say, "Spokesmen on both sides here may be in danger of making exaggerated claims. There will be those who will record Britain as economically finished if we are not in. There will be those who will predict an equal disaster if we are in." But Britain "survives and prospers in direct correlation to our own efforts here in this country, to our domestic policies — good or bad . . ." Right-thinking people regard Wilson as an unprincipled rascal, a fate often reserved for those unkind enough to point at the nakedness of emperors and empire.

If Wilson could not get worked up over Market membership, he was deeply and profoundly concerned over the zealots on both sides of his party. The division was both embarrassing and a hindrance to government. Labour, like the Tories and other major parties in democratic Northern Europe and the United States, is essentially a coalition embracing a spectrum of views. To survive, each faction or wing must tolerate and compromise with the others. But the Market issue had become theological, stirring deep passions among MPs if not common voters. After his February victory in 1974, moreover, Wilson commanded less than a majority in the House. If his minority party was to govern, the coalition had to be rebuilt and the Market issue dissolved. So Wilson contended that if membership was indeed a historic decision, it must now be submitted to the people for ratification. Let us, he said, have a referendum, the device used by all the other newcomers, Norway, Denmark and Ireland.

This two-pronged approach, insistence that Heath's terms were inadequate and that a national referendum must approve the decision, was a device pure and simple to heal Labour's internal wound.

The equally detached and practical James Callaghan, foreign minister at the time, was sent around to Luxembourg, Brussels and other points on the Community map to "renegotiate" the Heath terms.

The exercise perplexed and angered Britain's partners and most orthodox newspapers, who saw it as evidence of British insularity and Wilsonian treachery. When the French battle for higher wine prices to take care of their growers and the Germans agree in return for higher wheat prices for their farmers, everyone is supposed to understand the domestic political problems involved. But somehow this sympathy stops at the cliffs of Dover, at least when a Labour government is in power.

In due course, Wilson extracted some minor concessions.* Now he could go to the country, as he had intended all along, and urge a yes vote in the referendum. Neither Wilson nor Callaghan ever shared the imperial or industrial dreams of the genuine Market enthusiasts. They simply recognized a fact. Having gone in, departure would create intolerable strains with European allies. Staying in, they reasoned, would cost little if anything.

The issue put to the voters — whether or not to stay in on the terms Wilson had negotiated — was debated at length on television and in the newspapers. But the public at large seemed indifferent. Posters, stickers and streamers were slapped on billboards, cars and windows. The pro-Marketeers, who could draw on substantial funds from large corporations, were the most energetic. Even so, few citizens could be aroused. There was another debate in Parliament.

---

* These were nailed down at a summit meeting of the nine Market leaders at Dublin in March 1975. A breathless press in Dublin Castle waited for Wilson to announce whether he was satisfied, but he refused to play to the "historic" moment. Instead, he came out, saying, "Final outcome" — pause — "Leeds 1, Ipswich 1." This was considered very bad taste by Market journalists, the trivializing of an Important Question. The earnest if humorless journalists missed the point, that the "renegotiation" was a shadow play, that membership was something less than the Second Coming.

It did not quite prove Marx's dictum that history repeats itself a second time as farce. But the rhetoric on both sides was stale and unconvincing.

Perhaps its most remarkable moment was supplied by Foot, now Wilson's employment secretary. Britain had already been among the Nine for more than two years, time enough to assess the terrible damage to sovereignty he and others had predicted. To the uninstructed eye, Parliament was still in place, still functioning, still making Britain's laws.

But Foot saw it otherwise: "Even more speedily than might have been expected, the British parliamentary system has been made farcical and unworkable by the superimposition of the EEC apparatus . . . parliamentary protection for the people is impaired, and perhaps fatally . . . It is as if in 1940 we had set fire to the place as Hitler did with his Reichstag . . ."

And what were those burning brands that had reduced the Palace of Westminster to ashes? Alas, Foot declined to describe them, preferring imagery to fact.

Foot and the other Market foes did recite the catalogue of economic woe that had overtaken Britain by 1975 — high inflation, rising unemployment, a worsening balance of payments and a declining pound. The fact that non-Market nations like the United States, Japan and Canada were suffering from similar disabilities, all victims of global stagflation, failed to stem the rhetoric even if it impaired the logic.

Anyway, nobody paid much attention and it was Callaghan who explained why. Like Wilson, he had embraced the renegotiation-plus-referendum formula as a political expedient in 1971. Now, like his leader, he favored continued membership. After all, he had personally conducted the "renegotiation," an effort that brought forth a tiny but politically useful mouse. In effect, Callaghan urged the House to vote yes because the Market did not matter very much. All its offensive features had either died or been removed. There was the grandiose plan for an economic and monetary union with rules to prevent Britain from changing the parity of the pound. Dead. There was the proposal that EEC officials in Brussels, not London, determine the size and shape of subsidies to depressed industries in Scotland and Wales. Dead.

"We can make of the Community what we and the other members will that it should be. It can be as strong as we like. It can be as weak as the member Governments decide. What is more, they must decide unanimously." In foreign affairs, the Community does not matter either. It has not stopped Britain from "improved . . . bilateral" relations with the Soviet Union or anyone else. It has not "prevented a return to our familiar intimacy with the United States of America."

This last was the touchstone for the faithful Callaghan. Money from the United States or its international affiliates has always been the heart of his public policy. As chancellor of the exchequer in the mid-sixties, Callaghan had vainly and stubbornly tried to hold an overpriced pound at $2.80. Repeated loans from the International Monetary Fund, an institution heavily influenced by the American Treasury, had been wasted in this effort. Later, as prime minister himself, he again turned to Washington and the IMF for another unnecessary loan to prevent an underpriced pound from falling further. An imagined threat to the money pipeline in Washington was Callaghan's public reason for challenging Market membership in 1971; by 1975, he acknowledged the threat was unreal.

So, Britain's next prime minister argued, since there isn't much to it, vote for it. And they did, 396 to 170.

In the country at large, strong feelings were confined to a handful. Left-wing trade union leaders were passionately against and large corporations passionately for. The national press, except the Communist *Morning Star*, was all for staying. The overwhelming majority of Tory, Labour and Liberal politicians were for staying. Britons are not Norwegians and many agreed with Callaghan. The polls showed they would have voted against when Heath took them in without consultation in 1971. Now the electorate went along with the established order. The national referendum upheld continued Market membership by two to one, 17.4 million to 8.5 million.

There is often a time lag between an event and the public perception of its meaning. So it took two more years before Peter Shore, perhaps the shrewdest of Wilson's anti-Market ministers, openly pronounced that the membership issue was dead. "It would not be sensible, it would indeed be frivolous to raise the question again," he said, "unless there was clear evidence" of a national will to get out. In effect, Shore conceded that Wilson had achieved his aim, killing the divisive membership issue inside the Labour party and the nation.

What the EEC Really Does

What was it all about? What had engaged the energies of leading politicians, civil servants, business and financial leaders, trade union chiefs and publicists of high and low estate for much of the previous fifteen years? The Community's founding fathers — Jean Monnet, a former French wine dealer and later councilor to the mighty; Robert Schuman, premier of France; Konrad Adenauer, chancellor of Germany; Alcide de Gasperi, premier of Italy — believed they were building nothing less than a United Europe. Its constitution was the Rome Treaty of 1957. That joined six Continental states in the European Economic Community. The Community was endowed with an impressive array of officials, mostly at its headquarters in Brussels. There was to be a commission of eminent statesmen to propose fresh steps for the six to move more closely together. Under the commissioners, there would be departments of bureaucrats enforcing the regulations that had been adopted and inventing new ones for approval by ministers of the member states. A court of justice would interpret the treaty, superior to any national judiciary. There would even be a European parliament at Strasbourg, a powerless assembly in its infancy and youth that one day would become a genuine legislature for Europe, or at least the Community's member states.

Out of all this, the founders thought, would emerge a new world power, a United or at least a Federal States of Europe. It would wipe out obsolete national boundaries. With its large and advanced population, it would be rich enough, technologically advanced enough, to rival the United States and the Soviet Union. Having inherited the rich European culture and experience, it would civilize and tame the two new and crude rivals for world dominance. For the immediate future, the new institution would serve as a bulwark against extremes of left and right, forge an effective European defense against the Russian menace and seal France and Germany into a permanent alliance.

Apart from strengthening the links between Germany and France, little or none of this grand vision has been realized. There is, moreover, no reason to think that it will be, given the present set of circumstances in Europe.

The Common Market is essentially a set of rules governing trade between the members and those outside the club. It abolishes tariffs or import taxes among its own. A ton of steel produced in a Luxembourg mill can be sold duty-free in France, Germany, Holland, Belgium or Italy, or, more recently, in Britain, Denmark and Ireland. Similarly, a Fiat, a Jaguar, a Peugeot or a Volkswagen can be sold anywhere in the Nine without a buyer paying an import tax. (In fact, each of these cars will run up against "safety standards" and other local rules partly designed to preserve some of the home market for homemade cars. The Community's free internal trade is more often notional than real.)

In addition, the Nine erect a common tariff wall against

the products of all outsiders, a device to favor the goods that the Nine produce and discriminate against the rest. If the Nine agree to tax widgets, the same levy is imposed by each against all beyond the EEC pale.

These two devices — free trade within the Community, or notionally free trade, plus a common tariff wall against the products of outsiders — are as old as the first customs union. Indeed, it is simpler and more accurate to regard the Market as a customs union, nothing more and nothing less.

Like many trade agreements between nations, the Community has adopted a vast number of regulations to wipe out hidden trade barriers, techniques that give the products of one member an advantage over those of another. So the Community attempts to make uniform subsidies and rebates, government handouts that would give a French toolmaker an edge over a British competitor or vice versa. The Community, for example, has been wrestling with the size of trucks. Britain limits them to a weight of 32 tons, but the Continent's "juggernauts" are bigger. So the Commission has proposed a uniform limit of 40 tons. As long as Britain resists, the French and German monsters are shut out of Britain's carrying trade. Five years after Britain joined, this one still hadn't been settled, but it reflects Brussels' efforts to make competition equal.

The Market's rules are no different in principle from those prevailing in the global trade pact, the General Agreement on Tariffs and Trade. This code governs exchanges among the United States, Japan, the Common Market and virtually everyone else outside the Communist bloc. The Brussels machinery has simply ground out more rules for its members.

When the Market was first set up, the French especially feared that reviving German industry would crush rival firms in Lille, Lyon, Alsace and Lorraine. Even defeated Germans, it was thought, would be too efficient, too advanced, too hard-working for their partners. So something special had to be invented to offset the German advantage, to make membership more attractive to France.

The something special was the misnamed Common Agricultural Policy. It is an elaborate price support system, complete with elastic tariffs that go up and down quarterly, weekly and some even daily — all to protect and increase the incomes of farmers. France has lots of them, as have Italy and Holland. (As late as 1976, the percentage of the French labor force in farming was 11.6, Italy, 15.8, and Holland, 6.6.) The system was designed to provide these farmers with ever-rising incomes at the expense of consumers in general and the Germans in particular. The policy insures that no foreign beef, butter, wine and much more can be sold inside the Community until the Community's farmers have exhausted their supplies.

There are two principal methods of protecting the farmers' income. Most economists would argue that the more rational is the one employed by Britain before it joined the Community. It is the free market approach vainly proposed for the United States by former agriculture secretary Charles Brannan. This tells farmers to sell their goods freely in the market, letting supply and demand determine the price of eggs, beef, beans and everything else. Consumers are free to buy food produced at home or abroad, wherever it is cheapest. If domestic farmers do not earn an adequate income, they receive direct cash subsidies to make up the difference. Farmers don't like this because their subsidies are open for all to see.

The second system, employed by the Community and a close cousin to United States farm price supports, fixes target prices for each product. "Surplus" produce — output that can't be sold at these prices — is bought and stored by the EEC. This creates the mountains and lakes of butter, skimmed milk, wine, beef and more. Farmers prefer this system because their subsidy is hidden in the prices consumers pay and is thus less vulnerable than a direct subsidy to political attack. Big farmers like it most of all since the device yields its largest rewards to the largest producers.

Well-off consumers are also bettered by price supports. All consumers, rich and poor alike, pay roughly the same price for a pound of beef or a head of lettuce. They are contributing equally to the price support subsidy. Direct subsidies, however, are paid at least in part from income taxes, which fall more heavily on the best-off.

By 1977, the surplus mountains had reached such staggering heights that even the Brussels commissioners were seeking a halt. A bold one, Finn Olav Gundelach, proposed a compromise system, a mix of price supports and direct subsidies to check the mountainous growths. But this threat to a system that makes the worst-off pay relatively more to support big farmers was not given much chance of success.

Perhaps the most ingenious feature of the French invention is the way some of the subsidy costs are shifted from the French to foreigners. Countries like Britain and Germany that still import food from outside the Nine must pay the levies imposed on foreign produce. These funds go to the Brussels machine and are redistributed back to Community farmers.

The EEC, then, is a customs union attached to a complex price support system for farmers.

There is still another peculiar and seldom-discussed characteristic of the Community that bears heavily on the claims of its prophets. Just as the EEC tries to spare farmers from the rigors of competition, so too does it work to diminish market forces in other industries. Indeed, the French fears of an overpowering German rivalry now appear to have been more fanciful than real. The Community's roots, as John Vaizey of Brunel University has observed, lie in the prewar cartel of steel and coal producers, L'Entente Internationale de l'Acier. This typical German device, with headquarters in Luxembourg, embraced potential competitors in France,

Belgium, Luxembourg, Germany and, from 1935, Britain. Like any cartel, it suppressed competition, fixing prices and carving up market shares.

Unsurprisingly, the very first Franco-German institution set up after the war was the Coal and Steel Community, born five years before the Treaty of Rome. Its changeless nature was reflected as recently as 1977, when Community officials under Viscount Étienne Davignon were busy trying to bring steel producers together to limit output, share a market and keep out Japanese and other competitors. Brussels finally produced a scheme copied from the United States, fixing a minimum price below which foreign steel cannot be imported. Like the elastic tariffs for agriculture, this is potentially more protectionist than either quotas or conventional tariffs. A foreign seller can get through the first and under the second but a "minimum price" set high enough can squeeze him out entirely. In much the same way, rising minimum prices were fixed for Community-made steel, insuring that no producer suffers and consumers pay for this security blanket.

Every EEC document contains brave words about the joys and benefits of competition. The Community even maintains a Directorate General for Competition that does curb some restrictive trade practices. But like U.S. antitrust laws, this is a fig leaf. The undressed body, the Community in practice, is cartelism for factories and mines as well as farms.

Apart from steel, the EEC has been busy trying to fix up cartels for shipbuilding, oil refining and more. It wants the shipyards to recognize that orders will fall and so cut back on their capacity. This, of course, could be done only if each agreed to take a given share of estimated demand, which is what a cartel is about. The Commission has had no luck "rationalizing" oil refineries; its scheme to carve up the market fell apart when the British stubbornly insisted on refining the bulk of their North Sea oil in the United Kingdom. This policy implies expanding rather than freezing capacity levels, and the Continental refiners would not accept that. However, the seven great international oil companies, experienced cartelists themselves, may well do the EEC's work for it. The seven dominate the world's refineries and have no interest in any enlarged capacity that would threaten to reduce prices.

Just how such practical business arrangements were to evolve into a grand political structure, a Federal Europe, has always been obscure. Monnet told a long succession of politicians and prominent journalists from both sides of the Atlantic that the evolution was simply inevitable. Many believed — because they wanted to believe — that trading rules would compel member states to adopt first parallel and then identical economic policies. This in turn would forge common foreign and defense policies. But there was nothing inevitable about any of this. Nations, like citizens, embark on a radically new course with reluctance, under the compulsion of overwhelming fear or the lure of an irresistible prize. In the Community's first twenty years, neither was obvious.

This does not mean that the EEC is exclusively a set of business arrangements with no political implications. The politics, however, are much less than the Founding Fathers foresaw. One clear dividend from the arrangement has already been noted: the web of economic links woven between France and Germany that makes war between these two great former rivals virtually unthinkable. The Community has provided, as Heath argued, a framework for peaceful German energies.*

Indeed, the Community might have evolved further if

---

* Old memories die hard, however, as an important Gaullist politician reminded me as late as 1966. I had teased him about the Force de Frappe, the French nuclear deterrent. "Why, you have to refuel your planes over Poland," I said. "How can you expect them to reach Moscow?" He looked at me, smiled and replied, "My dear friend. You do not realize those planes need fly only as far as Germany."

only the Russians had cooperated. When the original six signed the Rome Treaty, most Europeans believed with John Foster Dulles that the Soviet Union was determined to expand by force. There were genuine fears that Russian tanks would roll across the North German plain any day, that World War III was imminent. Had this fear persisted, the sovereign states of the EEC might well have surrendered national decision-making to a supranational body, might have ordered the Brussels machinery to produce a common set of foreign, defense and economic policies. By the time Britain joined in 1973, however, fears of armed Soviet expansion had receded. The prevailing view was and had been for a dozen years that, although the Russians insisted on absolute mastery over their side of the World War II divide, Moscow would not move overtly across this line — at least as long as NATO was in place and the U.S. nuclear arsenal was pledged to Western Europe's defense.

Once the fear of Russia dissolved, the motor of political union stalled. There was no compelling need for any further pooling of defense and economic arrangements. The North Atlantic Treaty Organization provides — or is seen to provide — common defense enough, particularly since it rests on the U.S. deterrent. (NATO includes all EEC members except Ireland and France. Paris enjoys a characteristically unique status — in the Treaty, out of the Organization, engaging in common maneuvers, but not in setting common targets.)

In addition, a large complex of arrangements — the International Monetary Fund, OECD, the General Agreement on Tariffs and Trade, the EEC itself — provide rules for more or less orderly trade and economic support. EEC countries could see no reason why they should do more, why they should give over national decision-making in the economic sphere to Brussels. Stagflation only confirmed this view. In this time of stress, the best answer from the Brussels Commission was an arrangement to fix the rates at which currencies exchanged for each other. Had this peculiar affair survived, Britain, France and Italy would have been forced to undergo a terrifying deflation simply to stay abreast of the German mark. The consequences in lost jobs and output could have plunged Europe into misery matching the Great Depression. The Commission's remarkable rigidity may have killed any prospects of a common economic policy, perhaps for a generation at least.

The Community, in brief, was and is a limited commercial affair, an elaborate system of rules governing trade between four middle-sized and five small nations. Given this fact, it is not easy to understand the lofty claims made for membership. How could Heath, Jenkins and the other ardent pro-Marketeers believe the EEC was a glittering political opportunity? Indeed, they suffered from twin delusions. Not only did they believe the Community would become a political force in the world, they were also convinced that late-joining Britain must captain the team. An astonishingly complacent sense of superiority underlay this notion, that somehow Britons, with their vast imperial experience, would rise to dominate French, Germans and others by assent.

Heath, Jenkins and the rest hankered for lost glory. They had misread the lesson of empire and thought Britain was better when bigger. They identified the nation's well-being with their own. They saw themselves commanding a powerful bloc, a Community of 260 million, enjoying influence on a world scale like the British politicians of a century ago. In this strange vision, nine rich and united nations — under British aegis, of course — would be a power and not a suppliant in the Middle East, resolve energy problems, meet the United States and the Soviet Union as an equal, straighten out international monetary disorders, settle little local squabbles like those between Greece and Turkey over Cyprus or between blacks and whites in southern Africa.

They were urged on by the skilled and frustrated diplomats in the Foreign and Commonwealth Office. As Vaizey

observed, "Increasingly those who have risen in the Foreign
Office have taken the view that the Common Market has
been the only hope for Britain's maintaining a role in foreign
policy." All these people, Vaizey tartly concluded, were
"taking part in some enormous collective Western European
folk myth." Just as actors who once enjoyed the limelight
endlessly prolong their farewell appearance, Heath, Jenkins
and the others dreamed of re-creating the parts of Palmer-
ston, Gladstone and Disraeli. It was somehow fitting that
Jenkins ended up playing president of the largely powerless,
frequently snubbed Common Market Commission.

There were, of course, more prosaic soldiers in the pro-
Market camp. Tom Boardman, later Heath's industry minister, and the Confederation of British Industry spoke for
them. They saw membership as the road back to past economic glory. Refreshed by a shower of competing products
from French, Italian and German industry, Britain's sluggish businessmen would somehow revive. They would mod-
ernize technologically backward factories. They would
expand. European investors would bring their vigorous style
to Britain, setting up new plants on the offshore island. The
bankers, brokers and insurance firms in the City of London,
armed with skill and cunning, would overpower Paris,
Frankfurt and Amsterdam, perhaps outstrip New York as
the world's key financial center. Bothersome, left-led unions
would be squelched. The Common Market's paper assur-
ance of a free flow of capital would enable any owner to pick
up a strike-troubled plant and put it down in the Ruhr,
southern Italy or the Loire Valley.

At the start of the debate, Professor John Williamson of
Warwick even quantified the putative gains. He calculated
that economies from longer production runs, the pressure of
competition on managers and the growth of investment in
plants and machinery would add £750 million a year to the
British economy by 1977 — a gain of 1.5 percent in total
output. Another expert, Christopher Layton of Bath Uni-

versity, calculated that industrial workers would become 5 percent more productive if Britain joined the Community.

The economic realists were also victims of cherished belief. The Common Market was much less competitive than advertised. In any event, British industry did not suffer from a lack of investment, from technological backwardness or from strike-prone, leftist unions. To be sure, productivity was and is lower than on the Continent, but the evidence suggests, as we have seen, that this reflects a collective if unavowed choice. Britons appear to prefer a more leisurely life than the Germans and French. Adherence to a set of trading rules was not likely to change any of this.

If the friends of entry were visionary, their foes were apocalyptic. Michael Foot and Enoch Powell cried from every podium that entry would rape the Mother of Parliaments. MPs in the Palace of Westminster would no longer fix Britain's taxes or the spending levels of its great departments. Depressed areas and industries in Scotland, Wales and the English northeast would no longer be succored by Parliament but left to the dubious mercies of the Brussels machine. Parliament would no longer have power over Britain's economic life.

The Socialist foes — Foot, Peter Shore and others — saw membership as a desperate device to prop up a dying capitalist order. Once in, a Labour government could no longer nationalize an industry, plan an economy. The Market's rules for trade and competition would prevent all this.

Finally — and perhaps more plausibly — membership meant the end of an era of cheap food (although, as it happened, the world boom in commodity prices in 1972–73 put an end to this era well before the EEC's rules began to bite). Britain could no longer import from the cheapest world market but would have to take the bulk of its imported food from the Community and its crazy-quilt of protective levies.

What the EEC Did to Britain

Five years after Britain took the plunge, the great debate had all but died away. From time to time, anti-Marketeers fitfully emerged to blame Britain's plight on membership. Nobody paid much attention.

Even more striking was the almost total absence of anniversary literature — of books and articles assessing what membership meant. Five years offered a nice, round period for which editors could order a balance sheet, weighing the benefits and the costs. But the editors were not very interested. This was odd. If entry was to have restored Britain's imperial role, should not this transformation have been celebrated? If membership was to have brought a prosperity unrivaled since the Crystal Palace Exhibition of 1851, why did no one describe it? Conversely, if Parliament had become an empty shell, if press and public attended the performance of a eunuch at Westminster, should not this sad state have been lamented?

The deafening silence is easily explained. The simple fact is that it is very hard to credit or blame the Common Market with making much difference if any to Britain. The country is still a second-rank power among second-rank powers, making a modest impact on world affairs and calling in the big American partner for serious problems like rebels in Rhodesia or large loans to tide over the reserves until North Sea oil flows. Only the most fanatic opponents think the Common Market is responsible for Britain's uncomfortable mix of stagflation, inflation and unemployment.

In the same way, visitors to Parliament Square still find Foot, Powell, Heath, Shore and all the other familiar faces very much in business (only Jenkins and Tugendhat have left, for those better-paying jobs in Brussels). MPs are still ratifying or amending decisions of a cabinet that attempts to determine the shape of British life. Parliament still votes taxes, approves spending, pushes funds into depressed areas and nationalizes the occasional industry, usually one entirely dependent on government orders or about to go bust. It isn't socialism under Labour. But then it never was, and membership has not changed much of anything.

Two little-noticed books have tried to summarize Market membership for Britain and they reveal far more than they intend. Both are written by entrenched supporters of the Community and both concede that there is less here than meets the eye. One, *The Effects on the United Kingdom of Membership of the European Communities,* is published by the research department of the European Parliament, a Community institution. Buried away in the dense thicket of its bureaucratic prose, it makes this remarkable but accurate estimate: "It could even be asserted that the aversion of Britain's anti-Marketeers results, in a way, from their tendency to take Community decisions too seriously, something for which not they, but the Community must take the blame. In past years, it has all too often been the case that the Council or a Summit Conference formulated ambitious plans only to find that they could not be implemented."

Exactly.

The Hansard Society for Parliamentary Government, a private research group, has issued an equally revealing document, *The British People: Their Voice in Europe.* ("Europe," it must be recalled, is the inflated Brussels term for the nine Western European states — of twenty outside the Soviet bloc — who adhere to the Rome Treaty trading rules.) The Hansard team is pleased that British farm and big business groups lobby in Brussels, but it deplores the lack of serious discussion about the EEC in Parliament and the absence of lobbying by trade unions.

"It must be recognized," the anonymous Hansard authors write, "that up to now the Community has not been successful in making a common response to problems like unemployment, inflation, pay and working conditions, multinational companies and so on, which concern trade unions and their members most directly and forcibly. As a result unionists normally think that they have far more pressing questions to deal with than Community affairs, and the Community institutions are not nearly so important to them as national governments." In other words, national governments — cabinet and Parliament in Britain — still decide all the economic issues that matter most. Trade unions with limited resources must work on them; the Community can be safely ignored.

Again, with unusual frankness, the Hansard volume, pro-Market in sympathy, sadly concludes: "All these facts tend to suggest that the Community is becoming a stale and untopical subject for the majority of people."

A Heath, a David Owen, a Jenkins, who dreamed of a powerful third force in Europe, could have read that their hopes were doomed on the very day Britain signed the Treaty of Rome. In a symbolic assertion of national sovereignty, the French refused to let the Commission's president sign the document, an act that might have implied he was on a par with elected heads of government.

In Britain's very first year as a member, two interlinked crises — the Middle East and oil — amply demonstrated the disunity of the Nine. During the October War in 1973, Market member Britain had refused to allow U.S. planes carrying arms to Israel to refuel. Prime Minister Heath was fearful of offending Arabs. Market member Germany, however, had permitted the U.S. planes to touch down. Bonn was fearful of offending Washington. Regardless of who was right, the point is that there was no policy in common.

The Market's disunity was exposed again a few months later when the Arab nations announced an embargo, supposedly stopping oil to Market member Holland. Holland's eight partners did not rally around. They did not offer to pool and share their supplies. Quite the contrary; each, and especially Britain and France, tried to ingratiate itself with oil-bearing Arabs and insure its own flow. Heath even sent his close friend Lord Aldington to Saudi Arabia and Lord Balniel to the Gulf states hoping to win barrels of oil exclusively for Britons.

Later, on the initiative of the United States, the West did work out an emergency scheme to carve up limited oil supplies in the event of some future and genuine Arab embargo. The scheme could not be designed in the Common Market, where the rule remained each for himself. It was, instead, negotiated in the Organization for Economic Cooperation and Development, the Paris-based grouping of twenty-four mostly rich nations. France is a member of both the OECD and the Common Market. Nevertheless, France stayed out of the newly created International Energy Agency, fearful again of annoying Arabs.

On issues charged with economics and politics, the Market had proven impotent and irrelevant. The EEC could and did issue proclamations, asserting, for example, the right of Palestinians to a homeland. But this hardly affects the course of events. After he became foreign minister, Owen was to tell a *Sunday Times* interviewer: "I think increasingly the Nine see major *statements* on the Middle East as being part of the framework of European political cooperation. Primarily, the responsibility is that of the United States. They hold the power and the influence. I strongly believe it is a British responsibility, and I believe it is of the Nine as well, to be supportive to the United States" (my emphasis).

Not long after Owen's remarks, the EEC found it could not even speak, let alone act, on the Middle East. The Belgian foreign minister proposed that his colleagues salute as a "courageous initiative" the astonishing visit of President Anwar Sadat to Israel. The French would have none of this, however, calling it "premature" and thinking of their other, offended Arab friends. So the Nine stayed mute.

In other crises Labour had stumbled on to the very formula that Dr. Owen was to prescribe. In the summer of

1974, Callaghan was still foreign minister and he tried and failed to undo the Turkish invasion of Cyprus, an island whose uneasy peace was a British responsibility. He then turned not to his partners in the Nine but to that far more consequential ally, the United States. Again, when blacks threatened the white status quo in what was still in law the British colony of Rhodesia, neither Callaghan, now prime minister, nor his successor Owen at the Foreign Office sought aid from Brussels. They turned to a more plausible partner, the United States, to keep a lid on Southern Africa. Once again, Owen was remarkably candid about this. "I would not have involved myself in this renewed effort to achieve a negotiated settlement over Rhodesia," he told *The Sunday Times*, "if I had not done this in partnership with the United States."

The study by the European Parliament on the effects of British membership boldly insists: "Had Britain not been a member of the Community, she could never have hoped to cooperate with the USA on the basis of equality."

This remarkable judgment is not likely to be echoed by successive British foreign ministers who have enjoyed EEC membership, from Alec Douglas-Home through Owen. If they are in any doubt, Denis Healey, Labour's chancellor of the exchequer, can tell them. He went to Washington — not Brussels — to relax the terms of a $4 billion loan that Britain anxiously sought from the International Monetary Fund at the end of 1976. It was Henry Kissinger, the secretary of state, caring little for economics, who got Healey the money on terms Healey could afford politically. What impressed Kissinger was not the nonexistent strength of the Nine but fear that the harsh terms the IMF and the U.S. Treasury were ready to impose would make impossible any deal to restrain union pay demands. In other words, Kissinger acted to strengthen Britain's internal political stability; unlike the Nine, he had power to do so.

There is one notable exception to this record of political

impotence. It involves East-West relations, the area where Market founders once thought the impetus for union would arise.

Beginning in 1970, high-ranking diplomats from each EEC member began meeting monthly. Under Viscount Davignon, then head of the Belgian foreign service, envoys — nine of them now — worked closely to hammer out a common position for the Helsinki Conference on East-West Security. The Russians had promoted this gathering, largely as a ceremonial ratification of the borders established after World War II. But the shrewd diplomats from the Nine demanded something in return. They insisted on a code promising free movement of information and people between states, guaranteeing certain human rights by all the signers, and a series of so-called confidence-building measures, permitting observers from East and West to attend each other's military maneuvers. The Nine not only drafted the language, they insisted on its adoption at Helsinki. The Russians, perhaps unaware that the loftiest of words can sometimes move people, reluctantly agreed. The effect on the political life of Europe, particularly the code's support for dissident humanists in the East, has been striking and positive.

This incident is a unique example of the Nine working as one, exerting influence, making their collective weight felt. It was achieved, however, by representatives of nine sovereign states, without the participation of the Market's Brussels bureaucracy.

Common Market enthusiasts might argue that this account is incomplete, that it omits the united front the EEC displays in trade negotiations. Both in the Kennedy Round of tariff bargaining that ended in 1967 and in the drawn-out Tokyo Round that was still unfinished at the start of 1978, the Community members bargained as one, under a Brussels official. But this hardly qualifies as an example of collective weight in foreign affairs. Tariffs and other obstacles to trade are precisely what the Brussels customs union is all about. Their agreement would fall apart if each member was free to make his own tariff deal with outsiders. Collective negotiations in trade lie at the heart of the Rome Treaty.

Even in this area, national self-interest has forced open a sizable loophole in the "common" policy of the Nine. For years, the French, Germans and others had been making economically useful and politically profitable trade deals with the Soviet Union and other East Bloc nations. The Russians, naive believers in the political claims from Brussels, regard the Common Market as a dangerous power bloc and they have refused to deal with it as an entity. Moscow, moreover, is run by a conservative bureaucracy. It knows how to barter Russian gold and fur for French chemicals or German machine tools, but it does not know how to do such things with six or nine countries at once.

So the Russians insisted that trade pacts be conducted on a bilateral basis, between Moscow and one other national partner. The French liked this; they thought it gave them special political influence. The Germans got most of the trade, so they were satisfied; and the two EEC countries that mattered were content.

Smaller Market nations and the Brussels bureaucrats were not. Bilateral trade deals seemed to strike at the Community's soul, a common and uniform trade policy. The Nine agreed that all these bilateral deals would end in 1975. They would be replaced by Community-wide pacts with the Soviet world.

In 1975, the deals did end; they were simply replaced by "cooperation agreements," just as two-sided as the agreements that had been foresworn. The name of the arrangement changed; the substance did not. Common Market honor was preserved. So were the bilateral deals between the Russians and the French, or the British or the Germans or anyone else. The episode was a neat illustration of the Market's limited reach.

By 1977, however, the Community — crying for a political role that only Davignon's committee had fulfilled — was at last presented with a genuine opportunity and in its own back yard. Three Mediterranean nations, Greece, Portugal and Spain, had recently thrown off dictatorships and established new if uncertain democracies. Now they were seeking entry to the Community. This was precisely the sort of political opening that Heath, Jenkins and the British Foreign Office had held out as a prize. Britain by herself could do little to prop the new Mediterranean democracies. But if London led a Nine to give them shelter, London would play a historic role, building bulwarks against authoritarianism, strengthening NATO's southern flank.

Membership in the Market is incompatible with a totalitarian order of either left or right. Neither a Communist nor a Fascist regime could easily accept the Community's rules — no matter how circumscribed — demanding free movement of workers, capital and goods across national borders. The Community, moreover, may not have produced high politics, but its members assume theirs is a club of democracies. Under Franco and Salazar, neither Spain nor Portugal could even attempt to apply (although the French and Germans would have liked to bring in Franco's Spain; they simply could not overcome Dutch and Belgian vetoes). When the colonels seized power in Greece, her associate or limited membership in the EEC was frozen for seven long years. Now, if the three were admitted as democracies, potential coup-makers of the right or left would be discouraged. A revived dictatorship would threaten their countries with expulsion and a renewed isolation. Membership for Greece, Spain and Portugal would strengthen democratic forces in all three.

Instead of greeting the new democracies with open arms, however, the EEC responded to the applications with alarm and dismay. The French and the Italians cried over the threat to their Mediterranean producers of olives, peaches, wine, lemons, oranges. These things were produced in Portugal, Spain and Greece and might compete more cheaply. If the newcomers were admitted, Paris insisted, additional income support must be given to the Mediterranean growers.

The Belgians and Dutch had a different concern. Decision-making among nine was difficult, they said; among twelve it would be more so. The big Germans, French and British would then gang up to run the Community. A new system for making decisions — something like majority instead of unanimous voting — must be adopted before the trio could be let in.

The Germans were also suspicious of the newcomers. Wouldn't they flood Europe's labor markets with jobless migrants seeking work? Wouldn't they all need big subsidies so their developing industry could compete against the French, German and others? And who, if not rich Germany, would have to pay the bill for all this? Bad business.

At the receiving end of German money, the Irish were unhappy too. Greeks, Portuguese and Spanish would all demand a share of the limited welfare funds on offer in the EEC.

Even the several thousand bureaucrats in Brussels were unwelcoming. They were just getting used to dividing their comfortable, undemanding and highly paid jobs among nine member states. Newcomers would require that these splendid positions must be carved up among twelve countries and some bureaucrats might be pushed out. Even rich golden handshakes or outsized severance payments could not make up for this loss.*

---

* By the end of 1977, the Common Market salary scale was topped by President Jenkins' tax-free $120,000. Eurocrats fresh from university with no working experience started at $26,200. Middle-level secretaries enjoyed $18,860 — all free of national taxes. Pay is tied to inflation rates and perquisites abound. There are subsidies for wives, children and schooling. Eurocrats buy their cars free of tax and enjoy a supermarket that slices 25 percent off

The British had none of these worries. But somehow the cherished dream was not realized. The British could not shake their partners by the shoulders and cry out, "Forget your parochial problems. There is a great democratic order to be built, a genuine political goal to be won. Let us seize the day." The British had too many narrow concerns of their own in the Nine to do anything so romantic as that.

At the start of 1978, the fate of the Mediterranean three had still not been settled. In Brussels, it was said on all sides that, no matter the difficulties, the three could not be denied. Even the most narrow-minded capitals are said to recognize that the political stakes are too large, that the refusal of Greece, Portugal and Spain would carry too great a risk. So, in the end, Brussels expected that the Mediterranean trio would be admitted, that the Nine would become the Twelve. But none of the member states — including Britain — acted as if it were faced with a glorious political opportunity. Each behaved, rather, as if it had been handed a very poisoned fruit.

The European Parliament concluded its report on Britain's membership with this rueful observation: "It may be argued that membership of the Community has since January 1973 equally not endowed Britain with notably greater economic or political power."

Not Heath or David Owen, ambitious Foreign Office diplomats or the serious writers of the Establishment press could argue with that judgment. Jenkins, the high-salaried president of the Common Market, might have some personal reason for rejoicing in Britain's membership. But that hardly seemed to be what he was suggesting when he made those eloquent speeches in 1971 and 1975.

The hardheaded businessmen who had poured money and

---

local prices of filet mignon, salmon, caviar and other staples. If any officials are displaced by, say, new entrants, they enjoy at least 60 percent of their pay until age sixty, when a generous pension begins.

energy into British entry were also disappointed. Membership did not revive British industry; it did not provide a stimulating shower. Entry did not even lessen the power of unions. It is much harder than some had thought to pick up a chemical or a machine tools plant and move it to the Continent. Anyway, the businessmen soon discovered that wages and social costs were even higher abroad than at home.

The foes of entry, the Powells and Foots, had a superficially better case for Britain's first five years. Membership had coincided with a world stagflation that hit Britain with especial force. But only the most blinkered could blame the phenomenon on Britain's entry into the Community. The report by the European Parliament was somewhat nearer the mark when it suggested that Britain's plight had more to do with currency decisions in Zurich, the effect of weather on crops, the price mandates of oil company boardrooms and OPEC ministries than anything done or undone in Brussels.

Some foes of membership made great play of the rising imbalance in Britain's trade with the Market. The Continent was selling Britain far more than it bought. "We had to get rid of our high tariffs on imports of manufactured goods from the EEC six, and . . . higher food prices have pushed up labor costs. That is why we have had such an influx of cars, steel and electrical goods . . . The flood of manufactured imports from the EEC has worsened the problem of British manufacturing industry, and the result has been factory closures, declining investment and the loss of hundreds of thousands of jobs."

That was the gloomy verdict of the Labour Common Market Safeguards Committee, a left group. It was supported by statistics showing that Britain's trade deficit with the EEC's original six had been only £496 million on the eve of entry in 1972 but rose nearly five times, to £2410 million, by 1976.

It was an argument an eighteenth-century mercantilist would have enjoyed. In fact, the figures meant that Britain was receiving real goods from its partners in exchange for bits of paper, pounds or IOUs. This enabled living standards in Britain — the consumption of goods and services — to fall less rapidly than they otherwise might.

To be sure, the other countries would not pile up bits of paper indefinitely. They didn't. The used them to buy vacations, insurance, shipping and banking in Britain. Tourism and other "invisibles" rose and the total deficit was much smaller than the figures for trade in goods alone suggest.

Finally, there is little reason to believe that the gradual disappearance of tariffs between Britain and the other EEC members had much to do with anything. On the eve of entry, successive rounds of international tariff bargaining since World War II had already reduced to 10 percent Britain's average levy on manufactured imports. The remaining few percentage points could not have affected much trade. Anyway, if Britain had not joined, nearly all the opponents of entry said they would have sought a simple trade deal with the Market. Such a deal would have wiped out virtually the same tariffs that the Market abolished.

By 1977, the deficit problem had disappeared in the flood of North Sea oil. Britain had moved into a balance of payments surplus. There were unlikely to be further deficits until the oil ran out.

The foes of membership also asserted that the promised outpouring of Continental investment in British plants had never taken place. Indeed, the reverse had occurred. British ventures in the original Six far exceeded those crossing the Channel. For 1973 and 1974, Britons directly invested in EEC plants a total of £866 million; the Market members put only £177 million into Britain.

But the imbalance could have been greater had Britain stayed out. An Imperial Chemical Industries, fearing that tariffs might cost it Continental business, would have had an even greater inducement to set up in the Ruhr or northern Italy. A Ford would have little reason to plan an engine plant in Wales if its motors would run into tarriff obstacles at Hamburg. To make sense of their argument, Common Market foes must argue that a Britain outside the Community would impose such fearsome clamps on overseas investment that none would trickle abroad.

The foes of membership had warned repeatedly that myriad Community regulations to insure equal competition would strike down many British domestic props. There was particular concern for Britain's regional policy, funds poured into areas with obsolete industries and chronically high unemployment. There were warnings that Brussels would not allow Britain to grant tax privileges and other subsidies to draw plants to depressed regions in Scotland, Ulster and the English northeast. But once again the fears were groundless. EEC rules are always bent to accommodate a member nation with a determined will. The EEC's competition commissioner, for example, proposed the outlawing of Britain's subsidy to rescue the Chrysler company. It was most certainly a clear violation of the Market's "competition rules." But wiser heads prevailed, aware of how sensitive the issue was, and the competition commissioner was set to work at other tasks. In the same way, Britain's regional policy continues unruffled. London even dips into the limited sums that the Community provides for backward places.

This does not mean that Brussels' rule-making has no force, no effect. But the Market does not aim at its own dismemberment; any national scheme that does not nakedly discriminate against others can usually win approval.

Britain, for example, wanted to insure its shipbuilders against escalating costs, giving them an edge over competitive bidders from abroad. No problem, said Brussels, provided that the insurance is also granted to parts imported from others in the Nine and not limited to those made in

Britain. Again, Britain planned to give subsidies for the building of North Sea oil rigs. Fine, said Brussels, as long as any producer from the Nine also gets them. Not so good, said Britain. We only want to help our own rig builders. That quarrel was still unsettled at the end of 1977.

The point is that none of this is momentous. The rules neither make nor break Britain. Fulfilling the obligations of any treaty inhibits national sovereignty. But Common Market membership has not altered British institutions, behavior, weakness or strength in any noticeable way. Like any economic treaty, Britain's adherence to the Rome agreement has had some effect on the direction of trade, the way it is done, and the costs and benefits flowing from it. But only a scrupulous refusal to look at economic facts enables anyone to assert that membership — over the first five years — had much effect on Britain's economy for good or ill.

In one vital sector, however, the price of food, both foes and friends of the Common Market were certain that membership would have consequences and largely for the worse. Britain would be giving up a system under which it could import food from the cheapest markets for the Community technique that would compel the country to buy the bulk of the food it needed from abroad at prices fixed to subsidize the incomes of French, Dutch and other EEC farmers. In 1970, when Wilson was still bidding to bring Britain in, his government calculated the Brussels machine would lift British food prices by a substantial 18 to 26 percent a year. Heath's regime then forecast a slightly less dismal result, an ultimate rise in prices of 16 percent.

Both were wide of the mark. Once again, the Community's impact had been exaggerated. To be sure, there were some special reasons for this. The huge jump in oil prices imposed by the great international companies and their Arab collaborators led a global wave of inflation. At the same time, a series of poor crops around the world threw markets into a turmoil. The relative shortages of wheat and

sugar actually drove world prices in 1974 and 1975 above
those set by the Brussels machine. These were the first two
years of British membership. Moreover, the New Zealand
butter whose sale in the Common Market Wilson had strug-
gled to obtain simply was not available. All this led to an
unexpected result for British housewives. According to the
most careful calculation made so far — by S. A. Harris, a
business economist, and Professor T. A. Josling of Reading — Britons actually saved £109.4 million on their food
bill in 1973 because of and not in spite of their Market membership. Put another way, a Britain outside the Nine would
have had to pay £8,549,400,000 for the food it consumed.
Those swiftly rising world prices would have hit the housewives hard. Inside the Nine, Britain paid £8,440,000,000, or
1.3 percent less. The EEC had fixed its prices below the
world level.

Over the next three years, according to Harris and Josling,
the outcome was less perverse; Britain did pay more than it
would have had it bought in world food markets. But the
differences were trifling, far less than either friends or foes
had expected. For 1974, the EEC system added only 0.2
percent to household food budgets; it was 2.7 percent in 1975
and 1976. For living costs as a whole, it appeared that the
peculiar Common Market food price system was adding less
than 1 percent to British living costs.*

No doubt the Brussels arrangement was inefficient. The
stockpiles of butter, beef, wine and much more — bought by
Brussels to prop prices and incomes for Community farmers — all testified to the fact that there was a much better
way of doing these things. But the burden borne by Britons
was small. There was even something to the Brussels argu-

* More recently, some Cambridge economists provided a bit of cheer for
Market critics. They estimated that the complex farm support system would
cost British consumers in 1978 12 percent more than the old regime. The
Cambridge analysis, however, lacked the empirical underpinning of Harris
and Josling although it was strong in heroic assumptions.

ment that the inefficient system did smooth out prices for consumers — less sharp rises and falls — and did guarantee supplies of food to member states.

"EEC membership has been a disaster for the British economy," the Labour Common Market Safeguards Committee concluded. "None of the forecasts that were made about economic advantages have been fulfilled."

Like so much of the argument on both sides, this was half true, the last half, which correctly observed that great blessings had not flowed. But then neither had great curses fallen. Despite the prolonged and heated debates, staying in or out has made little difference.

Unlike the commentators and the politicians, most ordinary Britons sensed as much all along. The power game is sport for politicians and the civil servants who, at least in theory, serve them. A minister who is received abroad in great state, whose words echo around the world, who sees himself making history, understandably enjoys it. After all, power is what politics and politicians are about. Foreign Office and Treasury mandarins who write the briefs and pull global strings for ministers also enjoy a sense of well-being that their more modest counterparts in Copenhagen or Montevideo will never know. Much the same spirit animates a military bureaucracy pressing for every imaginable weapon, every imaginable base. Or a State Department promoting "commitments," asserting a "vital interest" in every remote and untamed corner of the globe. It is not clear what joy, if any, the man on the Clapham omnibus, the old lady in Dubuque or M. du Pont derives from this. So most Britons were not interested in a great-power role. They doubted, moreover, that heaven or hell could be attained by trading rules governing Continental commerce. They had a sober, modest sense of reality and were unswayed by the rhetoric. Repeated polls showed that Britons did not regard membership as an important matter. One taken for the

EEC itself in mid-1977 and not likely to understate enthusiasm for the Community showed fewer than two Britons in
five thought it a good thing, a larger number voted it "bad"
and nearly one in four had no opinion. This was about
right, more right than the expert economists, politicians and
journalists who saw Brussels as either the Beginning or the
End. This sense of proportion is not unlike — perhaps flows
from — the preference for leisure over goods. People who
will not strain for a second summer house, a bigger car or a
deepfreeze are not eager to see their rulers strutting on a
world stage or their industrialists striving to rationalize or
make workers work harder.

Even if the Common Market could have lived up to its
supporters' claims and given industry a shower, British
workers would have turned off the tap. Anyway, the Market
could no more do this than it could provide Britain with a
surrogate for empire. The very arguments that aroused
Heath, Jenkins and the business leaders bored most Britons.
In the same way, the rhetoric of a Foot or Powell was enjoyed as theater; it was hard to believe that joining the Nine
would burn down Parliament.

On the other side, the leftist leaders of unions, the Market's parliamentary foes, made much the same mistake as its
friends. Both took far too seriously the Community's promise to become a Federal Europe, a political force, a supranational regime. Both also suffered from the delusion that
membership would cause profound and far-reaching consequences for the ways in which people made their living, went
about their daily business.

It is not quite accurate to conclude that all British leaders
of opinion on both sides of the Market question — political,
press, union and industrial — debated in a dream world.
Certainly most did. But a few, generally labeled "cynic,"
like Wilson and Callaghan, appear to have had some
glimpse of realities. They dissembled; they said one thing

one day and another another. Like most citizens, they understood there was less to the Market than met the ear.

So Britain, as before, remains a middle power of the second order. It takes its place behind Germany in defense dis-
cussions with the United States. These three are generally
joined by France and Japan at meetings on major questions
of international economics. This is the way things were before Britain went into the Nine; it is the way things remain.
It reflects political and economic reality. If anything, this industrial directorate of one super and several middling
powers has become even more formal in recent years. Annual economic summits bring together government chiefs of
the five plus Canada and Italy. The Common Market is not
invited in its own right (although the Commission president
is allowed to sit in on a few sessions). Its largest member
states are present as sovereign entities.

At home, nothing much has changed either. The prime
minister, the chancellor of the exchequer, the cabinet
— with a group of high civil servants in the Treasury and
cabinet secretariat — fix British taxes, determine the levels
of British spending and try to tell the Bank of England at
what level to set the exchange rate of the pound. Over every
economic decision that really matters, British officials —
elected and unelected — decide; nobody would think of asking Brussels' advice let alone approval.

The Foreign Office still wrings its hands over Britain's limited influence in the world — Belize, Gibraltar and the Falk-
land Islands excepted. The foreign secretary frequently
meets his homologues in some agreeable Common Market
capital. But this is simply a convention. When in difficulty,
ministers turn to Washington, and it is there that serious policy is shaped. To be sure, the foreign secretary and his eight
Brussels partners frequently adopt important-sounding reso-
lutions on this and that around the globe. Almost invariably, they involve matters over which the Nine have little or

no influence — supporting that homeland for Palestinians and the like.

Parliament is still alive, as powerful (or powerless in the view of those who regard British government as prime ministerial or cabinet-based) as it was before January 1, 1973. It rarely debates Common Market matters and then only at inconvenient times when few show up. This is adequate recognition of how little they matter. It is Parliament and not Brussels that gives assent to the great matters of politics at home and abroad.

In 1977, one Common Market question again reached the front pages of the more solemn journals. But this was almost atavistic. At issue was the method by which delegates would be elected to the European Parliament at Strasbourg. Since that Parliament is virtually powerless, it was hard to arouse any but the most dedicated over whether Britain would elect delegates by a system of proportional representation or by the first-past-the-post technique used in Britain and the United States. The outcome most certainly could affect the fate of some of the participants — Strasbourg delegates are to get a handsome salary, perhaps $60,000 a year, for their ill-defined labors. Nobody else could care very much. (Liberals did, however, because they saw proportional representation at Strasbourg as a hopeful omen for Britain itself. In the event, they lost.)

The pro-Marketeers, unwilling to see so much energy expended for so little, would retort, "Just wait." The institution is young. Britain has been a member for little more than five years. Give us time. We will yet build a United States of Europe. Perhaps, but the skeptics have the better case. If someday there is a genuine threat of a U.S. military withdrawal from Europe, if there are real signs of an expansionist Soviet Union menacing the Western nation-states, then, perhaps, fear will drive the Nine closer together, make them willing to surrender control over their affairs to a common organ. But without such threats, there is little reason to believe that the Community will become more than it is now, a customs union with a complex price support system attached, chiefly for the benefit of farmers in Holland and France. Ordinary Britons, who have enjoyed prosperity since the end of empire and income levels that make leisure more attractive than goods, demand no more from their membership in the Nine.

V. Wound in Ulster

Subverting Law and Justice

God, Whose absence in Britain is deplored by the editor of *The Times,* is omnipresent in one part of the United Kingdom, the six offshore counties of Northern Ireland. There, His adepts and His temples can be found in abundance, perhaps overabundance. Ulster, to give the place its historic, euphonious name, is more intensely Protestant than Britain or Sweden, although both are buttressed by state-established Protestant churches. It is more passionately Catholic than Catholic Italy, France or Austria, if devotion can be measured by church attendance.

Men, women and children in Ulster are so attached to their separate religions that they have sporadically burned, bombed, shot and maimed those of the other persuasion for more than three hundred years. To be sure, they have done so usually in the name of a national ideal, "loyalty to the Crown" or an "independent Ireland." Ask an Ulsterman his address and the chances are you will know at once to which faith he subscribes. "Prods" and "Taigs," as they unlovingly call each other, mostly live apart in segregated ghettos, or villages, with fellow worshipers at the same shrine. A gunman from the IRA or a Protestant paramilitary gang who enters the rare plant where Catholics and Protestants work easily side by side knows how to spot a target even without asking an address. He simply opens a potential victim's shirt to see if he is wearing a Catholic medallion. The killer then

fires or withholds his fire depending on whether or not he
and the potential victim share the same ikons. Despite this
feverish concern with religious identity, it cannot be said
that the six counties are blessed with a happier condition
than godless Britain.*

The current round of Troubles, as the murder, mayhem
and arson are euphemistically described, can be dated from
August 1969, when Ulster's overwhelmingly Protestant police poured into the Bogside, a Catholic enclave in Londonderry. The police, swinging their batons or clubs freely
against the largely unarmed Bogsiders, served as an advance
guard for a mob of riotous Protestant youths. Two days
later, the Royal Ulster Constabulary improved on their
baton charge in Derry† by turning machine guns against
Catholic rioters in Belfast. Both events compelled the British government in London to send in 10,000 troops, largely
to protect the Catholics from the wrath of their Protestant
neighbors, particularly the Protestant forces of law and
order.

In the following eight years, 1794 persons were blown up,
shot, burned or tortured to death. Another 20,000 were
blinded, mutilated, lost a limb or otherwise wounded. In
Belfast, the grimly industrial and political capital of this
stricken land, 60,000 families have "moved"; the vast majority have been driven or fled from their homes at the urging
of neighbors from the other religious persuasion. About one
third of the province is Catholic, but Catholics have contributed most to the tide of refugees.

To the world at large, the televised spectacle of suffering
in Ulster has become monotonously familiar. Weeping

---

* In Ulster's 1961 census, only 384 of 1,457,000 identified themselves as free-
thinkers, atheists or humanists. The census taker is supposed to have replied,
"Yes, but are you a Protestant or a Catholic freethinker?"
† Everything in Ulster, even a name, has a Protestant and Catholic dimension. The city divided by the River Foyle (and much else) is known to Catholics as "Derry," to Protestants as "Londonderry." The names will be used
here interchangeably.

mothers, tense soldiers; burned and flattened homes, pubs and factories; commemorative funerals, parades, cries for vengeance and justice — all have become stale with repetition, an O'Casey drama with no last act. Even in Britain, separated from Ulster by only twenty-two miles of the Irish Sea, there is a numbing weariness with the place and its endless atrocities. The Irish of Ulster, like those of the Republic to the south and west, are regarded as a savage, inexplicable people, little more comprehensible than warring factions in Angola or Zaire.

The British Army engraves superbly detailed and accurate maps of the Catholic and Protestant enclaves in Belfast and Derry. Officers refer to those as "tribal maps," an expression of the contempt they feel. At a critical moment in the 1974 strike of Ulster's Protestant workers, Prime Minister Harold Wilson inflamed an already dangerous situation by calling the people of the province "spongers." They vote in United Kingdom elections too, but Wilson, more politician than statesman, was talking to Britons, his real electorate. He knew what would appeal to them.

Unhappily for Britons, the Troubles are not confined to Ulster. Apart from the IRA's sporadic and short-lived bombing campaigns in Britain itself, an insidious poison has spread across the Irish Sea. With some justice, Britons regard themselves as civil, humane, fair and tolerant citizens in a society of law rather than one of arbitrary edicts by men. But London's belated efforts to govern ungovernable Ulster since 1969 have begun to corrode the essential decency of British life. In trying to suppress terrorists (guerrillas, freedom fighters, patriots, gangsters — all apply), Britain has surrendered some of the quality that makes it civilized. Just as worrisome, it has given its army a political task and, inevitably, politicized an army that has traditionally been seen as the obedient servant of civilian masters. There is, it turns out, something after all to the dark forebodings of Sevareid and Friedman, although it is unlikely they thought of Ulster as the instrument for a Chileanized Britain.

Even now, Britons as well as Ulstermen are living under a law that temporarily suspends habeas corpus, permits arrest without warrant and penalizes some forms of expression with up to five years in jail. This is the Prevention of Terrorism (Temporary Provisions) Act of 1976, a measure that a Labour government put through the Commons with virtually no dissent. Of course, it is aimed at those who "belong . . . solicit . . . assist . . . or further the activities of, a proscribed organization." And the IRA — the Irish Republican Army — is, as of this writing, the only organization "proscribed." But there is an argument that rights are indivisible, that once civil liberties are breached for those suspected of adhering to a single group, no matter how noxious, the rights of all others are diminished. The act was first passed in 1974 after an IRA bomb in a Birmingham pub killed twenty-one young men and women, murdered at random. It gives the authorities draconian powers. Like most such laws, it has not noticeably inhibited the terrorists. But it has warped British respect for civil liberties. If a person can receive five years for "further[ing] the activities of a proscribed organization," speech or the distribution of literature becomes an offense. The act allows police to arrest, hold and question for seven days anyone a constable "reasonably suspects" to be guilty of any offense under the law. The "suspect" can and will be kept from his solicitor for the seven days and as many nights, a temptation to extract incriminating admissions by force that even some of the notably restrained British police might find hard to resist. The wearing of the uniform of a "proscribed" organization — for the Provisional wing of the IRA, black beret, black turtleneck jersey and dark glasses — can bring six months in prison. (This section was modeled after the 1936 act, which prohibited Oswald Mosley's followers from sporting their black shirts.) Just as remarkable, the home secretary can keep out or throw out of Britain anyone he thinks is attempting "the commission, preparation or instigation of acts of terrorism."*

No trial is required for such exclusion orders. The only appeal is to the same home minister who issued the edict, not the courts.

It must be said at once that there is no convincing evidence that these extraordinary powers have been abused by the first two home ministers endowed with them, Roy Jenkins and Merlyn Rees. Both are liberal, compassionate men, extremely sensitive to questions of civil rights. But the act is there, on the books. Like many such measures, it is even called "Temporary." But as the French have noted, it is the temporary that often endures. In the hands of a minister of strong passions, a home secretary less concerned with civil rights, crude abuses could become the norm. If this minister and his government, moreover, are exercised about "subversives" of the left (or right), the number of proscribed organizations might be enlarged. The sweep of the act could become far broader. This has not yet happened; it need not but it could, thanks to Northern Ireland.

In the first half century of Ulster's existence as a separate, self-governing, almost autonomous province of the United Kingdom,† there was little rule of law as it is generally understood. The place was endowed with all the trappings of a legislature, cabinet and even prime minister. But they simply legitimated a dictatorship of the majority. It was, as Lord Craigavon, one of its designers, said, a "Protestant par-

---

* This is aimed at Ulstermen who come to Britain. It simply throws the suspected terrorist back into Northern Ireland, which presumably has a surfeit. A companion provision aimed at suspects from the Republic enables the home secretary to bar them from either Ulster or Britain.

† The place names can confuse. "Britain" is Great Britain, the ancient kingdoms of England, Scotland and Wales, the island off the coast of the European continent. The formal name of the state is the United Kingdom of Great Britain and Northern Ireland, incorporating — at least in law — the six Ulster counties under the Crown and simultaneously recognizing their separateness.

liament for a Protestant people." The province's half million Catholics took what they could get. What they got, as Lord Cameron, a Scottish judge, observed in a dry report to the Ulster government, was wholesale violation of the Universal Declaration of Human Rights. The province's Protestant parliament gave its largely Protestant police — and their even more Protestant auxiliaries — the power to make "arbitrary arrest"; infringe a person's "right to be presumed innocent until proven guilty"; interfere "with personal privacy, home or correspondence"; and abuse "freedom of opinion and expression." (In the nature of things, a few Protestants also felt this lash; but Craigavon's Protestant machine chiefly ground up Catholics.)

That, of course, was in the bad old days before the British Army went in and returned effective control of the place to London. But it was not long before London, provoked by a revived IRA, began behaving much like the local regime it had pushed aside. On the night of August 8–9, 1971, the army, acting under orders, smashed its way into 342 homes and seized the men inside. They were suspected of IRA membership and, inevitably, all but a handful were Catholic. They were the first of 2158 who were to be interned over the next four years. They were imprisoned indefinitely — never charged with a crime, never tried and never sentenced. They were penned up in barracks and on suspicion with no right of appeal to any court of law. By the time Merlyn Rees ended this practice in December 1975, the interned population had altered a little. About one in twenty was now Protestant, suspected of belonging to one of the paramilitary organizations that had sprung up in response to the IRA.

Detention without trial had been a familiar instrument in Northern Ireland (and indeed in Dublin, capital of the independent Republic to the south). It was something new, however, for British soldiers, politicians and administrators to

wield in the United Kingdom. The peculiar flavor of Ulster
had overcome the new masters.

The soldiers and police who "processed" those seized were
understandably eager to extract information from them. In
the fall of 1971, they subjected at least twelve of the detainees to five unusual techniques. A man would be spread-
eagled against a wall, his full weight on his fingertips and
toes for up to six hours at a time. His head was covered with
a black hood to increase his sense of isolation, to "disorient"
him. An electronic machine sounded a continuous whining
note. He was deprived of sleep and given bread and water
every six hours.

The British press, notably *The Sunday Times,* suggested that
this was improper, even for IRA suspects. So Reginald
Maudling, then the home secretary, asked Sir Edmund
Compton, Britain's former ombudsman, to look into it.
Maudling in person is a kindly, amiable man, although his
failure to meet the Commons' unexacting standards for conflict of interest has earned him a mild rebuke from his fellow
MPs. In this affair, and with unintended irony, he insisted
that the remarkable methods were "necessary not only for
reasons of security and control but also *to protect the lives of
those being interrogated*" [my emphasis]. Ombudsman Compton was a shade more censorious. The techniques, he found,
constituted "physical ill-treatment." They weren't brutal or
cruel, however, because "cruelty implies a disposition to in-
flict suffering, coupled with indifference to, or pleasure in,
the victim's pain." There was no evidence that the army
and police enjoyed their work. Therefore, they were neither
brutal nor cruel.

More than four years later, the European Commission on
Human Rights declined to see the distinction. It held that
the five techniques "constituted a practice of inhuman treatment and torture." For good measure, the commission also
found that other detainees who had simply been beaten by

their captors had suffered "inhuman treatment" as well. (A Solomonic European Court of Human Rights then split the difference, declaring that the practices were "inhuman and degrading" but somehow fell short of "torture.")

Almost four years before the Human Rights Commission finally sliced through the sophistry of Maudling and Compton, the British sense of fair play and decency had put an end to the more outrageous practices. Prime Minister Heath ordered the spread-eagling, hooding, electronic noise and the rest stopped as early as March 1972. There is nothing to suggest that they have since been renewed. The IRA, however, regularly complains that arrested suspects are still beaten by the Ulster police, still an overwhelmingly Protestant force, and by the army. Although the IRA had a vested interest in seeking sympathy, the Protestant police and the soldiers have a strong interest in information and conviction. There has been independent confirmation that men taken in are at least sometimes treated more harshly than the law would allow. Mistreatment of those arrested had become so routine by 1977 that the police surgeons in Ulster were reported to be meeting privately to consider what they might do to halt the practices. Ulster's chief constable, Kenneth Newman, counted 215 complaints of brutality in the first nine months of 1977 alone, one in every seven his men interrogated. In a 1978 report, buttressed by medical evidence, Amnesty International described the systematic beating and intimidation of those hauled in by the police, including men and women against whom no charge could be lodged.

Most striking of all, perhaps, is that the British government actually acknowledged and paid no fewer than 473 claims for false arrest, false imprisonment and assault and battery between August 1971 and January 1975. Another 1193 claims were still outstanding. It is hard to imagine any other country that mistreats people on a large scale, admits it and compensates for it.

Despite this rectitude, however, the direct involvement in

Ulster has weakened some strands of British humanity. Soldiers and police responsible to London have become experienced in peculiar practices and the mistreatment of civilian prisoners. Given what may be regarded as sufficient provocation, all these techniques could be employed again.

In much the same way, Ulster has warped the judgment of judges. Every government inevitably tries to disguise and excuse the errors of its servants. Because of Ulster, some of those charged with uttering justice in the state have corrupted language to hide unpalatable truth. Compton, who as ombudsman had been responsible for protecting citizens from the abuses of government, invented the Jesuitical distinction that converted "inhuman and degrading" into "physical ill-treatment."

Similarly, the Honorable Mr. Justice (Leslie) Scarman of the Appeal Court was asked to report on the riots of 1969 in general and in particular on the behavior of the police, the Royal Ulster Constabulary (RUC). "Undoubtedly mistakes were made and certain individual officers acted wrongly on occasion," the Honorable Justice concluded. "But the general case of a partisan force co-operating with Protestant mobs to attack Catholic people is devoid of substance and we reject it utterly. We are satisfied that the great majority of the members of the RUC was concerned to do its duty which, so far as concerned the disturbances, was to maintain order on the streets, using no more force than was reasonably necessary . . ."

Since Scarman's own report also described how baton-swinging RUC men had preceded a Protestant mob into the Bogside, and how other RUC men opened fire on Belfast Catholics with machine guns, Scarman's verdict was extraordinary. It was no more so, however, than that reached a few months later by Lord Chief Justice Widgery, the highest judge in Britain's criminal courts. He had been called to examine "Bloody Sunday," January 30, 1972, when British paratroopers killed thirteen unarmed civilians in the Bogside and wounded thirteen others. This climaxed a civil rights march that the local authorities had refused to sanction. Widgery absolved the paratroopers, a notoriously vigorous force, of any general misbehavior, although he acknowledged that there was a bit of "firing [that] bordered on the reckless." None of the victims, he conceded, "is proved to have been shot whilst handling a firearm or bomb . . . but there is strong suspicion that some . . . had been firing weapons or handling bombs in the course of the afternoon." (Not a paratrooper suffered a scratch from these "weapons," which suggests that their victims were "handling" them in a state of advanced rigor mortis.)

The "strong supicion" rested entirely on the facts that lead particles had been found on the left hands of four of the dead and that four bulky bombs containing nails had been found in the pockets of another. This last was a find that two doctors who had separately examined the man first had somehow overlooked. Widgery rejected entirely the obvious suggestion that this "evidence" had been planted by the paratroopers who carted away the corpses.

Such documents from eminent juridical figures are a remarkable blend of careful fact and implausible conclusion. As Conor Cruise O'Brien was to say of one, they were "a characteristic 'British official' mixture of integrity and hypocrisy." At the very least, British justice is ill served when its judges are enlisted to endorse official lies, an inevitable consequence of Ulster.

A Political Army

Perhaps the biggest danger to Britain's political health is the evolving character of the army. Since 1969, when it was called in to spare Catholics from Protestant authorities and citizenry, the army has effectively run the province. It is the real source of authority, not the civil servants nor even less the ministers who sit isolated in Stormont Castle, three miles from the Belfast streets where Ulster's life is lived. The soldiers are in the streets every day, incongruously patrolling in combat uniforms, rifles at the ready, while housewives with babies and workers stroll by. Armored military vehicles race up and down main avenues and back streets of Belfast, Derry and smaller towns. The British minister nominally in charge almost never ventures out among his subjects, although occasional delegations troop out to his suburban fortress. He commutes between Whitehall and Stormont, lifted by helicopter from the green lawns surrounding the castle to a distant airfield and an RAF plane. He sees Belfast city almost exclusively from the air.

Unsurprisingly, an army assigned a political role becomes interested in politics. Its officers are quickly contemptuous of elected politicians, believe they know better and become an independent rather than a subordinate force. This is an inevitable consequence of wars against insurgents, of guerrilla wars. The army in Ulster sees itself engaging in a war against insurgent guerrillas like those in Kenya, Aden, Cyprus and Malaysia, where soldiers must act on both political and military fronts. The army's leading theoretician in Ulster, Brigadier Frank Kitson, has said as much.

So when Merlyn Rees, then the minister in charge of Northern Ireland, ended internment without trial, the army did not hesitate to speak out in defense of a system that had inflamed virtually the entire Catholic community and served as a recruiting magnet for the IRA. Lieutenant General Sir Frank King, the commander of the British troops, delivered a speech complaining that Rees had made his task more difficult. "In another two or three months," the general contended, "we would have brought the IRA to the point where they would have had enough." Rees' policy threatened to block King's light at the end of the tunnel.

Rees, a mild man, decided that the appropriate course was a soft rebuke. "The General made a mistake," Rees explained to the House of Commons. He has "expressed his regrets to me."

The incident need not be magnified but it was symptomatic. General King's objections did not reverse the policy. But the fact that a very high-ranking British officer believed he could publicly criticize the political policy of his civilian masters suggests strongly that Ulster is a potent brew.

Like most events in that unhappy province, there is ample historical precedent for the affair. On the eve of World War I, the British Army virtually mutinied rather than enforce a policy ordained by its political overlords.

Herbert Asquith's Liberal government, in alliance with MPs from Ireland, had finally agreed to Home Rule, a measure of local self-government, for the entire island. In those days, both North and South, all thirty-two counties, were still part of the United Kingdom. The Protestants, concentrated in Northern Ireland, saw that their dominance over the Catholics would be destroyed; even worse, the Protestants would become an outvoted minority in any Home Rule scheme covering the entire island and might be threatened with the treatment they had administered. So the Protestants, led by Edward Carson,* simply said, "We will not have Home Rule," and signed petitions to that effect by the tens of thousands. They demanded that the six northeastern counties, where Protestants then as now enjoyed a two-to-one majority, must be exempt.

More important, the Protestants formed their own army, the Ulster Volunteer Force, under the command of a retired British general. By March of 1914, the UVF had 100,000 men under arms, with British reserve officers drawing half-pay to stiffen them.

British officers on active duty were unwilling to put down the threatened rebellion. Then as now most army officers

---

* It is of some symbolic importance that a statue of the rebellious Carson, arms outstretched, still dominates the mile-long drive through the park to the entrance of Stormont, the seat of Ulster's civilian government.

were Protestant; Catholic Irish were regarded as inferior, primitive, a shiftless breed, disloyal to King and Crown. Even George V took the Protestant side.* Would it be wise, he asked Asquith, to strain the loyalty of his troops by asking them to enforce the government's decision, even though it had been ratified by Parliament?

The director of military operations at the War Office, Sir Henry Wilson, worked with opposition Conservative politicians and the leaders of Ulster's Protestants to insure that the government would get no help from the army. In an unprecedented gesture of sympathy, the War Office permitted officers living in Ireland to excuse themselves from putting down Carson's incipient rebellion. The commander of the cavalry brigade and fifty-nine other officers in the Curragh Camp exercised this option. It was, wrote Robert Kee in his magisterial history, *The Green Flag,* "a major Army mutiny." Prime Minister Asquith saw the point and exempted the six counties from his Home Rule Bill. "The Army was shown to be too unreliable" for any other course, Kee wrote. The Army's threat of revolt, vetoing the decision of the elected government of the United Kingdom, created the border that exists between North and South today. If there were any remaining doubts, Carson's UVF imported 24,600 rifles from Germany just four months before Britain went to war against the Kaiser in August 1914.

The full record of the army's political behavior in more recent times remains obscured. But there is enough evidence to suggest that Ulster has once again weakened an essential prop of any democratic society, civilian control of the military. To be sure, the struggle between Protestants and Catholics in the offshore counties is not the sole reason for in-

---

* Sixty-four years later, his granddaughter unwittingly displayed similar sympathies. Queen Elizabeth's Silver Jubilee visit to Ulster was limited to a pair of remote and overwhelmingly Protestant towns. To be sure, IRA threats made it unwise for her to venture among her Catholic subjects, but the tour amply demonstrated whose Queen she is.

cipient mutiny. Army officers in Britain as in most industrial countries tend to be conservative in politics, to deplore
what they think is the outrageous power of unions and to be
shaped by a hierarchical, authoritarian order. The coal
strikes of 1972 and 1973–74 that humiliated the Conservative Heath government also inflamed feelings in officers'
messes. They inspired waves of wild talk. But it was only in
Ulster that talk could be and was translated into action.

The current manual for British Army tactics against civilian Britons was written by Brigadier Frank Kitson in 1971.
Unsurprisingly, he had just returned from commanding the
39 Brigade in Derry before settling down to *Low Intensity Operations*. Stripped of its tortuous prose, the message of the
brigadier, a rising star in the army, was this: It is unlikely
that British soldiers will again have much chance to fight
traditional wars, against the soldiers of enemy nations.
Modern technology has made the traditional army obsolete.
But do not lose heart. We still have a role to play, combat-
ting subversion at home, "political and economic pressure,
strikes, protest marches and propaganda . . ."

Ulster is a current example, Kitson continues, but the
army is so strong there that it is "unlikely that it will be involved in exactly this task between 1975 and 1980." The
conflict will be over by then. "Even so there are other potential trouble spots within the United Kingdom which
might involve the Army in operations of a sort against political extremists . . . such a situation could arise . . . at a
time of apparently unrivalled affluence . . . [It] might result from a significant drop in the standard of living."

The heart of the brigadier's matter is a proposal that the
government use the army "to keep the country running during a prolonged period of strikes and civil disturbance." To
do this, the army must train "specialist individuals or units"
to "run ports, railway stations, power stations and sewage
works as well as *supervise the operations of mines and many types of
industrial plants*" (my emphasis).

In short, Kitson urges that the army save itself from technological obsolescence by turning its bayonets on striking British workers. The brigadier also calls for army "intelligence" and propaganda teams to spy on civilian "subversives" and manipulate the mass of the citizenry.

This could be put down as the fantasizing of an overeager officer who had misread his Ulster experience — except for one remarkable fact. The book carries a foreword by General (now Field Marshal) Sir Michael Carver, chief of the general staff and Britain's top soldier at the time. Sir Michael extols Kitson as "above all a realist, in spite of being both an idealist and enthusiast." The chief of the general staff concludes: "This book is written for the soldier of today to help him prepare for the operations of tomorrow. It will be of the greatest possible help to him, and I hope it will be read by all those concerned with training the Army."

Suiting action to words, Sir Michael posted Kitson to command the Warminster Infantry School, the chief training ground for fighting officers, Britain's Fort Benning.

The book triggered a few outraged cries from Labour politicians and union leaders. Kitson disappeared from public view and wiser generals, more conscious of public relations, minimized the importance of his manual. They suggested that Sir Michael really had not read it. Perhaps not, but the Labour government did. When firemen staged a national strike against the third year of pay restraint in 1977, thousands of troops replaced them. They did the job so well, a contented sergeant could say, "Next week, when the dockers go on strike, we'll unload the ships. When the miners go on strike, we'll dig the coal, and when the railways go on strike, we'll take the stuff to the power stations." He was running a bit ahead of the facts, but the doctrine had clearly percolated down.

As chance would have it, the army was given a splendid opportunity to practice Kitson's theory, in Ulster and on behalf of legitimate civilian authority. It came in May 1974, when Ulster's Protestant workers staged a paralyzing general strike to destroy a project designed to win the allegiance of disaffected Catholics. This was the short-lived power-sharing regime, a provincial government that placed Catholic politicians side by side with Protestants in charge of executive departments. The strike was organized to bring this government down.

But instead of responding to the Kitson-like opportunity, the army staged the equivalent of a second and more subtle Curragh mutiny. Like the largely Protestant police, soldiers in Ulster stood by and watched as gangs of men, frequently armed and masked, erected and manned barricades in the streets of Belfast and other towns to block or frighten away those who wanted to go to work. Later, leaders of the successful strike said that if the army had ordered the barricades down in the first two days of the stoppage, the strike would have failed and the power-sharing regime might have survived. The army did no such thing. It went further. It deceived its civilian masters, telling them that the barricades had been withdrawn when in fact they were still standing.*

According to Robert Fisk of *The Times,* whose book *The Point of No Return* is the authoritative account of the strike, the Defense Ministry in London collaborated with the strikers, too, delaying the dispatch of reinforcing troops. To be sure, the indecisiveness of London's principal minister in Northern Ireland, the gentle Merlyn Rees, made it easier for the army to play its game. But play it it did, killing for the indefinite future any prospect of a joint Protestant-Catholic regime.

The lessons learned from all this were summarized by a

---

* Once during the strike I had a luncheon date at isolated Stormont Castle with Stanley Orme, the Labour government's deputy minister for Northern Ireland. I apologized for being late, explaining that I had been held up at half a dozen street barricades in East Belfast on my way out. Orme looked at me in disbelief. The army had told him, he said, that all the barricades had come down before eight that morning, when citizens go to work.

serving officer who called himself Andrew Sefton in an article for the *Monday World,* a publication of the extreme right fringe of the Conservative party. "In retrospect," he wrote, "1971 can be seen as the year in which the Army accepted its role as the only effective force of law and order in the Province and started to take on routine police tasks. The Army was getting closer to the grass roots of the routine of actually running a country than it had ever been before in its history."

"Sefton" continued: "Then there was the Ulster Workers' Council strike. The unwillingness of the Army to act to bring about the end of the strike . . . and the subsequent confrontation between the military and the politicians must be the most significant event of recent years. For the first time the Army decided that it was right and that it knew best and the politicans had better toe the line." For the future, Sefton concluded:

The Government has at its disposal an Army with an experience in counter urban guerrilla warfare greater than any comparable force in the world. In an era when industrial action has become a threat to the very existence of the country, and when the possibility of having to use troops to maintain that existence has become a probability, then it must be a cause for considerable concern that the Army and the [Labour] government are not in a relationship of mutual trust . . . The Army . . . has shown a considerable distrust of Socialist politicians . . . It has emerged, in fact, as a force that has to be reckoned with in political circles.

This then is the most insidious of Ulster's legacies; a politicized army that thinks out loud and in print about taking over a strikebound Britain, with or without the sanction of elected (but mistrusted) politicians.

There is no need to exaggerate the danger. Nineteen seventy-four, when Sefton wrote, was also the year that striking miners and Heath's three-day week turned the Tories out of office. There was a lot of Sefton's talk and Kitson's thinking in British officer ranks. It was a year when retired generals like Sir Walter Walker and adventurous ex-colonels like David Stirling were organizing "private armies" of volunteer strikebreakers, enlisting ex-officers, stockbrokers and other patriotic types. It was a year when Prime Minister Harold Wilson — at least according to *The Observer* — could bring himself to believe that MI5, the domestic spy service, was plotting against him.

But the fact remains that twice in the lifetime of some living men the British Army had staged a passive mutiny on behalf of Ulster Protestants, defying lawful, elected authority,* the express will of Parliament.

If another great crisis occurs in Ulster, Parliament cannot depend on the loyalty of the officer class. Although it is farfetched to conceive of a military coup in Britain, if one ever takes place, the chances are strong that its leaders will have been trained in Ulster and that events there will strike the spark.

The Protestant Worker

To a casual visitor, the six offshore counties and their towns look much like the British mainland. The lush green and rolling countryside, dotted with sheep and cattle, could be Yorkshire or the Scottish lowlands. The smoke-blackened brick of Belfast might be Glasgow, Liverpool or some other decaying industrial port. Behind the steel fences that seal off Belfast's bombed-out city center, shoppers pass through turnstiles manned by searching soldiers to buy at British chains — Boots the chemist, Woolworth's or the C & A department store.

---

* One of the many ironies in Ulster is that Protestants habitually refer to themselves as "Loyalists," a reference to their preference for union with Britain over submersion in the Catholic Republic on the rest of the island.

But Ulster is very different from the British part of the United Kingdom. It is inhabited by two unreconciled communities that identify themselves by religion, are in fact separated by caste, both uncertain of their allegiance and both afflicted with the siege mentality of a threatened minority. The "Loyalist" Protestants are a majority in Ulster but a minority of one in four over the whole island. To retain their dominance, to preserve their majority in a separate, six-county regime, they have demonstrated again and again that they will fight with arms. The Catholics are called "Nationalist" or "Republican" because so many yearn for one nation to rule all Ireland, uniting the six with the twenty-six counties of the Republic. If this happened, Catholics, a minority in Ulster, would be transformed into citizens of a majority. They too have thrown up armed fighters. Sometimes they defend Catholic enclaves in Belfast and Derry; sometimes they encourage Protestants and Britons with bomb, bullet and arson to yield to a union of all thirty-two counties. The struggle is not over religion; neither sect cares to convert the other. It is over power and rights, citizenship and nationality, the preservation or destruction of the border dividing Dublin's regime from Belfast's.

The Catholics descend from the native Gaels, who, in the sixteenth century, refused to obey the political strategy of Henry VIII and abandon their church for his new one. To subdue this rebellious peasantry, James I followed Machiavelli's advice for taming alien possessions and planted settlers among the natives. Ulster's Protestants descend from the 150,000 Scots and 20,000 Englishmen whom James successfully encouraged to emigrate and seize Catholic lands. This ancient history is very much alive in Ulster today. It is revived every July 12. Then Protestants turn out in their Sunday best, bowler hat, furled umbrella and orange sash to march proudly through the streets, commemorating the decisive victory in 1690 by the (Dutch) Protestant William of Orange over the (English) Catholic James II at the Battle of the Boyne. Indeed, the current Troubles began with a march by Derry Protestants in August 1969 to mark the town's successful resistance against James' siege in 1689. In accord with custom, the Protestants derisively threw pennies down from Derry's walls at the Catholics in the Bogside below. But that year Catholics were no longer supine. They responded with bricks and stones. So the Protestant police and attendant rioters moved in to teach the rebels another lesson.

The border between the six counties of Protestant-dominated Ulster and the overwhelmingly Catholic Republic was a compromise with brutal fact. On the eve of World War I, Protestants had made clear they would not accept the proposal of a single Home Rule government for the thirty-two counties. So Catholics, concentrated in the largely rural and poorer south and west, began an uprising in 1916 against any form of British rule. Their rebellion, pursued by forces calling themselves the Irish Republican Army and marked by ceaseless atrocity on both the British and Irish sides, more or less succeeded. Lloyd George completed Asquith's work and in 1921 signed a treaty giving twenty-six counties their independence. But he preserved the northeast corner of Ulster for the Protestants and the United Kingdom. Some in the IRA refused to accept the division and continued the struggle, but now against the newly established Irish Free State in Dublin. They were suppressed in a civil war that was again marked by exemplary cruelty on both sides. The IRA that fights on today can claim to be the heirs of the losing side in the Free State's civil war.

British politics had been periodically inflamed by the Irish question for more than a century and British politicians wanted to forget the place. This is why they endowed Ulster with an autonomy unique in the United Kingdom. The place was given its own legislature, complete with prime minister, cabinet and — perhaps most important — full control of the police and its armed auxiliaries. All these instruments of authority were safely Protestant. The "Loyalists" used their two-to-one majority to effectively exclude Catholics from political power, jobs in public and private employment and from the police, the sole "legitimate" possessors of armed force.

For half a century, London and its Parliament virtually ignored the place. The Protestants ran it to suit themselves. From time to time, guerrilla terrorists of the IRA "warred" on the province with bullet and bomb, reinforcing the Protestant conviction that all Catholics are potential rebels, justifying their exclusion from power and place. The IRA had and still does serve to reinforce the Protestants' siege mentality. What, after all, do the gunmen want? Nothing less than to force Ulster Protestants into minority citizenship in a Catholic republic that, until 1972, afforded the Roman Church a constitutionally privileged position; still bans, at this writing, divorce and the sale of contraceptives; and educates the overwhelming majority of its children in parochial or church schools. In Protestant eyes, then and now, Catholics are a work-shy, fast-breeding lot of welfare loafers, dirty, ignorant, Church-ridden. Then and now, most Catholics hold an equally unpleasant view of their Protestant overlords. They are seen as bigoted, mean, cold and oppressive. Little wonder that many Catholics long for union someday with the relaxed and cozy Republic of their coreligionists. However, only a handful believe that Ulster Protestants should be forced into such a union at the end of a gun barrel.

Few Northern Catholics ever ask how strongly they are wanted by their cousins in the South. It is not easy to give an unambiguous answer. There is in the Republic considerable sympathy for the plight of Ulster Catholics and a largely unexamined belief that the Troubles would end if unity were achieved. There is even a lingering undercurrent of sentimental feeling for the deeds of the IRA — of a half century ago, in the war for independence.

But this feeling stops well short of encouraging the IRA's

current crop of gunmen. Successive Dublin governments have competed with each other to harass and prosecute the IRA. On paper, at least, they have gone well beyond London in curbing civil liberties. Police and soldiers from the Republic systematically cooperate with their opposite numbers in Ulster to catch IRA fugitives seeking a haven across the border. Insistence on law and order has paid off for Irish politicians at the polls. If Irishmen south of the border are often as unaware as Northern Catholics of the fears of Ulster Protestants, they hold few illusions about the IRA today. Many see it simply and not inaccurately as a form of incipient fascism.

Dublin's support for union is also tempered, at least in part, by a recognition that the Northerners, regardless of religion, are different. They are tougher, more vigorous, more challenging. Even so, most in the South still hope that Northern Protestants will somehow see the light, understand the wisdom and necessity of union and join in a peaceful embrace. The very same Dublin political leaders who chase the IRA often fan this remarkable hope with equally remarkable rhetoric.

Left to their own devices after the 1921 treaty, Ulster Protestants ingeniously disenfranchised the minority on a scale to make a Boss Croker ("Government is Tammany: And Croker is its prophet") green, or perhaps, Orange, with envy. Derry was so effectively gerrymandered that a two-to-one Catholic majority in population was transformed into a local council of twelve "Loyalists" to just eight "Nationalists." Fermanagh County enjoyed a slight Catholic majority, 27,000 to 24,000. But the county council was rigged to give Protestants a 35–17 dominance. In Armagh, Catholics outnumbered Protestants almost three to two. But the Urban District Council reversed the ratio in favor of Protestants. And so it went throughout the province.

To achieve these splendid results, the majority employed

two devices. One was the classic gerrymander, drawing constituency boundaries to concentrate and waste Catholic
votes but maximize the Protestant electorate, giving it a narrow edge in most districts. The other trick was more direct.
In local government elections, the poorest one-quarter was
simply disenfranchised. Since Ulster's poor are predomi-
nantly Catholic, the losers in this game were predictable.*
When a new class of university-educated Catholics
emerged in the sixties, beneficiaries of Britain's 1944 education act, it is hardly surprising that they made "one man,
one vote" the chief demand of their new civil rights movement. It was this civil rights movement, inspired by events
in the United States and Les Événements in Paris — not the
dormant IRA — that lies behind the current Troubles.
Their marches and sit-ins, defying Ulster's Protestant authorities, made clear that Catholics would no longer accept
passively the diminished citizenship they had been assigned.
The Protestant monopoly of political power paid off
where it mattered, in public housing and jobs. For most of
this century, living standards in Ulster have lagged well behind Britain's, largely because the two industries that made
Belfast a landmark of the Industrial Revolution — linen and
shipbuilding — were dying or dead. So workers, Protestant
and Catholic, mostly lived in mean little row houses, "two
up and two down," as they say, meaning two cramped rooms
on one floor and another pair on the ground, no bath and
one freezing outdoor toilet in a tiny, garbage-strewn back
yard. Escaping from this to even the grimmest of public or
council housing tower blocks seemed to many like a new
world. But since local governments controlled the distribution of public housing flats and homes, an outsized share of
the new world was inevitably distributed to Protestants. For

---

* This stunt was accomplished by denying the vote to subtenants, lodgers,
servants and those over twenty-one living with their parents.

the first twenty-five postwar years in Fermanagh, two thirds of all public housing went to Protestants. Catholics, however, hold a slim majority of the population and, by virtue of their lower incomes, are in greater need. In brilliantly gerrymandered Derry, the Protestant authorities simply stopped building public housing for Catholics. There was no more space in the south ward where Catholics are concentrated; no sober Protestant would threaten his coreligionist's thin majority elsewhere by opening any place to an influx of fresh Catholics. Just before Britain abolished the Protestant regime in March 1972 and began ruling the province directly from London, this particular game stopped. Public housing is now distributed on the basis of points, reflecting family need.

The Protestant ascendancy also paid off in public jobs, and it is unlikely that even London's direct rule has very much changed this. Unhappily, with the decline of interest everywhere in Ulster's fate, the phenomenon is now rarely examined. But when the Troubles broke out, an attempt was made to find causes, and some interesting data emerged. In 1951, it was learned, Catholics held only 130 of 1095 white-collar jobs in local government, one in eight for a population measuring one in three. As late as 1969, Catholic Fermanagh supplied just 3 of 77 school bus drivers. No Catholics held senior local posts in the county; their "loyalty" was suspect, it was explained. In Derry, the two-to-one Catholic majority gained less than one in three of the clerical and technical posts. The police, the Royal Ulster Constabulary, then and now, are thought to be Protestant by a nine-to-one majority. Indeed, a study of the 1971 census found that just 10 percent of the police force was Catholic.* The

---

* Under London's rule, RUC commanders periodically urge Catholics to join the force. There is little response, partly because most working-class Catholics regard the Protestant police as the spearpoint of their traditional enemy, partly because they suspect the call is less than genuine. It serves a useful purpose, however; it enables London and the RUC to insist they do not dis-

notorious B Specials, the armed auxiliaries to the police, were almost 100 percent Protestant; their behavior was so scandalous, they were abolished in 1970; most either went into the newly formed Ulster Defense Regiment, a reserve unit under British Army control, or into the Protestant paramilitary* formations or both.

But the most critical and least understood area of discrimination is in the private sector, the factories and mills that are the basis of Ulster's economy. Ulster is a depressed region, and jobs, private and public, are critical for both a livelihood and status. In recent years, Ulster's rate of unemployment has typically run twice that of the high level in Britain; the Catholic jobless rate is twice again that of the Protestants. In other words, when unemployment is 6 percent in Britain, it is likely to be 12 percent in Ulster. This burden is shared "equally" between the communities. Six of every 34 Catholics who want a job can't find one and 6 of every 66 Protestants are in the same strait. This crucial fact gives Protestant workers an overwhelming interest in maintaining their monopoly or quasi-monopoly on jobs in the big plants.

There are no reliable figures for this practice. But observation by specialists and the folklore of the place hold that Protestants man 9600 of 10,000 jobs at Harland & Wolff, the province's biggest employer. This inefficient shipyard is gov-

---

criminate and to complain about their inability to patrol in many Catholic ghettos.

* The term "paramilitary" for the armed gangs of Protestant vigilantes, home defense units, assassination squads and protection racketeers is a gross misnomer. It suggests that these groups — the Ulster Defense Association, Ulster Volunteer Force (new model), Red Hand Commandos — and others enjoy a degree of legitimacy they do not have, although the British Army did covertly encourage the formation of the UDA, with which it has since had some occasional differences. But "paramilitary" has become so much a part of the language, to describe these lawless groups by any other word would be quixotic. It is, after all, no more misleading than "Irish Republican Army" for their Catholic homologues. The IRA does not recognize one Irishman in four — the Protestant — as Irish, is authoritarian rather than republican, and is less an army than an undisciplined band of guerrilla terrorists.

ernment-subsidized and, more recently, government-owned. But no London government, Labour or Tory, has ever dared to use its power to insist on open hiring. The Sirocco Engineering Works, a machinery plant, and James Mackie & Sons, a textile machinery maker, employ nearly five thousand between them and both are located in the heart of Catholic ghettos in Belfast. Both nevertheless have overwhelmingly Protestant payrolls.

In the sixties, a fresh breed of Protestant prime ministers in Ulster succeeded in attracting plants to a new industrial development in the east. Imperial Chemical Industries set up a synthetic fibers plant; Courtauld's, a knitted fabrics mill; GEC, a heavy machinery plant; and Rolls-Royce, an engine parts factory. The eastern Ulster belt is heavily Protestant, so it is safe to assume that the vast majority of the new jobs went to Protestants. Many Catholics believe that was precisely why the Ulster regime encouraged their establishment there. Workers at all four plants responded without threat or intimidation to the 1974 strike call by Protestant workers. This fact alone is strong evidence as to which side of the religious divide these workers stood on.

Most journalists in Ulster at one time or another write in despair that the quarrel is mad, that there is no difference between the cramped row houses on the Protestant Shankill Road or the Catholic Lower Falls, heartlands for the two communities in Belfast.* The cliché, supported by outward appearance, is belied by fact. Geoffrey Bell, whose *Protestants of Ulster* is acute, scholarly and restrained, examined the proposition. On the Protestant Shankill he found about twice as many foremen, compared to the population, as on the Catholic Falls, twice the percentage of families with cars, twice as many families who owned and did not rent their homes.

---

* I fell into the trap once too, writing that the only difference was the portrait on the overcrowded living room wall, the Queen on the Shankill and the Virgin Mary in the Falls.

In both communities, a visitor is overwhelmed by the warm hospitality almost invariably offered. In the side streets off the Shankill or Falls, a strange reporter with impertinent questions is plied with tea and cookies; given the best chair before the electric heater or coal grate and urged to stay on to watch the color television playing continuously in the meanest homes. It is easy to think they are the same. They are not. The Protestants have used their two-to-one majority to stake out for themselves a two-to-one chance of living twice as well as their Catholic neighbors.

The Protestant control of the best jobs in the private sector is not merely a source of comfort for the here and now. It is seen as having consequences for generations to come. A welder at Mackie's, a stager at Harland & Wolff, expects that he will pass on his job or one like it to his son, his nephew, his cousin. He may have been introduced to the mill or the plant by his father or uncle. Maintaining a grasp on those jobs, particularly in the face of Ulster's chronically high unemployment, is both a legacy and an estate. This invests the Protestant quasi-monopoly with a strength that those outside the blue-collar, manual force rarely understand.

Within each Ulster community there is a sense of extended family, familial tie and obligation that reminds reporters who have seen both of villages in India. This is one reason why emigration from the province is small despite the daily bombings and killings. Any Belfast street, Catholic or Protestant, is an Indian village. Doors are left open, women can shop comforted by the thought that a close neighbor will keep an eye on the children. When the man in the home is "lifted" (jailed), the street rallies round with food, clothing, money and the nonmaterial comforts that make life endurable. Passing on jobs within the community is a sacred caste obligation, an integral part of the village life-style that holds people to the grimmest streets. For a Protestant to surrender his workbench (probably covered with Union Jacks or the bloodstained Red Hand flag of Ulster) to a Catholic is not only foolish; it is a betrayal of his extended family, of his close-knit village.

This feeling, these attitudes, and the very real material benefits that flow from them are the key to any understanding of the current Troubles. At every decisive point, it has been the Protestant blue-collar workers — not the IRA, brutish and nasty as it is — who have determined events. It is Protestant workers who have firmly vetoed every attempt at accommodation with Catholics. From the start, Protestant workers knew that yielding to civil rights would threaten those precious jobs. The assaults of Protestant workers, ably assisted by Protestant police from the same milieu, forced Britain to bring the army to Ulster in 1969. It was this group that revived the IRA's guerrilla war.

The IRA still existed in 1969, but it had largely become a talk-shop of half-educated teachers and others who mouthed an irrelevant Marxist jargon. When Catholic ghettos found they were helpless against Protestant assaults, their denizens turned on the talkers ("IRA — I Ran Away" was one graffito) and sought out old-timers in the movement to reorganize the community's "defense." The old-timers, and some youngsters, clerical, blunt and suspicious of godless communism, put together "active service units" of fighters. They soon exceeded their "mandate," however, insisting on the "historic" half-century mission, trying to drive the British out and force Protestants into a single Irish state. This was the origin of the divided IRA movement. The Official IRA is the old Marxist crowd, engaging in sporadic violence and much talk. The Provisional IRA, or Provos, are those who picked up guns, made bombs and now account for most of the violence from the Catholic side. More recently, some Provos have begun aping the Marxist phrases of the Officials. This does not endear them to those in the ghettos.

In the 1960s the Ulster Unionist party, the single and dominant party of Protestants, began throwing up more modern leaders. These provincial prime ministers — Terrence O'Neill, James Chichester-Clark and finally Brian Faulkner — each in his turn sought some way to relieve Catholic grievances, to cooperate with the Dublin regime, to end the quarrel over the border by giving Ulster Catholics a reason to remain loyal to Ulster. All three more or less well-meaning men were secure themselves, substantial landowners or, like Faulkner, a businessman-manufacturer. They did not, could not, understand the drives of Protestant workers, no more than could the British government. Each of the three was politically destroyed, driven from office. They were brought down by politicians who did understand the importance for Protestant workers of Carson's "No Surrender."

This fact was brought home with stunning clarity in the spring of 1974, when Protestant workers paralyzed the province, Europe's only successful political general strike since the war. Ever since, there has been no serious political initiative to resolve the hideous problem; that is precisely why they struck, to preserve the essential status quo.

Their target was the new and flimsy power-sharing regime that London had created for Ulster on January 1. Britain had been running the province from London since March of 1972 under the stewardship of William Whitelaw, a wise, shrewd and fatherly landowner from the north of England. The very embodiment of Tory good sense, Whitelaw, as Northern Ireland minister, had cajoled Faulkner, what was left of his Protestant Unionist party and the leading Catholic politicians, Gerry Fitt and John Hume, to agree on what seemed a historic compromise. They would all serve in a permanent coalition government for the province, dividing up ministerial portfolios or departments in rough accord with their numbers. Faulkner would preside as chief minister, Fitt was the deputy chief minister, Hume was put in charge of commerce and other portfolios were distributed with a fine sense of the politico-religious balance. To draw the heat from the border, the new Ulster regime would contain an "Irish dimension," recognizing the attachment of Catholics to their coreligionists in the Dublin Republic. Ulster and Dublin would create a Council of Ireland to discuss tourism, power generation across the border, fishing and other common matters. In time, if all went well, Catholics would have no reason to grieve, Protestants would lose their fear of a "disloyal" community, the gunmen would lose their support from both sides. The plan was a model of British justice, fairness and inventiveness. It was backed by all parties in Britain, by Dublin. In Ulster, it had the consent of politicians who commanded perhaps four Catholic votes in five and those Protestants who had traditionally led the Protestant party.

There was one fatal flaw. It did not have the assent of Protestant workers. How could it? Sharing power with Catholics who had been rigorously excluded for half a century threatened the heart of Protestant existence, the near-monopoly over jobs. If Catholic ministers sat at Stormont, the pressure to end discriminatory hiring at Harland & Wolff would be irresistible. Almost every other large Ulster plant runs with some kind of government subsidy, on taxes, exports, investment and the like. Inevitably, Catholics would move to Protestant workbenches at Mackie's, at ICI, at Courtauld's and the rest. Sons, nephews and cousins could no longer be guaranteed a place. A man's own job and his family's for generations were at stake.

So the Protestant workers called everybody out. Their remarkably skillful stoppage, with its slow, steady squeeze on the province's diminishing supply of electricity, paid scant attention and owed little to the familiar hard-line politicians. The best-known ones — Reverend Ian Paisley, the demagogue who every Sunday leads cheerful hymn singing on the Ravenhill Road before he launches into a fiery denunciation of the Pope; William Craig, the tough, blunt lawyer who had toyed with pulling Ulster out of the United

Kingdom and threatened Catholics with a pogrom; colorless Harry West, a farmer — were all dubious about the tactic. They scrambled aboard the strike bandwagon late in the day, still doubting it would succeed.

The strike's organizers were men unknown to politicians and journalists, but all figures of consequence in the Protestant working class. They were Harry Murray, a shop steward, or local union official, at Harland & Wolff; Billy Kelly, a convenor, or chief shop steward, at the Belfast east power station; Jim Smyth, an official of the Amalgamated Union of Engineering Workers; and others like them. It was Kelly who talked to Protestant shop stewards at depots where coal and oil are distributed. Others enlisted Protestant union officials at the shipyard, foundries, aircraft plant and the rest.

To be sure, they used muscle as well as consent. The paramilitaries — the Ulster Defense Association, Orange Volunteers, Ulster Volunteer Force and the other Protestant vigilante groups — threw up and stood by street barricades with clubs and guns to stop citizens from going to work. They were "pickets," mostly drawn from the same Protestant blue-collar force in whose name the strike was staged. At Mackie's, about one fourth of the work force (some may have been Catholic) turned up for work one morning. Masked gunmen drove them home. In Larne, I saw a band of about 120 men wearing fright masks, carrying clubs, marching up and down the principal streets to insure that strike "support" was total. It was all this the police and army quietly watched, lending the strike enforcers their tacit support.*

It took fifteen days before London, Faulkner and Fitt gave in. Threatened with a complete power blackout, confronted

---

* I saw one group of "pickets" at the entrance to a tomblike Harland & Wolff jump on the hood of a car carrying two executives and their secretaries. The paramilitaries threatened to turn the car over unless it turned around. Two armed RUC constables looked on with amusement while the car's occupants were effectively terrorized.

At another point, an armed RUC man in Stormont Drive asked me where I with an army that insisted it could not — despite Kitson — run power stations, the nominal authorities surrendered. Choking back his tears, Faulkner resigned and power-sharing ended after just four months. The Protestant workers, who saw themselves as descendants of Derry's besieged three centuries earlier, had closed the breach, preserved their ascendancy. More than three years later, nothing had changed. Not a single new political step worth recording had occurred in Ulster. London was still in charge but the Protestants had their jobs.

This insistence on the primacy of Protestant manual workers and their jobs is not a popular interpretation. Protestant workers themselves are reluctant to duscuss it, at least with outsiders. They usually maintain that there is no discrimination, that men simply work near their homes. (Which does not explain why the Short Strand, a Catholic enclave next door to Harland & Wolff and to Short Brothers and Harland, supplies few workers to either, or the Protestant domination of Mackie's and Sirocco's, both in West Belfast Catholic ghettos.) In public, leaders of the Protestant workers insisted they were most concerned about the innocuous Council of Ireland. Despite its lack of power and built-in vetoes, it was portrayed as an attempt to force "loyal" Protestants into a wastrel, evil Catholic republic. As for sharing power with Catholics, that would deny "democratic" rights.* These were the lines adhered to rigidly. But they are explicable. If, as a loyal Protestant, I deny the very existence of discrimination, I can hardly acknowledge that I strike to preserve it.

---

was going. I told him I had an appointment with Orme, the deputy minister who was trying, with the help of the British trade union movement, to break what he called a "Fascist" strike. "I hope they kill that bastard," said the policeman of the man whose life he was supposedly guarding.

* Jim Smyth, one strike leader, told me that power-sharing was the same as "saying in the U.S. that you must have a black mayor." Apart from the politics, this was an interesting insight into the Protestants' racial view of Catholics.

Two authors of indispensable books on Ulster, the American professor Richard Rose of Strathclyde University and Conor Cruise O'Brien, editor, critic, biographer, essayist and sometime Dublin politician, reject my view entirely. In *Governing Without Consensus,* Rose concludes from a questionnaire that class plays little part in Ulster, that the Protestant middle class is as likely to disobey an elected government as workers. There is, he insists, "a limited influence of class on political outlooks." O'Brien agrees in *The States of Ireland* and other writings.

It is hard to quarrel with two men who have written so sensibly about the place. But history, recent experience and repeated observation on the scene have convinced me otherwise. The very income figures from Rose's questionnaire undermine his position. They show that 43 percent of his Protestant families were making more than £21 a week in 1968 compared to only 28 percent of his Catholics. Since his average Protestant family had three children and his average Catholic four, it is likely that a higher percentage of Catholics had more than one wage earner to bring in these sums. In other words, Protestants dominated the better-paying, more skilled jobs — those at Harland & Wolff, Mackie's and the rest.

Early in 1978, and for the very first time, an official agency attempted to measure the advantages of the Protestant working class. The findings of the newly created Fair Employment Agency for Northern Ireland document the thesis offered here. Based on 1971 census data, the agency found that the Protestant jobless were an uncomfortable 56 in every 1000. But the Catholic rate was a cruel 139 per 1000, two and a half times as large. In the mills and factories, Protestants dominated the best-paying jobs and Catholics were consistently underrepresented in metal manufacturing, metal engineering, instrument engineering and electrical engineering.

Catholics held only one job in seven in the gas, electric

and water utilities, the power base for the Protestant strike. In shipbuilding and marine engineering, Catholics held slightly fewer than one job in twenty, 4.8 percent, striking statistical confirmation of the folk wisdom about Harland & Wolff.

"It is clear," the report said, "that the Protestant is most likely to be a skilled manual worker while the Roman Catholic will be an unskilled manual worker."

Skeptics about class differences in discrimination will find some support from a table showing Protestants dominate the better white-collar as well as blue-collar jobs. Working Catholics outside manufacturing and construction run pubs, wait on tables, dress hair, work as servants and nurses, teach (parochial) primary and secondary schools. Middle-class Protestants are company secretaries, policemen, chemists and biologists, engineers, managers and senior government officials.

But these tasks can't be handed down from father to son like those in the plants. Some are awarded as a result of examination, at least nominally open to all. So the table simply illustrates the continuing fact that Catholics are an underclass rather than weakens the belief that it is Protestant manual workers who have the greatest stake in keeping things as they are.

It is quite true that the Ulster workers' strike was, in the end, backed by virtually the entire Protestant community. But in the crucial early days, when its outcome was in doubt, many Protestant shopkeepers, small businessmen, teachers, nurses and others tried to continue working. They were the ones who lined up outside the Hawthornden Road villa that served as headquarters for the strike movement. They queued for "permits" to work, buy gas, pass through the barricades. They were more or less reluctant supporters of what was from start to finish an affair by Protestant workers for the preservation of Protestant jobs.

Three years after the successful stoppage, there was fresh

evidence of its real object. The Reverend Paisley, whose constituency as well as his congregation is essentially lower middle class, tried to stage his own general strike. He wanted, he said, sterner measures brought against the IRA. Apart from those in his home base of Larne, few turned out and the whole affair was a dismal flop. It was led by a man from the wrong class and for no genuine purpose — in sharp distinction to a walkout aimed at destroying a regime that had threatened job control.

Here then is the crux of the dilemma in Ulster, the source of endless deadlock. Catholics will no longer accept passively the second-class citizenship of the old Protestant hegemony, will no longer tolerate systematic discrimination in politics, housing and jobs. To the extent that there is a popular British concern with Ulster, the Catholics enjoy public support for these limited goals. But Protestant blue-collar workers will not give up their dominance of the better-paying, more secure, more skilled tasks. They can and will veto every effort to put Catholics on an equal footing. They will say they are struggling against immersion in a popish, foreign republic; they are defending in fact what they consider a family heritage. The Protestant middle class, petty and grand, can and will accept equality; they are not threatened by it. But the squirearchy, the business community, no longer determine the fate of Protestants and the province. Since Catholic aspirations must be frustrated, Catholics turn to their coreligionists in the South and revive the old cry for Irish nationhood. This further inflames Protestants of all classes and strengthens their belief in the fundamental disloyalty of the minority. As Professor Rose concluded, *"The problem is that there is no solution"* (his emphasis). This is because the minimum Catholic demand exceeds the maximum that Protestant workers will yield.

The Men with the Guns

If this is not reason enough for despair, there is still more. Despite the political deadlock since the 1974 strike, the shootings and bombings by guerrilla terrorists in both camps go on. Their pace may slacken from time to time as they did in 1977, but they can and will continue.* They have little political point because politics in Ulster have reached a dead end. Nevertheless, every few days brings a fresh atrocity, although it no longer rates more than a few paragraphs even in the British press. The violence goes on quite simply because its practitioners have now developed a vested social, psychological and pecuniary interest in it.

On the Catholic side, the Provisional IRA can still claim some support for the role it first played when it emerged in 1969–70 — defending the community from "aggression." Catholics, like Protestants, feel themselves besieged by a hostile majority. In enclaves like Andersonstown or ghettos like Ballymurphy, the IRA is seen by a substantial number as defense against pogrom. Army units periodically search these places for arms, smashing down doors and frightening sleeping families in the small hours of the night. This too creates clients and sympathy for the Provos (who now rarely attack soldiers in prolonged firefights and are content with picking off the odd trooper every few weeks just to keep their franchise).

The Provos justify terror as a legitimate political instru-

---

* The Callaghan government and the press rejoiced in the diminished level of violence in 1977. That year, there was one killing every three days compared to a daily murder in 1976; nearly two persons were injured seriously each day against four the year before; shootings fell from five a day to three and bombings from two to one. It is doubtful that this provided much comfort to the citizens of Ulster, and it is notable that when Callaghan visited the troops before Christmas, he slipped in and out of the province unannounced and virtually unseen by its citizens. Security, not cowardice, dictated his caution, recognition that the terror was still very much alive.

ment. They are, they say, wearing down the British will to remain, or when Marxist types mouth the line, destroying British capitalist-imperialist interests by blowing up a hotel or a shop. All this, of course, is in the name of reuniting the nation, returning the six counties to their rightful place, in the Dublin Republic. The enemy is Britain, it is said, not Protestant Ulstermen. In fact, of course, the Provos are blind to the existence of the one million Protestants, their will, their fears, their desires. But this too is traditional. Even James Connolly, the most gifted thinker in the Republic rising of 1916, the movement's Socialist theoretician, managed never to see what mattered most. In his *Labour in Irish History*, Connolly avoids any discussion of Belfast, the industrial center of the island. To touch on Belfast would have forced him to consider the Protestant workers, whose nonexistence is crucial to the stated aims of the IRA.

Despite this intellectual bankruptcy, there is no reason to think that the IRA will be unable to draw fresh recruits for its depleted ranks, attract the fourteen- and fifteen-year-olds who graduate from stone-throwing to running messages to the sniper's rifle and the gelignite bomb. Life in Ulster, particularly in the towns, is grim, drab, pleasureless. The joy of fighting for a dangerous "national cause," perhaps becoming the hero of those instant ballads that celebrate some imagined feat, is an irresistible lure for some.

There are more tangible benefits as well. The illegal drinking clubs that flourish in both communities, particularly since most pubs have been bombed out of existence, are a source of steady income. By 1977, in the Catholic ghetto of Ardoyne, for example, the Star Club was understood to be paying the Provos £200 — nearly $400 — each week as a "contribution" to the cause. Every cab driver plying the Falls Road was paying a "tanner," £10 or nearly $20, to keep rolling. The Provos collect payoffs from some businesses — said to be up to $2000 a month — and run others, including grocery stores. Any reluctant contributor knows that at best he will lose his business to a bomb. The payoffs are in goods and services as well as money. Gunmen drive cars, usually stolen Ford Cortinas, take their girls across the border for rest and recreation and generally enjoy a status in communities where the jobless rate can run over 30 percent.

Martin McGuinness, who when I knew him was the "commander" of the "Derry Brigade," is a case in point. In 1972, he and his "staff" were headquartered in a shabby house near a chapel in the Catholic Bogside. McGuinness was relatively secure and easy to find then because the Bogside was a "no go" area, left untouched by the watching army. A visitor was struck by the young girls, some in camouflage jackets, sprawling on the doorstep, IRA groupies. McGuinness himself was unprepossessing. He was twenty-two and had been a butcher's assistant in the nearby Creggan; acne scars were still visible on his pale face. He was playing with a toy gun, a peculiar taste for a young man who commanded several score of the real thing. He was cool to me because he had not liked an article I had recently written.* But he talked because I came from the American press. Was he not worried lest his bombings subject Belfast Catholics to a terrible retribution?

"The people of Belfast are in a minority," he replied. "Possibly they will be subject to attack from Protestant extremist groups."

The key word, of course, was "people," meaning Catholics. Protestants, in the view of McGuinness, a cold, me-

---

* Both actors and bit players in the Ulster drama follow their notices in the press and on radio and television with an almost manic avidity. They sometimes give the impression of staging everything for the media. I could always tell, for example, whether Maire Drumm, the president of the Provos' political front, had recently been sent a clipping from *The Washington Post*. If she had seen something she did not like, she would talk to me at her Andersonstown doorstep; if she had been pleased, she would invite me in for tea and cookies. At bottom Mrs. Drumm was a motherly woman, although she, her husband, daughter and son had served time frequently for their IRA activities. That, of course, was before she was murdered in her hospital bed by gunmen from the Protestant camp.

chanical youth, a William Faulkner Popeye, were not "people."

But the central point is that McGuinness, the former butcher boy, was now a figure of consequence. Adoring girls at his doorstep, sought out by the world's press, a "patriot" in a "national cause," he and his kind are not likely to give this sort of thing up easily to go back to a shop in the Creggan.

On the other side, the Protestant paramilitaries are a carbon copy. They too are mostly workers escaping a dreary, colorless life. They too emerged first as local defense communities against "Republican" assaults. Cabbies on the Shankill Road pay off the same tanner each week as those in the Catholic Falls. One UDA bar alone is said to gross £60,000 a year, more than $100,000. The organization also runs a betting establishment and collects "contributions" from small merchants. It hijacks trucks with television sets, cigarettes and liquor — commodities quickly turned into cash or arms. The same peculiar blend of "patriotism" and interest animates Protestant gunmen.*

A representative leader was Dave Fogel. When I knew him, Dave was in his twenties, friendly, pleasant-looking, a bit of a confidence man. He had been discharged less than honorably from the British Army. There had been some difficulty about another soldier's transistor radio. Fogel had married a girl from the Protestant enclave of Woodvale and settled down there on the dole. When the Troubles began, the neighborhood turned to the ex-soldier to organize a defense, and Fogel soon became a figure in the UDA. More than that, he would walk a reporter through the neighbor-

---

* Sometimes the pecuniary interest becomes too conspicuous. One of my regular contacts was Tommy Herron, a thin, blond garage manager of thirty-four who affected a natty dressing style when he was the number two man in the UDA chain of command. Unhappily, his mother took to driving all over Belfast in cabs, paying them off in grand fashion from a thick roll of bank notes. Tommy was administered the ultimate penalty, almost surely by his own side.

hood to hear all the citizens who sought help — with the police, city hall and other institutions. Fogel had become a political boss. More than that. He found a vacant building and turned it into a clubhouse and discotheque for the neighborhood's idle boys and girls, starved for recreation. Fogel liked to do his serious talking over the bar there, complaining that the middle-class Unionists no longer represented Woodvale's workers, insisting that "we're poor here. We need social amenities, a stronger voice in the corridor of power. We're no better off than the Catholics."

This sort of thing is attractive, too, certainly better than lying listlessly around a cramped house, watching television and waiting for the weekly dole check.

In time of course, UDA politics and Fogel's old habits caught up with him. He had to flee from the wrath of his colleagues and seek refuge in Britain. But his life-style too is irresistible. The fate of a Fogel (or a Herron) does not discourage new recruits.

The two forces, IRA on one side and Protestant paramilitaries on the other, enjoy a peculiar symbiotic relation. Each needs the other to justify its own existence. Catholics who peep out from the Short Strand to watch the UDA march in the Newtownards Road count on the IRA to defend them from assault. Protestants in Sandy Row supply fresh recruits to the UVF when another IRA bomb goes off in the Belfast city center.

The two, moreover, make an unlikely accommodation even more remote. Each bombing, each killing, each maiming, only reinforces the feelings of hate by one side for the other, stirs passions that need no further arousing. Every atrocity is seized on by each side to confirm its darkest suspicions. "How can you live with them after so many killings?" I have been told again and again, on both sides of the sectarian line.

Even the army, as far as one can tell, likes its duty in Ulster. "We're doing what we're paid to do," a sergeant once told me. "It's a lot less boring then the BAOR" (British Army of the Rhine). The soldiers have now become so skilled that few are killed anymore. The IRA prefers softer targets — civilians, policemen, lone members of the Ulster Defense Regiment, the reserve unit. If no conclusive result emerges, no matter. The army is getting splendid training in the very tasks that Kitson said it must fulfill in the future, running a country, grappling with insurgency. Families of soldiers, moreover, exert little if any political pressure to bring the boys home. An all-volunteer army — no draftees — is an army of professionals who have chosen this life as a career.

Eight years after the Troubles revived, no end was in sight. Nor should one be expected. President Carter had held out the promise of American investment when a solution is reached "which will command widespread acceptance throughout both parts of the community." That, of course, was the point. There is none.

In London, key figures in the Labour government sometimes talk of "pulling out," of leaving Ulster to Ulstermen. But nobody can figure how to do it, to whom power would be turned over. In the past Britons have walked away from colonial possessions and left behind two divided communities eager to slaughter each other. India, Cyprus and Palestine are examples. But Ulster's majority, although it flirts with the idea of independence from time to time, does not want to leave Britain. The IRA can ignore Protestants; London cannot.

The province, however, is a sinister danger to Britain. Ulster and its consequences are the most subversive force in the United Kingdom. It stimulates dangerous political ambitions among some officers, erodes civil liberties and develops a calloused official attitude toward outrage and untruth. There are many in Ulster, particularly on the Protestant side, who believe that Britain is already withdrawing, slowly, quietly, without announcement, fading away like the Che-

shire cat, leaving behind a ghostly smile. British ministers in
Ulster rarely talk of power-sharing anymore; instead they
speak of turning over the "police" burden from the army to
the RUC. Or, like Roy Mason, who became Ulster minister
in 1976, they talk of a "devolved" provincial government
"which the majority of all parts of the community can support and sustain." Although there are repeated public deni-
als of any intent to leave, more and more in Ulster are
convinced this is where London is heading. They could be
right.

What would happen then? In 1972, Conor Cruise O'Brien
offered this "benign model" of Ulster's future:

> The offensive of the Provisional IRA will falter and fail as a re-
> sult of the increasingly hostile mood of the Catholic people; the
> "water" poisoning the "fish" . . . Catholic elected representatives
> to enter into serious discussion with the British Minister . . . The
> end of IRA hostilities will permit the elected Protestant representa-
> tives to enter into similar discussions . . . Out of these discussions
> will emerge new structures with which both communities can
> live . . . The British Army will be withdrawn from all responsi-
> bility for policing . . . the British government will invest in a
> massive reconstruction program . . . Dublin . . . will agree to
> contribute . . . and will invite the friends of Ireland in America
> to do likewise. Religious discrimination in job appointments will
> be progressively eliminated (immediately in relation to new jobs
> created). Catholics will be convinced that their major grievances
> are being disposed of; Protestants convinced that the end of these
> practices does not entail the end of the world, i.e. Catholic power
> over Protestants.

But even if the IRA is worn down, O'Brien's happy ending is far from assured. Protestant workers will continue to
fear for the end of their world as long as there is any threat to
the network of practices that preserves their jobs, the discrimination that not even the most peaceful Catholic will

now tolerate. Like so many others, the "benign model" ignores Ulster's crucial class.

O'Brien also sketches an alternative scenario, the "malignant model":

> The Provisional offensive will continue . . . It will provoke an escalating Protestant counter-offensive . . . followed by massed Protestant assaults on Catholic ghettoes . . . The British Army comes under armed attack from both communities. With increasing casualties and no solution in sight, the British public clearly favours a policy of withdrawal. A British government announces its agreement to the unity of Ireland . . . and begins a withdrawal of its troops. Mass meetings of loyalists . . . acclaim "no surrender" . . . Armed Loyalists move en masse into these ghettoes to get rid of the IRA . . . and to punish Catholics generally. Thousands of Catholics are killed and scores of thousands fly south in terror . . . The Irish Army takes over in [border] Catholic areas. Its efforts to penetrate the Protestant hinterland are held off, or beaten back . . . a United Nations force [would] patrol the cease-fire line; the new border.
>
> Ireland would be left once more with two States . . . [one] homogeneously Protestant without the tiniest Catholic crack or crevice for a new IRA . . . [the other] with its massive ingestion of embittered and displaced Ulster Catholics would be an uncongenial environment for Protestants . . .
>
> Both states would be under right-wing governments, scruffily militarist and xenophobic in character. The principal cultural activities would be funerals, triumphal parades, commemorations, national days of mourning, and ceremonies of rededication to the memory of those who died for Ireland/Ulster.

A Hungarian proverb holds that the difference between an optimist and a pessimist is that the pessimist is better informed. Eight years after the Troubles revived, O'Brien's pessimistic scenario — details aside — still appeared better informed.

VI. Disorder at Home

Exploiting Color

Discrimination and violence, Ulster's birthmarks, are not unique to the six offshore counties. From time to time, Britain's calm is disturbed by nasty street riots occasioned by the presence of nearly two million citizens with black and brown skins. The ugly fact is that these people, mostly immigrants from the West Indies or South Asia, are abused because of their color. Their victimization — psychological, economic and sometimes physical — disturbs the model of a just, tolerant and humane society. Unlike the imaginary ills attributed to Britain by popular commentators — excessive welfare spending, selfish unions, the loss of empire — race relations are demonstrably sick and potentially dangerous. Minorities in Britain have suffered neither slavery nor the social indignities endured by blacks in the United States. But they do run up against barriers in jobs and housing that bear a family relation. After Ulster, race, with the complex of white British feelings attached to it, is the greatest source of tension in the national life.

Indeed, the nation's official thinkers have warned that race reflects Ulster. A report by the Central Policy Review Staff in 1974 declared that "there are uncomfortable parallels between the situation of Britain's coloured population and that of the Catholics in Northern Ireland. For 50 years, British governments condoned discrimination and deprivation in Ulster, and in the end Ulster blew up in their face. We believe that not only for reasons of social justice but also to preserve social stability . . . more should be done to deal with the problems of race relations in this country."

For a generation now, there have been sporadic clashes with color as the trigger in decaying sections of London and other cities. Even so, these have been only pale imitations of the mass rioting and looting that have shaken American towns. But Britain contains relatively fewer colored people and they have been there for a much shorter time. If racial tension in Britain is on a much smaller scale than in the United States, it has nevertheless provoked some brutal behavior, provided a platform for vicious demagogues and strained the sense of community that is a British strength.

There were few colored persons in Britain until the middle 1950s. Then stick and carrot drove and pulled successive immigrant waves. Race and religious hatred in some newly independent African and Asian countries, coupled with a chauvinist tide in the United States, was the stick. The lure was Britain's booming demand for cheap labor.

The first arrivals were black, West Indians mostly from Jamaica and Barbados, driven to Britain by the McCarran-Walter immigration act of 1952. This remarkable law slashed the number of West Indians allowed into the United States. So the more ambitious, the underemployed and the jobless sought a new haven. Before the act was passed, about nine in every ten who left the Caribbean went north to the United States. Now the ratio was reversed and nine of ten came to Britain instead.

Independence for India and Pakistan had touched off massive religious pogroms, slaughtering millions of Hindus, Moslems and Sikhs in the Punjab. Vast numbers were forced from their homes and these refugees were another source of the immigrant wave. Still a third stream, also Asians, came from the newly independent states of Africa. Kenya and Uganda in particular celebrated their freedom in time by expelling Indian shopkeepers and other Asians who had played a central part in the commercial economy.

Until 1962, all these people, citizens of British colonies, enjoyed a British nationality of sorts and there were no obstacles to their entry. Indeed, at first they were welcomed by the government and British employers, largely because they would do jobs that white Britons would not at wages white Britons refused.

London Transport, running the buses and subways, contracted with the government of Barbados to recruit local labor. It was hard to find whites who would work nights and weekends, but West Indian blacks could not afford to be so choosy. In the Midlands, textile mills were installing new, modern machinery. To make them pay, these looms were run around the clock. Again, Asian immigrants filled the jobs, accepting night work and split shifts.

Apart from color, the newcomers were set off from their neighbors in other ways. Those who spoke English spoke it with strange-sounding accents. Many from South Asia could neither speak nor write the language. As late as 1977, it was estimated that three of every five Asian women and two of every five Asian men spoke English slightly or not at all. The Asians further distressed their white neighbors by peculiar dress, strange religions, different cooking odors. Many young Asian girls were separated from white schoolmates because they were not allowed the same freedom to pair off with boys. Both the new black and brown communities shattered what had been a more or less homogenous British society; they were different and differences breed suspicion, even hostility.

A prolonged riot between blacks and whites in the Notting Hill section of London in 1958 forcefully impressed these differences on the country at large. Britain discovered that there were popular limits to tolerance, and pressure began to cut off the immigrant inflow, to curb the quasi-nationality that had been extended. Successive Conservative and Labour governments responded to this pressure, sometimes reluctantly, sometimes with almost indecent haste. When Kenya threw out its Asians, a Labour government took only a week to shut Britain's door against them, sharply limiting the arrivals. Since 1971, the flood of colored immigrants (the barriers are porous for those from white Commonwealth nations like Australia, New Zealand or Canada) has been reduced to a steady but narrow stream of about forty thousand a year. Most of those now allowed in are dependents — children, wives and parents of those already settled in Britain. The high persistent unemployment of the 1970s has ended the need for more imported colored labor.

By 1977, there were an estimated 1.8 million colored citizens in Britain, about one in thirty-three. They "faced a very substantial amount of unfair discrimination when seeking jobs and housing . . . tended to live in very poor accommodations and to be doing manual jobs that were often below the level of their qualifications and experience." This summary came from the most intensive survey made of their plight. It was produced by Political and Economic Planning, a private research group on whom Labour governments have relied to frame reforming laws.

Like blacks in the United States, the colored immigrants often huddled together in inner-city enclaves or ghettos. This is partly choice; newcomers from a Punjabi district or a Pakistani town seek their own people. It is partly necessity; the enclaves are run-down and cheaper. Better houses are simply not rented or sold to colored citizens. Some, particularly Asians, scrimped and saved to buy homes in modest suburbs like Southall, the industrial bedroom community west of London. There shop signs, movies, restaurants and newspapers are in Hindi or Gujurati. This "Little India" comforts the newcomers but enrages the longer established whites.

Whatever their disabilities, however, colored Britons still appear to be far better off then American blacks. None of the immigrants have mounted a sustained protest against their condition, suggesting it is not intolerable. In 1963, for example, the jobless rate among black and brown Britons was four times that of whites, a painful difference. But the gap has been closing rapidly and by 1975 the colored jobless rate was almost the same. In the United States, in contrast, the black rate is invariably twice the white.

The pay differences too are not as wide. In 1974, the median pay for white British men was £40.20 a week; for colored men, £36.70. The gap was 9 percent, far less than the 35 percent in the United States. To be sure, the gap in Britain was markedly greater than 9 percent for the best jobs, but white and colored pay for blue-collar workers was roughly the same.

In housing, the Race Relations Act of 1968 forbade discrimination. Although bias still exists, it is not as severe as it had been. Perhaps the most painful area of discrimination is in subsidized public housing, for which there are long waiting lines almost everywhere in Britain. There are clues suggesting that colored immigrants are steered to the poorest buildings and, in some towns, wait longer to get in than whites. But an astonishing three of every four Asians have sweated to buy their own homes, a far higher proportion than the 50 percent for Britain as a whole. The PEP survey did show, however, that colored homes are shabbier than those of whites, are far more crowded and much less likely to boast a bath or toilet that is not shared with another family. The immigrants, moreover, are penned in their ghettos; building societies rarely give them mortgages on homes in white neighborhoods.

In addition, the colored population must work far harder to maintain their pay and living standards. About one white worker in six labors on a night or divided shift; for the colored it is almost one in three. The Race Law bars discrimination in hiring; but an ingenious PEP test, using teams of black and brown actors, revealed that many firms ignore the law, refusing to take colored applicants.

White Britons are pulled two ways. Most are clearly uneasy about prejudice, at least in the abstract. One poll showed 80 percent oppose discrimination in jobs and 70 percent discrimination in housing. These feelings enabled the government in 1968 to outlaw a wide range of discriminatory practices. The law, however, relied largely on persuasion and contained virtually no means of enforcement. So it was strengthened in 1976 and — at least on paper — offers greater prospect of redressing wrongs through the courts.

For an American observer, the passage of this act was astonishing. There was almost no political pressure for it, least of all from the immigrant groups. If anything, the better part of political wisdom in Britain is to "protect" whites from both black demands and immigrants. The new law was a living expression of Britain's liberal nineteenth-century reforming tradition, a judgment by an elite that a wrong needed righting. Roy Jenkins was then the home minister and responsible for race relations. He was determined to push the measure through and he succeeded. For Jenkins, it was an appropriate farewell to British politics and his assumption of the Common Market Commission's presidency.

The failure of the immigrants to organize politically, to exert pressure of their own, is a continuing and puzzling feature of the troubled racial scene. There is no colored civil rights movement of consequence in Britain. There are neither organized militants like the American Congress of Racial Equality, moderates like the National Association for the Advancement of Colored People or even conservatives to match an Urban League. Among the Caribbeans, about 43 percent of the colored, small groups of black militants appear briefly and locally, then disappear. The Indian Workers Association has many branches and sometimes tries to organize voters in a constituency, but has little impact outside the Asian community. Almost single-handedly, David Pitt, an Edinburgh-trained doctor from Grenada, has tried to arouse black political consciousness. He has failed. A bright man with a sharp sense of irony, his own inability to win a parliamentary seat for Labour has not been an inspiring example. Pitt has calculated that immigrants hold the balance of power in at least thirty Labour constituencies. But blacks have ignored his repeated pleas to join ward and constituency organizations, where the choice of candidates is decided. If immigrants were represented in the Commons as they are in the population, they would hold twenty seats. Their concentration in enclaves should make it even easier to win. In fact, not one West Indian or South Asian sat in Parliament at the end of 1977.

Dr. Pitt is now Lord Pitt, a peer. But his personal success underlines his political failure. He sits in a chamber that is largely honorific.

Pitt blames the lack of political action on immigrant suspicion and fear of authority, the ghetto psychology that warns people to keep their heads down. These traits are common among any first-generation immigrants. But a second generation is now reaching maturity, those who came as infants in the 1950s and 1960s and those who were born in Britain. They may not suffer the disadvantages, the indignities, as meekly as their parents.

The absence of political identity is so strong, however, that immigrant traits can't fully explain it. There simply appears to be no widespread sense of outrage among Britain's colored citizens. The PEP survey turned up an astonishing 46 percent of the colored workers who declared themselves "very satisfied" with their jobs. This was not far behind the white level, 53 percent. No less than 82 percent of the immigrants announced themselves "satisfied" or "very satisfied" with their housing; the white figure was 88 percent. While three West Indians in four were aware of job discrimination, fewer than one Asian in two thought it existed. This is not the stuff of political protest.

More recently, there have been signs that colored youths are rejecting the docile ways of their parents. But it is street violence rather than Lord Pitt's call for political action to which they are drawn. The high unemployment of the 1970s has sharpened their sense of grievance. Until late in 1977, there were no reliable estimates of joblessness among colored youths. But the unemployment rate for all those under twenty-five was a worrisome 13.5 percent, twice the national average; even more alarming, the number of the colored youths on dole queues was growing more than three times as fast as the number of whites.

In the working-class East End of London, a black militant publication was urging residents who came from what is now Bangladesh to organize full-time defense groups. Immigrants there had been beaten up frequently by marauding white youths, and the police were charged with indifference. *The Times* described how Bengalis in Tower Hamlets were frequently punched, stabbed, kicked and struck with stones, eggs and tomatoes by local whites. Chief Inspector John Wallis, the "community liaison officer," said, "There is a great deal of exaggeration about the extent to which they suffer." On a quiet spring Sunday in 1978, scores of white youngsters ran through the community with clubs, bottles and stones, crying "Kill the black bastards" and smashing shop windows and cars. London's city fathers briefly considered segregating Bengalis for their own protection in high-rise blocks. It had become harder to sustain the Inspector's dismissive "exaggeration."

Two summers before, in Southall, similar complaints were raised against the police. An eighteen-year-old Asian had been stabbed to death by white youths in a brawl outside a pub, but police insisted race was not involved. A mass march by protesting immigrants on the police station lifted community feelings to a high pitch. All through Southall, young men were insisting that they must organize their own defense.

One was Harvinder Rai, a nineteen-year-old student of electrical engineering, whose father is president of the local Indian Workers Association. Young Rai told me: "The youngsters think the oldsters have an inferiority complex since they came here. They've been pushed around. We don't want any more troubles but if there's any more trouble, we have the capacity to retaliate."

Some of this may be bravado; none of it is political action. The assaults in Southall stopped and no more was heard of vigilante groups. But the relative passivity of Britain's immigrants could be deceptive, particularly if high unemployment persists.

Lord Pitt, the very embodiment of moderate conciliation, once warned me: "We could find ourselves in a hell of a situation. We could have a pretty rough scene here, even riots. It's the next generation one has to worry about. Their parents are prepared to take any job, but the young blacks and young Asians now coming out of school are not prepared to tolerate the posture of their parents. They despise them for it."

Pitt may be right; Harvinder Rai and the militants of the East End may yet touch off passions to rival those unleashed in Detroit, Washington and Chicago. As things are now, however, this looks unlikely. Prejudice among British whites is not yet respectable on a wide scale; immigrant disabilities are real but not overwhelming. Resentments exist on both sides of the color line, but unless they are deliberately cultivated they need not overwhelm the predominant mood of fair play and reform.

Aggro

This tolerant spirit inevitably is at its weakest among the working-class neighborhoods next door to the new enclaves of Indians, Pakistanis and Jamaicans.* The whites near the bottom of the economic ladder, often living in grim, high-rise towers, struggle with the upward spiral of prices and look down on strange people with peculiar skins and curious folkways. The white citizens of Stepney or Tower Hamlets in the East End, those of Southall in the West, or Ladywood in Birmingham are ripe targets for stereotypes. The new-comers are seen as lazy welfare scroungers (much like the Protestant view of Catholics in Belfast), although the Asians in particular are a notoriously hard-working group. The immigrants are described as "blacklegs" or "scabs," breaking union wage rates. In fact, the percentage of union members is higher among colored workers than among whites. There is no doubt that immigrant homes give off different odors; curry smells different from fish and chips. But the stereotype translates this to mean that immigrants are dirty.

Unsurprisingly, a handful of would-be leaders have emerged. The most notorious are found in the National Front, put together in 1957 by John Tyndall and Martin Webster, alumni of Britain's minuscule Nazi party. The Front stands on a single-issue platform: drive all persons of color from Britain; make Britain white.† The Front de-

---

* Although the more virulent forms of racism are largely a working-class af-fair, it must not be thought that the best-off and best-educated are immune from crude prejudice. Sir Richard Dobson, the former chairman of British Leyland, delighted a score or so of fellow business executives by sneering at "blackish" (meaning Asian) strikers in North London; asserting the "perfectly respectable fact" that Leyland is "bribing wogs" (dark-skinned Arabs) to win sales abroad; and complaining that "some urban schools are grossly overbur-dened [with] immigrant children." Sir Richard, who, *The Times* had said, "talks with the force and the precision of the classical scholar he once was," was forced to resign from the government-owned car company when a recording of his speech reached the newspapers. But it is likely that his atti-tudes are commonplace in the business world.

† Its formal program does contain some other, populist-nationalist elements: take Britain from the Common Market, drive the multinational oil companies from the North Sea, fire "Communist" schoolteachers and the like. But these are decorative rather than substantive. Race supremacy is what matters.

mands not only a complete ban on all immigration from colored nations but also the forced repatriation of people already in Britain. A second and minor theme is anti-Semitism, but Tyndall and Webster are careful to voice this sentiment in muted form, limiting themselves to anti-Jewish sneers at indoor, semiprivate rallies. There is clearly a working-class audience for attacks on people of color. But anti-Jewish feeling is largely confined to a narrow group of Britain's best-off who regard the Front as plebeian.

Webster is a pudgy, jolly salesman who works a crowd for contributions with chants — "If they're black" — and responses — "Send them back." Tyndall is a stiff, humorless man who affects a military bearing and whips himself into a staged lather over the "degeneracy of the British stock." Neither appears to have the personality or style for successful mass leadership. The politics of race hate in Britain has not yet thrown up a figure of great appeal, a George Wallace let alone a Hitler. Nor, unless world stagflation worsens, is one likely to emerge in a society that is relatively stable, comparatively free from large-scale discontent.

But the Front does draw a fluctuating fringe vote that has sometimes reached disquieting proportions. It carefully picks its spots, presenting candidates for Parliament or local city councils in run-down Labour areas. Decaying city sectors or dreary industrial suburbs, where urban "redevelopment" has destroyed stable neighborhoods and replaced houses with soul-chilling tower blocks, provide the Front's most fertile ground. In by-elections for vacant parliamentary seats, the Front typically gets 4 or 5 percent of the vote, although once, in 1973, it scored a remarkable 16 percent in West Bromwich. At local elections for council members, where the turnout is invariably small, the Front has picked up as much as 30 percent. But in its first ten years, the Front failed to elect anybody to anything. Its best showing came in the local London elections of 1977, when it drew 119,000 votes for its 91 candidates, 5 percent of the total. Martin

Walker, who has written the most detailed account of the Front's internal leadership squabbles, estimates it could receive 750,000 votes in a national election, about 2 to 3 percent.

So far, then, the National Front is an ugly excrescence rather than a force. It is less a harbinger of fascism in Britain than a reflection of despair at the bottom of white Britain's social ladder. Could this boil erupt, could a low-grade infection become a raging fever if it were inflamed by a charismatic medicine man? There is no simple answer to this question because no such leader has appeared. So far Establishment politicians have all shunned the Front and most have vigorously condemned it. Indeed, only one politician of consequence, the maverick Enoch Powell, has consistently exploited the politics of race and he is too fastidious to embrace the Front.

Powell is a curious figure, a mystic nationalist whose anti-Market tirades riveted the Commons, a brilliant scholar who became a full professor of Greek at twenty-five, a one-time rising star of the Tory party. He was the minister for health as early as 1960 and had every reason to think he might one day lead his party to power. But Powell was sidetracked while others, who in his view must have been lesser men, competed successfully for the top prize. In his disappointment, he suddenly discovered the immigrant menace in 1968 and lashed out with a now notorious speech at Birmingham.

"In fifteen or twenty years' time, the black man will have the whip hand over the white man," he cried. Britain is "busily engaged heaping up its own funeral pyre." He told a scarifying story of an aged widow in Wolverhampton who refused to rent to blacks and found excreta shoved through her letterbox. (Journalists later tried but failed to find the aged widow, who apparently was a creature of political license.) And then, in a famous peroration: "Like the Roman, I seem to see 'the River Tiber foaming with much blood,' " Powell cried.

There is no doubt that he struck a responsive nerve; immigration laws were tightened; the government even now provides cash for those who want to return, just as Powell urged. But Powell's manipulation of these dark feelings exiled him from Establishment politics. Edward Heath dropped him from the shadow cabinet. In time, Powell left the Conservatives to represent an Ulster Protestant party in Parliament. He never turned his considerable talents to form a race movement of his own and he keeps a long distance from the National Front. But he has given and continues to give its line a degree of legitimacy, of quasi-respectability. In the late summer of 1977 he was back at the old stand, declaring on television that immigration will "go on until a third of Central London, a third of Birmingham and Wolverhampton are colored, until the civil war comes." Powell paves the way for a lesser Powell who might transform the Front from an unpleasant nuisance to an ugly danger.

Today, the Front is a recurrent focus for street violence in Britain. It has copied its technique from Oswald Mosley and his British Union of Fascists who, in the 1930s, marched through the Jewish East End of London to battle residents there. Today, the Front regularly assembles several hundred stalwarts carrying Union Jacks and anti-immigrant placards to march through Asian and West Indian enclaves. Typically, Tyndall and Webster notify the police in advance. In the name of free assembly and speech, the police provide the march with an escorting phalanx. Through 1977, few immigrants rose to the bait, despite the calls for self-defense groups. But marginal leftists have eagerly filled the vacuum, seizing the chance to "defend" working-class immigrants by assaulting the Front marchers and the police.

At one Front march I attended in North London, the leftists hurled only smoke bombs, beer cans, bottles and bricks. There were a few fistfights and sixty arrests. But sometimes the "Anti-Fascists" — organized usually by a grouplet called the Socialist Workers party — have used clubs and even knives. These affairs leave everybody pleased except the police. The attackers not only appear as champions of down-trodden minorities but make the police — the state — look like defenders of racism. The Front, in turn, takes on the character of a law-abiding body under brutal assault from a mixed bag of "Communists" and blacks. After each clash, both groups invariably get the publicity they seek. So far, however, neither side has been able to convert this attention into votes. The test came at a 1977 by-election in a run-down Birmingham constituency, splendid demographic material for both extreme right and left. The balloting, more-over, was held just a few days after two well-publicized riots. Even so, the Front collected only 888 votes, a mere 6 percent, and the Socialist Workers party a derisory 152 votes, 1 per-cent. The politics of race, violence and extremism seemed to appeal only to a narrow fringe on a distant margin.

The Front's appeal to workers, however, was strong enough to arouse the Labour party and the TUC, the federa-tion of unions, late in 1977. Abandoning their traditional ostrich posture, they organized an open campaign against the Front, damning its "merchants of hate" in leaflets and a political broadcast. At the very least, this was tacit recogni-tion that the Front mattered, particularly in the council housing blocks, where disaffection runs high.

Early in 1978, Margaret Thatcher, the Tory leader, also recognized the Front's appeal and radically changed the complexion of British racial politics. In a televised bid for some of Labour's unhappy supporters, she repeatedly prom-ised "an end to immigration." She coupled this with the re-markable observation that "the British character" which "has done so much for democracy, for law" might be "swamped by people with a different culture." Her message was clear: citizens with black and brown skins are un-Brit-ish. Mrs. Thatcher even flirted with the Front's followers, deploring their organization but sympathizing with their feelings. If she didn't go as far as Powell and bluntly call for an all-white Britain, Mrs. Thatcher had surely widened the limits of acceptable hostility toward those of color.

Leading Labour politicians first responded by harshly criticizing the Conservative leader. But on second thought, at least some concluded she had struck a popular chord. A Select Committee of MPs from both major parties unanimously urged measures to cut off "as expeditiously as possible" further immigration from the Indian subcontinent. Blacks from the Caribbean were less of a concern; they were leaving faster than they were coming in. The Callaghan government, clearly on the defensive, issued waves of statistics to show that all colored immigration was falling. The leaflet campaign against racism was interrupted.

But Mrs. Thatcher seemed to go from strength to strength. Her deputy leader, William Whitelaw, popularly regarded as a humane keeper of the Tory conscience, publicly blessed her works. He placed his party behind an even more stringent program than the one the Select Committee proposed. It would put finite limits on the number of immigrant dependents from South Asia who could follow their relatives to Britain and would impose yearly quotas on the total allowed in.

All this drastically changed the public debate. Respectable politicians were no longer asking how to assure equal rights and reduce tensions in a multiracial society but how to curb if not reduce the number with dark skins. In time, this may yield a counterreaction, politically mobilizing the hitherto dormant immigrant community. It could stir others in all parties who fear Mrs. Thatcher is encouraging latent feelings of race hostility among whites. She and Whitelaw insisted they were simply trying to quell legitimate anxieties; but they ran the risk of stimulating fresh and even violent attacks on Britain's immigrant minority. After all, Mrs. Thatcher had said that these alien citizens threatened British democracy and British law.

The very fact that street riots take place in Britain is a dissonant counterpoint to the dominant theme of a civil nation at peace with itself. The country takes quiet satisfaction in its belief that police go unarmed, that most citizens regard policemen as friends. After one street clash in 1974, Lord Justice Scarman wrote: "The principle that lies behind the Metropolitan [London] Police method for the maintenance of public order is that it is the job of ordinary policemen operating without firearms, without special equipment, but enjoying the support and, if necessary, the cooperation of the general public. The method assumes a society united on essentials."

Since then, more and more police have drawn pistols and rifles for special tasks — guarding embassies against terrorists, coping with a rising wave of bank robberies, chasing the IRA. The street riots, moreover, have led to something new: police assigned to demonstrations now carry body-length plastic shields to ward off missiles. This is a defensive tool but, because of its grotesque and provocative appearance, it causes dismay among both citizens and police.

Even so, Britain is still, in Scarman's words, a "society united on essentials" and most police continue to make their rounds unarmed. The National Front and its leftist partners are only a remote threat to this unity. But their existence, no matter how limited their support, is a disturbing symptom in Britain's body politic.

Ritual violence in Britain is not confined to extremist politics. One of the strangest national customs is performed every Saturday afternoon, from late August through May, when professional soccer teams play. Young men, wearing their team's colors in scarves around their necks, wrists and waists, travel with their club to another city. They roam through these "foreign" towns, smashing windows, tearing up fences and gardens, assaulting those who resist. They seek out supporters of the rival team, similarly clad, and engage in "aggro," or "aggravation." This can be an exchange of anything from insults to fists to clubs and knives, and the outcome is sometimes fatal.

Only a minority of the supporters at any game are involved and not every club carries its band of "soccer hooligans." But on any Saturday, the numbers engaged can reach into the thousands and stretch the resources of hard-pressed police.

The affairs have a predictable, tribal quality. They are touched off by taunts from the other side, by attempts to fence off one group from another, by the memory of past insults or losses, by the cry that "they" have one of "us." The participants are unlikely to be jobless because theirs is an expensive pastime. In 1974, it was estimated that a fan traveling to all the twenty-one away games his side played would spend £200, roughly $400, on train and game tickets, scarves and other paraphernalia.

A sensitive BBC "Panorama" program caught the mood of the trouble-seekers. "All we are going for is a good game of football; a good punch up and a good kick up . . . it frightened the fucking arse off Tottenham . . . Best Saturday in years that . . . I am not going away for some dirty Northern ponce to spit all over me. I'll put a fucking plate glass on his head . . . They've got the reputation, you know. The reputation of being a hard team . . . Supporters, hard supporters . . . You don't want people to turn around and say 'What's up with him? Look at him over there, he's a coward.' "

Just as important, the BBC found Webster of the National Front quick to spot the potential fodder in this working-class pasture. "I think there's a lot you can do with a soccer hooligan," Webster observed. "I think people resort to mindless violence and vandalism because they have not been given by society a point and a meaning to their lives. People do like to identify. They do like to associate themselves with something which is big and glorious and noble which they, the little individual, can associate themselves with and feel proud that they somehow belong. And we feel that the very, very fanatical adulation by supporters for their particular clubs is a sort of sublimated patriotism."

"So it's a case of Millwall today and National Front tomorrow?" the BBC man asked.

Webster replied, "We hope so."

The government's response, typical and less acute, was a complaint from Denis Howell, the sports minister. He said that the program was "irresponsible."

Police and soccer authorities have been trying and failing for years to end the staged soccer riots. They have come up with a dozen different schemes, all futile. Their frustration was nicely illustrated by Brynmor John, a junior minister in the Home Office. During a brief Commons debate over the damage done by Manchester United's notorious supporters at Southampton in February 1977, John said:

> I offer my hon. Friends my deepest sympathy and the determination of the Government to ensure, as far as is practicable, that people can live in peace and watch in peace on the occasion of so-called sporting events. However, it is not an easy problem and it is not susceptible to simple remedies . . . It is time that people took responsibility for the behaviour of their young people when they go away. It is time that they gave them the example, the upbringing and teaching that would bring back the pleasure to sport instead of the present gladiatorial attitude to it, not only on the field but off it.

The bizarre cult of soccer violence, as regular as the calendar, suggests something more complicated than parental neglect, however. The rioting youths seek a pleasure, a joy that they do not find during the week at jobs or school or on the weekends in the drab city quarters from which they come. These are the children of *A Clockwork Orange* whose inarticulate grievances are gratified by blood lust.

In a peculiar way, the welfare state may have built a hothouse for these youths. In the rush to throw down the old slums and throw up new housing, postwar Britain created towering blocks of impersonal and subsidized flats. Only now is it widely understood that the slums — like the mean terraces in Belfast — are organic communities, places where people feel some sense of responsibility for each other, where all can look out to see what is happening in their street, more or less orderly and self-policing places. Orwell recognized this forty years ago when he observed with some surprise that Wigan's slum-dwellers, shifted to new council housing estates, "miss the frowsy warmth of the slum." But government agencies are not likely to listen to novelists, so the huge towers were built, isolating families from their nearest neighbors, breaking down any sense of common concern.

There is a standard liberal formula to change all this — livable homes instead of grim high-rises; neighborhood swimming pools, discotheques, gyms, playing fields, libraries; jobs that develop instead of stifling personality; schools that engage, not cripple, minds. But even if the liberal formula worked — and there is reason to think that men and their darker impulses could resist it — its application in Britain must be limited.

All these things require money and change, demand a society richer than Britain's. The preference for leisure over goods may strengthen some of Britain's most agreeable qualities; it carries a cost as well: the inability to provide amenities on a scale large enough to absorb at least some of the violent impulses that recur with remarkable regularity.

VII. A Model of Sorts

Nanny Knows Best

The genuinely pathological features of British life — racism, violence, corruption, financial scandal — frequently burst on an unsuspecting public with little warning and less examination. Despite a press that is often vigorous and a television that is the envy of the world, Britons tend to be shielded from what they need to know. Indeed, the very refusal to examine real problems can make them worse. Dilip Hiro, whose *Black British, White British* is one of the more useful studies of race, suggests that the absence of open discussion has deepened tensions. "Appeals for frankness," Hiro writes, "do not seem to weaken the middle class belief that talking about a problem creates one." He cites a leading television executive, Jeremy Isaacs, who had acknowledged: "Television current affairs deliberately underplayed the strength of racist feelings for years, out of the misguided but honourable feeling that inflammatory utterances could only do damage. But the way feelings erupted after Enoch Powell's speech this year [1968] was evidence to me that the feeling has been under-represented on television, and other media."

In much the same way, William Deedes, a former Tory minister and later editor of the *Daily Telegraph,* ruefully discovered "the most damaging division" between a government sympathetic to the plight of immigrants and a hostile section of the governed. "To talk of a conspiracy of silence among national and local leaders is unjust," Deedes wrote. "More accurately, there has been . . . a shyness, a nervousness about the subject which has inhibited frank discussion." Deedes, a gentle man, is almost too kind. A strong elitist strain runs through the dominant layers of British life — the judiciary, ranking civil servants, government ministers, newspaper publishers, television executives, financial and business leaders. They see themselves as guardians of a society that cannot bear too much information, an overexposure to truth. They do not believe many citizens are capable of understanding what top people claim to understand; therefore common people must not be burdened with it. This is the adage, Nanny knows best. Its guiding rule is Don't make a fuss.

In one sense, these are curious rules for a society that pioneered social reform in the nineteenth century, reform based on the voluminous information in the famous bluebooks. These factual encyclopedias about life in slums, mines and mills provided a basis for change. But today the Bank of England's standard — Do not disturb public confidence — replaces blue-books. So when Slater Walker, a gigantic machine for manipulating stock prices, collapsed, the Bank persuades even a Labour government to prevent any public inquiry. With the aid of the courts, the principals, Jim Slater and Peter Walker, even succeed in delaying Charles Raw's carefully written book about their shenanigans until two long years after the Bank has bailed out their firm.

The style, of course, is self-serving. It enables civil servants and ministers to escape responsibility for the hundreds of millions of pounds wasted on the economically disastrous Concorde. It saves any government from coming to grips with the discriminatory hiring at the government-owned Harland & Wolff shipyard in Ulster.

But as Hiro, Isaacs and Deedes all suggest, "Nanny knows

best" can suppress pressure until it explodes with far more damaging consequences than if it had been allowed to escape naturally.

Roy Jenkins, properly described as a liberal reformer, went to the United States to look at its Freedom of Information Act. This measure opens up a vast array of government files to the press and other citizens. Jenkins came back appalled by what he had found. The act, he reported, "is costly, cumbersome and legalistic." What he meant was that governing Britons do not believe in trusting citizens with a close scrutiny of government's deeds. There will be no Freedom of Information Act in Britain, the liberal Jenkins explained, because: ". . . in our instinctively private, discreet and secretive society there has been little spontaneous acclaim for the virtues of the Fourth Estate, and still less tendency to construct an accepted theory of journalistic rights." The key phrase is "private, discreet and secretive." These qualities are surely marks of civilization for private individuals; when they are applied to the public business, however, it is not likely to be well done.

They enable a Sir Hugh Fraser to disguise the fact that one huge company he controls has made a bad loan to still another he controls and later dump his shares on an unsuspecting public before they fall through the floor. (To be sure, a Stock Exchange Committee concluded Sir Hugh had been sloppy, not greedy.) They allow an Angus Ogilvy, husband to a cousin of the Queen, to dicker with Rowland "Tiny" Rowland on behalf of a mining company and accept from Rowland a portion of the price that Rowland is to receive. Anywhere else this would be called a kickback, but Britain is discreet about such things. Just as remarkable, the company, with Rowland now in control, is advised by its own lawyers that it would have no defense against a charge of trading illegally with the white regime in Rhodesia. This trade becomes known to the highest civil servants in the Foreign Office, whose policy the company is violating. But the highest civil servants simply put a discreet word in the ear of Ogilvy that perhaps he should get out; no one would dream of publicizing or punishing the sanctions-breaching concern until years later.

"Muckraking" has been a term of praise for American journalists since Theodore Roosevelt first applied it to Ida Tarbell, Lincoln Steffens and the other contributors to *McClure's Magazine*. But in Britain, it is a badge of shame. Right-thinking people do not pry or poke about into the affairs of others, particularly if those others are prominent and well connected. That is a vulgar American habit. To keep the British press from prying, successive governments and the judiciary have designed an effective array of muzzles.

One of the sturdiest is the judicial device of contempt. On the surface, it looks merely like a safeguard to insure a fair trial. Press comment on a case before the courts is severely limited to prevent prejudicing the outcome. Violation of this rule is contempt, punishable by a jail sentence. The principle is reasonable enough, particularly in criminal cases. Indeed, some American journalists — myself among them — would welcome a British contempt statute for U.S. *criminal* cases, where too often defendants are victimized by a media circus. Before a criminal case comes to court in Britain, British newspapers — unlike those in the United States — are forbidden to discuss a defendant's past life and record, interview his family or that of his alleged victim, describe the charges in any words other than those on an official charge sheet. This is a much better guarantee of a fair trial than the relentless pursuit of American defendants frequently conducted by press, police and district attorneys before the victim gets his day in court. Unlike in the United States, a trial in Britain is almost never moved from the place where the crime was committed nor is a verdict set aside because publicity would or did prevent the accused from getting a fair trial.

But when the contempt doctrine is imposed on civil cases, the results are often grotesque and the public interest is poorly served. A classic case involved *The Sunday Times'* investigation into Thalidomide, the tranquilizer that produced mutilated infants. The newspaper had to battle its way past the Heath government and into the highest court to print even some of its findings about the Distillers Company, the near-monopoly in whiskey that made the drug in Britain.

Distillers had stalled a settlement with the parents of the mutilated children for twelve years, offering a meager sum. But the government and the lower courts insisted that the matter was still *sub judice,* before the courts, that Distillers' right to a fair trial of the issue would be threatened by *The Sunday Times* reports. In the end, *The Sunday Times* won its fight in part, published some of its findings and exposed Distillers to public indignation. The whiskey-makers promptly multiplied their offer by five times. But it took nearly five more years and an appeal to the European Commission on Human Rights before the paper could lift a High Court order prohibiting publication of the final chapter in the Thalidomide saga. The story, of course, told how Distillers had ignored scientists' warnings against use of the drug and instead promoted it vigorously. Needless to say, no government agency has ever examined this curious behavior, at least as far as the public knows.

Another restraint, just as effective as contempt, is the notorious Official Secrets Act and in particular its Section 2. This marvelous machine slipped past a sleepy Parliament on a quiet August day in 1911 during a recurrent scare over German spies. Its first section, which outlaws conduct that might be "useful to an enemy," bears some relation to the concern at hand. But Section 2 drops any reference to "enemy" and issues a blanket prohibition against giving or receiving any and every piece of government paper. Quite literally, a civil servant who delivers or a reporter who re-

ceives an unpublished government study of garbage collectors' wages in Ealing or a survey of tea-drinking habits in
Whitehall can be jailed for two years.

To be sure, the section is used infrequently to avoid complete ridicule. Since the end of the war, only twenty-seven
persons have been convicted under it. But it does not need
to be used to be effective. It stands on the books, a chilling
reminder to every civil servant and every journalist that he
risks jail by leaking or examining paper he is not authorized
to distribute or see.*

The sweep of Section 2 is so broad — Scotland Yard's
Special Branch once used it to seize papers of a trade journal
that had disclosed government plans to cut rail services —
that there are frequent calls for its amendment. Government commissions and ministers promise that it will be limited to defense, foreign policy and critical economic matters.
But somehow, this "reform" gets stalled; the simple fact is
that many in the bureaucracy and government like Section 2
as it stands.

Practical consequences flow from this. If it had not been
for the prohibition of Official Secrets, the press might have
discovered the actual and probably abundant state of Britain's coal stocks in 1973–74. The three-day week that top-
pled Heath might never have been ordered. In the same
way, a less chilling law could have enabled the public to
learn that the government had not audited the accounts of
Concorde until 1975. Taxpayers might also have discovered — before it was too late — that they stood to lose anywhere from $75 million to $89 million on every plane sold,
even after the huge development costs had been written off.

---

* Since no modern government can exist without leaks of its own, the law has
been interpreted to provide for "authorized" unofficial release. Certain unde-
fined and ranking officials are said to be self-authorizing — ministers, ambas-
sadors, top civil servants. In perfect safety, they can invite journalists to look
at unreleased documents. In a rare burst of cynical candor, Prime Minister
Callaghan once explained the difference. "Leaking is what you do," he said,
"and briefing is what I do."

If Parliament had had such information — it did not get it until 1977 — the wasteful project could have been stopped well before the 1978 date reluctantly fixed for its death.

There are still other devices to muffle press inquiry. Harsh libel laws do not, as they do in the United States, discriminate between the privacy afforded private citizens and that of those in public life. Reckless, inaccurate and defamatory writing is an unhappy feature of any free press; it is hard to quarrel with laws protecting ordinary citizens from such abuse. But it is equally hard to defend libel laws that obscure from public view the private business dealings of a Labour prime minister or a Tory chancellor of the exchequer. The lesser Truman doctrine — If you can't stand the heat, get out of the kitchen — ought to apply. Politicians who want protection from press inquiry into their private business dealings should resign and become private citizens.

Again, there are practical consequences. Peter Walker, Heath's minister of trade and industry, repeatedly denounced "insider dealings." This description applies to Sir Hugh Fraser, who, with inside knowledge, sold shares and avoided a large loss. If the libel law had not inspired a peculiar contract and a succession of court orders, Charles Raw would not have been delayed in publishing his exposé of inside dealings conducted by the company which bore Walker's name and which profited, among others, his prime minister, Edward Heath. Walker might then have won approval for the criminal bill he unsuccessfully sought.

Although *The Sunday Times* and its editor, Harold Evans, are notable exceptions, the British press does not struggle very hard against its chains. Indeed, the media submit voluntarily to still another curb, the D Notice. Invented on the eve of World War I, it aims to prevent the disclosure of material thought harmful to the national security. Newspapers or broadcasters fearful of disseminating something sensitive call the secretary of the Defense, Press and Broadcasting Committee, usually a retired admiral or general. He gives his opinion and they almost invariably abide by it. In addition, the committee issues guidelines that warn against publicizing certain weapons, plans and other subjects.

Again, on the surface it sounds quite reasonable. It is not. It is hard to think of an editor who would disclose material he thought might damage the nation simply for the sake of disclosure. It is easy, however, to conceive of many things that a Ministry of Defense would like to hide in the name of security — wasteful cost overruns on weapons; manufacturers' faults in planes, helicopters or tanks; brutality in a military prison; and the like. An editor's judgment may be unsound. But that is a risk worth running compared to the political abuse that D Notice invites. President Kennedy persuaded *The New York Times* to muffle its story of the proposed invasion of Cuba. Later he acknowledged that, had he not interfered, the United States could have been spared a painful and costly humiliation. D Notice violates a common-sense rule: the advantage of unfettered publication is likely to outweigh the cost of revealing some dubious secret to a potential enemy.

So the popular press, notably *The Sun* and the *Mirror,* expose the erected nipples of models; the *Daily Mail, Daily Express* and *The Times* largely limit their inquiries to the darker deeds of supposedly leftist unions or Labour politicians. More serious matters requiring public discussion are muted or ignored; journals that want to raise them are frustrated by courts and the law.

For those in power, the system works well and even helps them to survive. But it would be unfair to suggest that they are guided only by self-interest. As Andrew Shonfield once explained: "The element of arrogance should not be left out of the compound. Persons who carry high responsibility in Britain tend to assume that they cannot be expected to explain their actions fully to ordinary people, who would be unable to understand even if they wished to. This is the residue of old-fashioned aristocratic principle, which remains firmly embedded in British democracy."

This attitude, a view that only specialists can be trusted to understand special information, runs all through the civil service. It is reinforced by a system of recruitment that singles out for rapid advance a select group from Oxford and Cambridge, and particularly Oxbridge graduates from the more expensive private boarding schools. Self-selected philosopher-kings are not likely to share information with subjects, particularly when they recognize that information is power.

Another reason for the muffled quality of Britain's public debate, for the lack of candor in exploring genuine as opposed to mythical problems, is the absence of a leading paper. There is no daily vehicle capable of mounting a sympathetic challenge to government, the bureaucracy and the business or financial establishment on terms of equal prestige and almost equal knowledge. All these institutions, of course, are critically discussed in every paper from time to time; *The Sunday Times* is a persistent and consequential gadfly that works within the very Establishment it irritates. But Britain lacks a daily leader, a paper that matches the importance of a *Le Monde* for France or of a *New York Times* for the United States (more recently, *The Washington Post* could be said to share this role). Britain has no daily that sets a standard for serious disinterested reporting, that is willing to challenge the complex maze of press curbs, serving as a model for the rest of the craft.*

The Times, it is widely thought, once filled this space and, with justice, still recalls in advertisements the brilliant re-

---

* The *Financial Times* comes closest, but it addresses too special an audience to be regarded as a model. Its political reporting, both at home and abroad, makes it one of the world's most important journals. Interestingly enough, the financial and business reports that most appeal to its business audience are usually marked by the same lack of curiosity and relevant information that characterize the lesser national papers.

porting of William Howard Russell, who reformed an army
in the Crimean War a century ago. But the paper has never
recovered from its jingoism in World War I and its support
for "Herr Hitler" in the 1930s, its systematic suppression of
Germany's destruction of the Jews. *The Times* still matters. It
is the favorite reading of the higher bureaucrats, most MPs,
older professors, Church of England clergymen, other pro-
fessions and a fair sampling of executives in business and finance. But it is largely a house organ for these interlocked
groups, passing messages from one to another, stroking prej-
udices, rarely disturbing.

When, for example, two lecturers at Birmingham University produced a searching and pioneering study of the abuse
of criminal defendants by police, lawyers and judges, *The
Times* quietly buried its own scoop. The story was tucked
away on page four and began:

> A report suggesting that several barristers had improperly per-
> suaded their clients to change their pleas from not guilty to guilty
> is to be published in the summer in spite of strong opposition by
> the Bar Council, which has told the Home Office that its publica-
> tion in its present form would be against the public interest, dan-
> gerous and misleading.
>
> The dispute has, however, raised questions not only about the
> conduct of criminal cases . . . but also about the ethics of
> research . . .

A patient *Times* reader could, by laboring on, discover
some of what the devastating report said; the bulk are
warned away with the suggestion that the lecturers are in the
dock as firmly as "several barristers." (Five months later, a
Times leader did discuss the report's core — in an essay that
loftily criticized the researchers, judges and lawyers.)

Again, *The Times* can be counted on to reflect faithfully
almost any Civil Service view. In the fall of 1977, for example, Britain, the United States and thirteen other nations

reached an important agreement on a code to govern their exports of nuclear materials. This was a major effort to prevent the growth of bomb-making countries, and American papers claiming to be serious put the news on the front page. For reasons that are still obscure, the Foreign Office was more interested in advertising its local differences with the United States than with noticing the pact. The dutiful *Times* ran a brief story on page nine, and one of its "diplomatic correspondents" did not disclose the agreement until the fourth paragraph of his eight-paragraph essay.

This muffled voice does not simply reflect a taste for restraint, an abhorrence of the sensational. *The Times* may be written, more often than not, in a mind-dulling prose, but it is frequently as reckless as the most sensational sheet on the stands. It is reckless, however, in a very special way — toward those of whom it disapproves (unions, leftists) or who are helpless. The paper, for example, had no hesitation in running a five-column story on the top of page one and a substantial profile opposite the editorial page identifying a Cambridge professor, dead for sixteen years, as the man who had seduced Philby, Burgess and Maclean to join the Soviet spy network. This astonishing revelation was unsupported by a single fact or incident connecting the dead professor to either the three spies or the Russians. Since a dead man can't be libeled, *The Times* did not need to worry about letting itself be used to pursue the hobbyhorse of a retired Secret Service deputy. Two weeks later, *The Times* did apologize for its palpably fictitious yarn, but still insisted there had to be a fourth, "senior" man.

A year earlier, *The Times* had given much the same treatment to "Sheikh Ali Ahmed," described as a "mysterious" financier. The paper printed three long articles on the front page and two in its business section, hinting at something peculiar. But in 192 column-inches of type, *The Times* could not make clear what wrong, if any, the "mysterious" sheikh had committed. His evocative name disappeared from its columns as completely as that of the Cambridge professor.*

Just why *The Times* is no longer a standard to which other papers can repair is unclear. Its staff includes some of the ablest journalists writing in English, both at home and abroad. But somehow there is a lack of fiber at the top. *The Times* sustains large losses nearly every year and is supported by the Thomson family's profits from North Sea oil and other, provincial newspapers. *The Sunday Times,* far more vigorous, responsible in the best sense of the word, is also owned by the Thomsons, but it swings back and forth from loss to profit. Perhaps a completely kept paper, one that can't meet the market test, is inevitably soft and self-indulgent. Perhaps *The Times* appreciates that its audience does not want a fuss over anything involving them. Whatever the reason, Britain's lack of a flagship daily reinforces the will not to know, the prejudice against inquiry, an attitude that obscures any searching discussion of race, corruption, the inner workings of government — real as opposed to spurious concerns.

Parliament should but does not fulfill the watchdog's role, should but does not explore — except in the most perfunctory manner — real as well as fictitious problems. Some Americans unfamiliar with the system think that question time, the routine that compels a minister from a great department to answer MPs' inquiries for about forty-five minutes every four weeks, is a splendid device to insure

---

* Few papers enjoy criticism, but *The Times* is more stiff-necked than most. It once ran a front-page account of a "secret" CIA probe of British unions, Communist-led, of course, and bent on subversion. The paper had relied on a one-time CIA official to support its frightening tale, but he felt compelled to repudiate it in *The Times'* very own Letters column. I wrote a tongue-in-cheek account of this mishap for *The Washington Post,* an unforgivable lapse. Eventually, *The Times* struck back. On three mornings in less than a week I was savaged for "put[ting] a gun at the head of British reporters working abroad." The occasion for this was a long survey I had made of British intelligence, during which I had observed that some British foreign correspondents are interchangeable with agents — like Philby.

accountability. There is, it is often observed longingly, nothing like it in the United States. Moreover, question time subjects the prime minister himself to answer twice each week for fifteen minutes, responding to inquiries not from ill-equipped journalists but from his peers in the House. Those who actually attend at question time or read Hansard's, the account of debates, are quickly disabused. The MPs are ill informed; they lack the staff of a congressman. MPs are typically allowed only one follow-up or supplementary question; it is easy to avoid giving answers. Except for information the government wants to yield, question time is little more than an exchange of schoolboy political taunts. The government can even insist that some questions are, for one reason or another, entirely out of bounds. James Michael, an American authority on British secrecy, looked at the range of unanswered questions in one session and found they embraced such crucial subjects as the expected output from North Sea oil fields, the government's building standards, the extras or perquisites ministers receive in addition to pay and details of the loose contract with the maker of Concorde. Only the clumsiest of ministries need be much embarrassed by parliamentary questions.

Parliament does have committees that can and do go beyond the puerile question time. But not far. The 1977 inquiry of the supposedly powerful Accounts Committee into Concorde was characteristic. Civil servants were questioned deferentially. When they gave ambiguous or uninformative answers they were not pressed. The committee could and did conclude that the contract had been an invitation to escalate costs. It never found out but accepted imprecise answers to a crucial question: exactly how much will the taxpayers lose?

In part, this timidity reflects a structural defect. Parliamentary committees are assisted by a few professionals, usually drafted for the occasion, but they have nothing like the staff of a congressional committee, with its economists, lawyers, engineers, physicists, accountants and many more. Against the bureaucracy's defense in depth, a parliamentary committee is hopelessly outmanned.

That could be changed if there were a will to change. But there is not. The same reluctance to make a fuss, the same insistence on the privacy of public men, the same demand for secrecy in public business that castrates *The Times,* also inhibits MPs.

There is another and seldom-discussed reason for parliamentary timidity. The fact is that nearly every MP is daily engaged in a lawful conflict of interest. Apart from ministers and junior ministers, all the rest are entitled to, and most do enjoy, a second income from a private job. They work at advertising or public relations, practice law, serve in banking, insurance, real estate, manufacturing, construction and more. Parliamentary salaries are deliberately kept low — £6270 in 1977, or about $12,000 — to encourage members to seek other work. Sessions in the House begin at two-thirty, leaving an MP free to pursue his other business in the morning. Brian Walden, a promising Labour MP who abandoned his career for Peter Jay's television slot, once told me the system protected Britain from "professional politicians" like those in the United States. As an MP, Walden received a handsome retainer for serving as the parliamentary spokesman for the bookmakers, a common sort of role. But a part-time legislator, directly tied to business interests, is also unlikely to become a penetrating critic of things as they are. He develops a strong personal stake in boats that do not rock.

So spurious or marginal issues dominate public discussion. Genuine causes for concern are obscured or ignored until they burst on the public consciousness with uncomfortable force. A praiseworthy respect for privacy, for a civil and moderate discourse, becomes a style to evade, hide and bury.

A Post-Industrial Model

Throughout this book, I have insisted on distinguishing real and disturbing problems like Ulster, race, violence and secrecy from the notional ones posed by commentators —the end of empire, radical unions, lack of investment. But a lingering suspicion must still persist that the one acknowledged and evident economic failing, a low rate of manufacturing productivity, has been dismissed too lightly.

Is it really enough to say that this low rate reflects a preference for leisure over goods, to suggest that no baleful consequences flow from it?

By the end of 1977, even editor Rees-Mogg, lowering his sight to things of this world, had isolated low productivity as the key factor in "the equation of British poverty." "It has cost all of us the difference between the British standard of living and the German or French," he concluded in the first of two impassioned articles. "In times of slump, low productivity is not only damaging, it is very dangerous. If our response to a recession should be a further retreat into job saving and deliberate overmanning then that danger will certainly prove to be a disaster . . . All we have to do to double our standard of living is to become as efficient as the Dutch."

Beneath the apocalyptic prose is a grain of truth. The growing gap between the output of British and Continental workers — whether due to slack management or leisure-choosing labor — must shrink Britain's industrial sector. The rising costs of producing a Leyland car compared to a Datsun must not only reduce Leyland's share of markets abroad but also widen Datsun's sales in Britain. One alternative is to devalue the pound continually against the yen (and other currencies), thereby cheapening British exports and making imports dearer. Or, another form of the same thing, throw up tariff or quota barriers against foreign goods. Both these devices, however, must reduce the real standard of British living, shrink Britons' command over goods and services. There is historical reason to believe that Britons willingly settle for a slower pace of growth in incomes than citizens in Japan or on the Continent; there is nothing to suggest that Britons will accept indefinitely an absolute decline in living standards.

What then? Is Rees-Mogg right? Must Britons after all reverse their priorities to save steel mills, coal mines, auto assembly lines and machine tool plants?

I think not. There is, I believe, still another strategy and Britain is stumbling toward it. It is based on an insight of economics as old as David Ricardo: the doctrine of comparative advantage. In crude form, it urges nations to maximize their income by specializing in the production of things they do best. Indeed, the doctrine goes further. Even if a nation — let us call it Technomania — can produce every commodity cheaper than another — say, Povertyland — Technomania will gain from trade by concentrating its resources where its comparative cost advantage is greatest. Let Povertyland run textile mills, even if Technomania's are more efficient; Technomania will gain by trading its electronics or its television programs for Povertyland's trousers, shirts and sisal. (Povertyland will gain too, but our interest lies in Technomanian policy.)

Like most insights in economics, this is simply common sense refined. Moreover, we see it at work every day. In many developed nations, the white-collar labor force — clerks, scientists, bankers, teachers, computer operators, government workers and the rest — is now larger than the blue-collar. Workers in mills, mines and factories are a decreasing fraction of the working population. We properly interpret this as a sign of advance in the United States, Germany and everywhere else.

In some sectors — chemicals, specialized electronics, some machine tools — Britons are still efficient and productive, competing at a world level. In most manufacturing — notably cars, shipbuilding and steel — they are not. Ricardo's doctrine tells us that sound economic strategy calls for transferring resources — men, managers, engineers, capital and land — from the less efficient to the more efficient. In Britain's case, moreover, the transfer need not be from less efficient manufacturing to more efficient manufacturing, but to those areas where Britain has the greatest comparative advantage, into services like medicine, insurance, teaching and the arts.

Such a strategy seems to fit the tastes, if not the aptitudes, of most people. There is little joy working in a coal mine, a steel mill, a car assembly plant. Quite the contrary. These are tasks that deaden the spirit. Even in progressive Sweden, where Volvo is making an imaginative effort to transform a car assembly plant at Kalmar, conditions of work hardly enhance the human personality. They have simply become less unbearable, but the labor still offers no scope for creativity. The Kalmar plant is quiet, clean, sunny, cheerful; the assembly line has been replaced with moving platforms or pods; workers are free to engage in several routine tasks instead of being tied to one. But the tasks are still routine. Kalmar remains a factory, a place where only managers enjoy any sense of stretching their imaginative powers.

In effect, this is a suggestion that Britons stop worrying about declining industry and actually hasten its demise, give up the things its workers are reluctant to do for those they might willingly undertake.

Clearly, this is something that cannot be done overnight. A coal miner can't be converted into a television film splicer with a thirteen-week training program. But his son, properly educated, might. Gradual change is anyway almost always preferable to abrupt change except in the most desperate circumstances. So a government decision to bail out a Chrysler plant whose closure would destroy an entire Scottish town is understandable. But the argument here is that these bailouts — direct subsidies, tax relief, loans and the rest — should be recognized for what they are, techniques to ease a transition and not props designed to preserve industry forever, as if it contained some intrinsic value. The Heath government, with its resolve to abandon "lame ducks," was right in principle; so in practice was the Heath government that rescued Rolls-Royce and the Upper Clyde Shipbuilders.

It is less clear, however, that the Callaghan government had grasped the point. The prime minister himself personally wooed Henry Ford II to win a large engine plant for Wales. The government is putting up an estimated $133 million of the $350 million investment, an outlay of no less than $53,000 of taxpayers' funds for each of the 2500 jobs. At the same time, the government hesitated for months before making up its mind to invest in a remarkable new technique invented at the Post Office. The device, Viewdata, is a bit of microelectronics that would enable a television viewer to summon up and transmit an astonishing array of information. A subscriber could examine stock prices, sports results, the contents of encyclopedias and other reference books, unanswered telephone messages and virtually everything that can be coded electronically. Through the same device, he could book airline and theater tickets, order other goods and services, send telephone messages to absent recipients and much more.

Britain's scientific ability had given the nation a technological lead in a vast new market, but the government wavered over whether to exploit it. A car engine plant is familiar, big and solid (and employs union and Labour members) so the Ford investment in Wales was eagerly sought and subsidized; microelectronics and its development are not so obvious and nor are the political loyalties of its workers. In the end, the government did decide to provide money for Viewdata and its rich possibilities. But it was a close-run thing.

The fallacy of the useful I-beam and the worthless poem reappears almost as soon as a de-industrializing strategy is suggested. Surely Britain can't pay its way in the world by selling tourism, BBC films, drama, banking and insurance? How will the nation earn its food and raw materials if industry is allowed to decline?

The answer may have been given by the third Lord Cowdray, said to be Britain's richest man. His family's fortune underlines the doctrine of comparative advantage. Cowdray's grandfather, plain Weetman Pearson of Bradford in Yorkshire, was a late Victorian contractor in the grand imperial style. Pearson built a dam on the Nile, the great harbor of Vera Cruz, four tunnels under the East River for the Pennsylvania Railroad and wildcatted successfully for oil in Mexico. He made so many millions that he was ennobled with a hereditary peerage, the first Lord Cowdray. His grandson, the shy third lord, is probably even richer despite all those crippling taxes that are supposed to inhibit the accumulation of capital. Cowdray will hand on an even more stable fortune to his son because the family has shifted smartly into the things that modern Britain does best. So Cowdray controls Lazard Brothers, a leading merchant, or investment, bank; Penguin Books, perhaps the world's greatest paperback house; the *Financial Times,* Britain's most adult daily; *The Economist,* a profitable ornament among weeklies; Doulton & Company, makers of Royal Doulton and other superbly crafted chinaware; a rich string of provincial newspapers; Viking Press, a leading U.S. publisher. To be sure, there is also a substantial holding in Ashland Oil of Ohio. But the core of the family fortune depends on the sale of things of the mind — banking and publishing — and of the creative hand, china.

In 1976, this empire of words and services grossed a tidy £290 million, more than $500 million in 1977 exchange rates. Its profits were a modest but not unimpressive £14.5 million, or about $28 million. At least that was the sum declared to the tax collector. They key point is that more than half — 55 percent, or £11 of every £20 that the Cowdray empire took in — came from overseas: the United States, Europe, Africa, Asia and Australasia. Cowdray has not only made British words and services pay, he has discovered that the world will pay handsomely for them too. For an increasingly richer world also demands more leisure and relatively fewer goods. The appetite for books, tourism, entertainment, information and art is insatiable; there is a limit to the number of cars any one family will want to own. Cowdray has not entirely abandoned manufacturing; Grandfather Weetman would recognize the pottery mills. But the china plants that Cowdray keeps going exploit British skill and craftsmanship. Arnold Bennett would have been pleased, too.

Not everyone is as well placed to take advantage of Ricardo's doctrine as Cowdray, whose personal fortune has been estimated at £60 million, or nearly $120 million. But even in a notionally socialist-welfare society, the adaptation of this shrewd Yorkshire family is a model. Cowdray and the relatives who are succeeding him skillfully cultivate and profit from the things Britons do best, largely things of the mind and skilled hand. What he has done deliberately others are stumbling toward instinctively.

Oxford and Cambridge, whose older colleges sit on large piles of capital, have discovered there is a great thirst abroad for their product. Along with other British universities, they open their gates every summer to thousands of students from Europe and the United States. Oxford alone held more than a dozen summer schools for a thousand pupils in 1977 and collected about $1.5 million. After a summer's lecturing, A. J. P. Taylor, the historian, wrote: "These summer schools keep the colleges and universities of the country going. Our institutions . . . are transformed into boarding houses for American and European students and without them could hardly make ends meet."

At a less grand level, the hunger for instruction in English is worldwide and the British are uniquely placed to teach it. Thanks to the size and energies of Britain's former colonies in North America, English has become the universal tongue; and the able and ambitious everywhere — except in China — must master it. According to one estimate, 200,000 foreigners took language courses in Britain during 1977, spending a substantial $1 million. "Spreading words is a Growth Industry," crowed *The Times.*

In the same way Lew Grade — now Lord Grade — the impressario of Associated Television Corporation, an entertainment conglomerate, took full-page ads in leading newspapers to boast that he had sold "over 100 million dollars" of film to the United States alone in the first nine months of 1977. He listed another 106 countries that had also bought his firm's product. *Upstairs, Downstairs* is both entertaining and profitable. In the same way, the BBC makes money from *The Forsyte Saga,* sells its Shakespeare films to the United States for nearly $3 million and much more.

From Cowdray to Grade, from A. J. P. Taylor to English International (a language school that had to rent the wine cellars of a diplomats' club for its overflow students), the message is clear. Ricardo's doctrine works and promises Britons a useful, creative and comfortable future. Things of the mind and spirit — books, medicine, television, music, drama, education (as well as banking and insurance) — not only enrich the human personality but enable men and women to earn their way in a world whose material income expands. Tourism has taken on an unpleasant ring for those who deplore the package tours swarming over classical Greek sites or once unspoiled beaches. But mass tourism is a reflection of the great burst of postwar prosperity, and Britain — its climate notwithstanding — is splendidly poised to profit from this appetite as well.

Indeed, these ways of earning a living are so comparatively satisfying, they dissolve the characteristic British trait

found in factories. Anyone who has ever worked on a program with producers, writers, directors and broadcasters
from the BBC or commercial television; watched at work
correspondents from *The Economist, The Observer, The Sunday
Times, The Guardian* and others; seen Sir Peter Hall conduct a
National Theatre rehearsal or counted the hours that musicians labor for the Philharmonia, is struck by the intensity of
those involved. There is no preference for leisure over goods
when men's minds and spirits are engaged; rather, there is a
craft devotion to perform at the limit of one's ability. When
a man does a job he respects, he works hard.

Now we can answer the question of Britain's health with
some confidence. Far from being sick, the place is healthy,
democratic, productive, as stable a society as any of its size in
Europe. It is transforming the heritage of the Industrial
Revolution, shedding the plants, the mills and some of the
values that made them work. It is slowly becoming a post-
industrial society where a decreasing number of men and
women are concerned with the production of goods and an
increasing share with things of the mind and spirit — or services in the economists' accounting. This transition is eased
by the fortuitous discovery of North Sea oil, an old-fashioned
process of mineral extraction made possible by new and advanced technology.

To be sure, many service tasks are as numbing as any job
on an assembly line. A clerk in an insurance office is unlikely
to derive much more joy than a worker in a steel mill, even if
his collar is whiter. But electronic machinery is gradually
replacing the clerk and newer industrial states are threaten-
ing the steelworker. A post-industrial society, moreover,
won't wipe out all handwork or indeed all industry. There is
pleasure, profit and even foreign exchange to be earned from
a broad spectrum of skilled crafts. In an increasingly specialized world, there is a growing demand for men to repair machines that go wrong and to design and build new ones to go

right. An advanced society, moreover, will surely keep and
expand industries near the frontier of knowledge — nuclear
power, microelectronics, drugs and many more.

But more and more Britain will earn its way by trading its
skill with words, music, banking, education and leisure for
the products of more traditional societies. This can't and
won't happen overnight. But the day that the last mine, mill
and assembly line closes should be an occasion for national
rejoicing, not despair.

We can go further and answer Dean Acheson's implied
question. Britain is unlikely ever again to play a big-power,
imperial role. Gratifying for the few, global ambition imposes too great a burden on the people as a whole. To be
sure, and because of its past experience and present size, the
country will not slip entirely from history's stage. But inevitably Britain will take a supporting part at most, advising,
urging, counseling but not determining. However, this is not
the measure of Britain's future importance. As teacher of
the world's most nearly universal language, transmitter of
high and middle culture, Britain's influence will exert itself
in thousands of hidden ways. In Israel, India and Sweden,
Ireland, Poland and Brazil, South Africa, Czechoslovakia
and Chile — wherever one point of view is imposed on
broadcast news — serious citizens turn to the BBC short-
wave broadcasts. They are impressed not with propaganda — that is what they are escaping; they receive instead
the implicit message of a free society, acknowledging and
capable of righting wrong. In the same way, the tourists who
flock to Britain are drawn by and quietly impressed with the
civility they mostly experience. Post-industrial Britain semi-
consciously practices a new and more lasting empire of the
spirit, quietly insinuating the values it proclaims (and frequently practices) — tolerance, decency, respect for the
human personality.

Even the much maligned British welfare state — however
bureaucratic, costly and impersonal — is an object lesson. It

has achieved the Beveridge goal, providing a tolerable minimum of material well-being for virtually all citizens. What Britain did in the immediate postwar period, other Western nations, including the United States, have copied and frequently expanded. Thirty years after Britain put in place a comprehensive service of medical care, divorced from the ability (or inability) to pay, the United States is about to embark on the same momentous path. For all the criticism of the system, it has been accompanied by and may have even partly caused a vast improvement in health. This service is no more likely to be replaced by the old, fee-paying technique than the United States is to cling to its traditional ways.

In much the same way, commentators predicted that Britain could not stand 1 million jobless, that 1.5 million would lead to riots in the streets. Unemployment at that level has surely taken a toll of men's skills, dignity and self-assurance that no statistics can measure. But there have been no riots; unemployment has been made far more bearable than in the thirties because of the cushion of benefits. Men have not been driven to the barricades (although there is a link between high joblessness and the fears exploited by the National Front). The commentators were false prophets because of the provision of welfare.

Jobless benefits are not a British invention and they are far more generous in richer countries, where they have also served to dampen resentment, to keep "hot" summers cool. If Britain is not the model here, at least its values and its technique have played a substantial part in the widespread use of another device to prevent the social fabric from disintegrating.

It may seem willful paradox to assert that Britain's unions can stand as a model for anyone. But their extraordinary performance in the years after 1974 contains a lesson that will not be lost abroad. They demonstrated that free and vigorous trade unions, with a long history of independent bargaining, have come to understand there are limits they must impose on their own power. Union members see that their well-being now requires a measure of union restraint.

In the textbook world of classical competition, restraint and power are words outside the economic vocabulary. But in the world as it is, each industry is dominated by a handful of firms, exercising considerable power over output and price, confronting a handful of unions with considerable power over the price and supply of labor. If each exercises its power to the utmost, the result is unemployment and inflation. The indirect regulators of government — Keynesian spending and tax cuts to mop up unemployment or severe deflation to curb prices — only sharpen the other horn of the dilemma.

This state of affairs is not uniquely British. It describes the economic map in the United States, West Germany, Scandinavia and other industrial states.

Only the doctrinaire, political fanatics believe the problem can be solved by breaking up the unions and the large corporations, restoring the textbook model of innumerable competitors. Instead, modern societies are driven to seek other answers — wage and price guideposts or guidelines; national wage bargains; agreement on a division of the gain in the national product — all variants of what economists call "incomes policy."

Incomes policy was not invented in Britain either. A dozen years before Jack Jones accepted the "social contract," the Kennedy administration briefly flirted with it in the United States. The Germans and Scandinavians have been practicing forms of incomes policy for years. But, in the four years through 1978, the British unions demonstrated that incomes policy is workable in the nation believed least amenable to such devices. Wage restraint helped reduce a terrifying inflation to a tolerable level and prepared the ground for conventional, Keynesian techniques to expand the economy.

In the United States, George Meany has all but vowed that as long as he presides over the AFL-CIO, there will be no incomes policy. Despite appearances, his tradition is mortal; other, younger U.S. union leaders will have observed the British performance. So too will government and business executives. The unexpected success of the gamble by Britain's AFL-CIO has sharply enhanced the prospect that incomes policy will now travel across the Atlantic.

Britain has frequently been held up as a horrible example, a warning to others against letting this happen to them. But a cooler appraisal suggests that Britain — at least a Britain somehow shed of its running sore in Ulster — is precisely the contrary: a comfortable, decent, creative place, burdened with problems, as are all industrial societies, but moving hesitantly toward a more civilized life. By choosing leisure over goods, both as a life-style in factories and as a source of work, Britons have created a society that attracts many outside it. The tourist horde marvels at the patience, sense of fairness, of Britons who stand in queues for buses, theater, goods in a shop. Indeed, a few tourists are so impressed they even imitate the local custom. Outsiders notice too the remarkable courtesy, particularly among workers, that governs most transactions. The lady from the public housing project asks, "Have you a *News of the World*, luv?" The newsagent replies with a smile, "Here, dear." And she responds, "Thank you, luv."

The "dear" and "luv" are ritual, unthought, the common vocabulary. But they also suggest a kinship, a oneness, a decency that is not part of the ritual vocabulary in New York, Munich, Cleveland, Stockholm or Marseille. Some left-wing, politically aware workers in other parts of the world address each other self-consciously as "comrade." Anywhere in Britain, one worker calls another "mate," an unconscious reflection of a genuine fraternity.

There is no need to exaggerate. Britons can be as cold, hard, mean, tough, sly, self-centered, brutal, as people anywhere. But the foreigner's sense that British workers are likely to be pleasanter, easier with each other and with strangers, is not altogether wrong. The foreigner, however exasperated by the slower working pace, is likely to reflect that there may be a cause-and-effect relationship, that there could be something here worth importing.

Just as the working-class vocabulary expresses a concern for the individual personality, so too does the physical setting. There is a reason why so many regard London as the last inhabitable great city. To be sure, the skyline is pockmarked by the excrescences of the real estate speculator, huge and rude towers of glass, steel and cement. But it is not dominated by them. You can walk through miles of city streets where buildings are five stories high or less. These terraces do not crush the human spirit; they are built to a human scale. In strictly economic terms, profit and loss, they are no doubt an inefficient use of real estate that would be better exploited by some forty-story monster. The survival of a human skyline, however, is another aspect of the British choice, an insistence that things must not always take pride of place before people.

It is not inconceivable that other post-industrial states will make similar choices. As a matter of economic strategy alone, they are likely to leave conventional industries more and more to developing peoples in other parts of the world. They are likelier to pursue energetically the new knowledge-arts-entertainment sector. They will rediscover Ricardo. In the same way, post-industrial nations are looking for ways to make work more human, exact less of a toll. They too may find that some jobs can be humanized only by doing less of them, either by working at a slower pace or by abandoning them entirely. As rich societies insist on more satisfying work, they are likely to reflect on Britain. Then, instead of serving as a warning, Britain will teach a lesson, serve as a model of sorts in tomorrow's world.

Notes

Notes

Chapter I: Europe's Sick Man

PAGE

1 William Rees-Mogg, *An Humbler Heaven* (London: Hamish Hamilton, 1977), p. 55.

1-2 Peter Jay, "A General Hypothesis of Employment, Inflation and Politics," Sixth Wincott Memorial Lecture, December 4, 1975, p. 32.

2 Eric Sevareid, CBS News, May 6, 1975. Morley Safer, "The Second Battle of Britain," CBS, March 17, 1976; Cyrus L. Sulzberger, "Memories: IV — What Giants Leave," *International Herald Tribune*, December 19, 1977.

3 Vermont Royster, "Britain: A Model Study," *Wall Street Journal*, August 20, 1975; "Sick Man of Europe": R. Emmett Tyrrell, Jr., intro., p. 2; R. Emmett Tyrrell, Jr., ed., *The Future That Doesn't Work: Social Democracy's Failure in Britain* (New York: Doubleday & Co., 1977); Steffens' quote: *The Autobiography of Lincoln Steffens*, vol. 2 (London: Harrap, 1931), p. 799; Irving Kristol, "Socialism: Obituary for an Idea," p. 197; James Q. Wilson, "Crime and Punishment in England," pp. 64, 65.

3 Britain-Chile analogy: Milton Friedman, *60 Minutes*, CBS, November 28, 1976.

4 Friedman as adviser to Pinochet junta: Orlando Letelier, "Economic 'Freedom's' Awful Toll," *Nation*, August 28, 1976, p. 137; N. P. Barry, "Milton Friedman's Political Ideas," *Cambridge Review*, December 2, 1977; Lord Robens: Peter Webb, "Land of Hope and Glory," *Newsweek*, October 21, 1974; Cecil King, *The Cecil King Diary, 1965-1970* (London: Cape, 1972), pp. 173, 213, 270, 241; Lord Chalfont, "Who Says It Could Never Happen Here," Anglia Television, December 18, 1975; Robert Moss, "Anglocommunism?" *Commentary*, February 1977.

4-5 Margaret Thatcher, *Panorama*, BBC, July 11, 1977.

5   Tom Nairn, *The Break-up of Britain* (London: New Left Books, 1977), p. 287; democratic collapse: Samuel Brittan, "The Economic Tensions of British Democracy," in Tyrrell, *The Future That Doesn't Work*, p. 141; Peter Jay, "Englanditis," in *The Future That Doesn't Work*, p. 176; Engels, in Nairn, *The Break-up of Britain*, p. 37; Lord Chalfont, *Time*, September 30, 1974.

6   Eric Sevareid, CBS News, May 6, 1977; James Reston, "Britain's Costume Party," *International Herald Tribune*, June 2, 1977.

7   peak of GDP: *Economic Trends*, Central Statistical Office, January 1978, p. 6; unemployment by the end of 1977: *Economic Trends*, January 1978, p. 36; 1975 price rises: *Economic Trends*, November 1977, p. 42.

7–8 foreign exchange value: from Bank of England.

8–9 living standards since the war: real disposable income at 1970 prices £18, 766 million in 1948, £41, 460 million in 1976, *Economic Trends*, Annual Supplement, 1977, p. 16.

9   "ten years of steady national decline": "Adrift in a Deepening Crisis of Faith," *Time*, September 30, 1974.

9–10 Friedman, *60 Minutes*.

10   UK growth rate: *The United Kingdom in 1980: The Hudson Report* (London: The Hudson Institute Europe, 1974), p. 45.

11   Safer-Friedman thesis: Morley Safer, "The Second Battle of Britain," CBS, March 17, 1976; Milton Friedman, *60 Minutes*.

12   social and political fabric: *Time*, October 11, 1976, p. 6, Eric Sevareid, CBS News, May 6, 1975.

12–14 threats to democracy: Brittan, pp. 128, 129; Jay, pp. 169–179, in Tyrrell, *The Future*.

14–16 Peregrine Worsthorne, "The Trade Unions: 'New Lads on Top,' " in Tyrrell, *The Future*, pp. 5, 20.

16   Tyrrell, *The Future*, p. 3; Kristol, in Tyrrell, *The Future*, p. 197; Safer-Reid: "The Second Battle of Britain."

16–17 Jack Jones' power: Moss, "Anglocommunism?" p. 32.

17   Royster, *Wall Street Journal*.

17–18 Robert Bacon and Walter Eltis, *Britain's Economic Problems: Too Few Producers* (London: Macmillan, 1976), p. 24.

19   percent in manufacturing jobs: Robin Marris, "Is Britain an Awful Warning to America," *New Republic*, September 17, 1977, p. 25; Bacon and Eltis, *Britain's Economic Problems*, p. viii.

19–20 Exporters: *Britain's Economic Problems*, p. 25.

21   tourism and foreign earnings: *United Kingdom Balance of Payments 1966–76,* Central Statistical Office, HMSO London 1977, tables 2.2, 3.1, pp. 19, 27; 1967–77 tourist growth: *Annual Report of the British Tourist Authority* (for the year ended March 31, 1977), p. 4, and *Digest of Tourist Statistics,* no. 7, British Tourist Authority, April 1977, table 10, p. 14; tourism and the Queen: Joseph C. Harsch, "Queen's Jubilee," *Christian Science Monitor* News Service, May 16, 1977.

22–23 jobs in local and national government: Marris, *New Republic,* p. 25; Leslie Lenkowsky, "Welfare in the Welfare State," in Tyrrell, *The Future;* accumulation of wealth: p. 158; Britons' living standards: pp. 152, 153; cost of welfare: p. 150; welfare-prosperity relationship: pp. 159, 166.

23–24 industrial backwardness: "The Second Battle of Britain," *The Hudson Report,* p. 69; "Upstairs/Downstairs at the Factory," *Time,* September 15, 1975, cover story.

24   industrial investment: *Britain's Economic Problems,* p. 19; *The Hudson Report,* pp. 35–40.

25   politico-economic crisis: *The Hudson Report,* pp. 1–7.

26   strikes: Ibid., p. 28.

27   per capita GNP: Ibid., p. 15; quality of life: pp. 45–48.

28   North Sea Oil: Ibid., pp. 74, 80.

29   domestic oil consumption: estimates from U.K. Department of Energy. Later calculation in White Paper, *The Challenge of North Sea Oil,* March 21, 1978, p. 6, predicts balance in 1980 and exports in the 1980s; net exporter and balance of payments surplus: *Economic Progress Report,* U.K. Treasury, July 1976, pp. 1–3.

30   Peter Odell, "Indigenous oil and gas developments and Western Europe's energy policy options," *Energy Policy,* June 1973, p. 57.

30–31 Hudson's French report: *The Hudson Report,* p. 2.

31   indicative planning: Bernard D. Nossiter, *The Mythmakers* (Boston: Houghton Mifflin Co., 1964), pp. 200–205; peerages: *The Hudson Report,* p. 123.

31–32 Pentagon-Hudson: from U.S. Department of Defense.

32   Penelope Hartland-Thunberg, "The Political and Strategic Implications of Britain's Economic Problems," Center for Strategic and International Studies, Georgetown, January 4, 1977, pp. 1, 10.

33   Rees-Mogg, *An Humbler Heaven,* pp. 56–58.

33–35 Wilson, in Tyrrell, *The Future,* pp. 66, 67, 68; FBI index and British crime figures: from U.S. Department of Justice, FBI and Professor F. H. McClintock, Department of Law, Edinburgh.

35–36   Kristol, in Tyrrell, *The Future*, p. 197.

36   Dean Acheson: December 5, 1962, West Point, N.Y. Anthony Burgess, "Five Futures for Britain: Tucland," *New Society*, November 17, 1977; Harsch, "Queen's Jubilee."

36–37   V. I. Lenin, *Imperialism, The Highest Stage of Capitalism* (Moscow: Progress Publishers, 1975), pp. 13, 14.

37 ff   Tom Nairn, *The Break-up of Britain* (London: New Left Books, 1977); dependent upon empire, p. 13; Common Market illusions, p. 57; no other nation so dependent, p. 69; irredeemable decline, p. 45; New Imperialism, p. 21; peripheral nationalism, p. 70; neo-nationalism, p. 89; Scottish revolt, pp. 190–193.

40   illusion of oil: Moss, "Anglocommunism?" p. 33; barrels a day and foreign exchange savings: from U.K. Department of Energy.

40–41   Thatcher: *Panorama*, July 11, 1977.

41   along Communist road: Moss, "Anglocommunism?" pp. 29, 30.

42   Ibid., p. 29; Sevareid, CBS News, May 6, 1975; Harsch, "Queen's Jubilee."

Chapter II: Examining the Symptoms

45–48   Clive's reward: John Strachey, *The End of Empire* (London: Victor Gollancz Ltd., 1959), pp. 32, 33; estimate of East India Company's profits: pp. 62, 63; a test of imperial gain: pp. 44, 147–153.

48   annual growth in output, 1855–1945, computed from Charles H. Feinstein, *National Income, Expenditure and Output of the United Kingdom, 1855–1965* (Cambridge: University Press, 1972), table 6, T18, 19; for post-imperial period, *Economic Trends* Annual Supplement, 1977, p. 5 (1948–76).

49   income per head, 1865–1965, Feinstein, *National Income,* table 17, pp. T42, 43; Mill, in Strachey, *End of Empire,* p. 72.

50   Gunnar Myrdal, *The Challenge of World Poverty* (London: Penguin Books, 1970), pp. 286–302.

51   Third World's terms of trade: "Poor Countries Get Poorer," Washington *Post,* July 10, 1975; *Time,* September 15, 1975, p. 11.

52–53   Organization for Economic Cooperation and Development,

Studies in Resource Allocation, *Public Expenditure on Income Maintenance Programmes,* July 1976, p. 17.

53–54   government spending: table supplied by Statistical Office of the European Communities.

54–55   taxation: OECD, *Revenue Statistics of OECD Member Countries 1965–1975,* p. 80.

56   Confederation of British Industry, *The Road to Recovery,* October 1976, p. 40; Foreword by Prince Philip in the *Engineer,* November 1976.

57–59   Lord Diamond, *Royal Commission on the Distribution of Income and Wealth,* Reports No. 1, No. 2 (cmnd. 6171, cmnd. 6172), July 1975, and Report No. 5 (cmnd. 6999), November 1977; prewar and postwar personal incomes compared: Report No. 1, p. 36; Gini coefficient: ibid., p. 203; inclusion of benefits in data: ibid., p. 62; 1975 drop in wealth of top 1 percent: Report No. 5, pp. 76, 77; distribution of wealth: Report No. 1, pp. 102, 103.

60   CBI, *The Road to Recovery,* p. 40; Lord Diamond, Report No. 1, p. 68.

60–61   Malcolm Sawyer, "Income Distribution in OECD Countries," *OECD Economic Outlook,* July 1976.

61   French and Italian Communist vote: Thomas Mackie and Richard Rose, eds., *The International Almanac of Electoral History* (London: Macmillan, 1974), pp. 137, 219.

62–63   "Communist-dominated" unions: "Who Runs the Unions?" *The Economist,* January 19, 1974.

63   Robert Moss, "Anglocommunism?" *Commentary,* February 1977, p. 33.

64 fn   weekly pay: Treasury figures in written parliamentary answer, *Hansard,* Vol. 940, November 30, 1977, col. 259; Labour Government plans to inhibit union bargaining power: "In Place of Strife: A Policy for Industrial Relations," Department of Employment and Productivity, January 17, 1969.

65   stimulate union recognition: "The British at Work," *The Economist,* January 1, 1977.

65–66   special piece of law: The Dock Work Regulation Act (November 23, 1976).

66   wage restraint: *The Economist,* June 11, 1977; "Wage Curbs Essential Wilson Tells Britain," Washington *Post,* July 12, 1975; "British Unions, Government Trade Pay Curb for Tax Cut," May 6, 1976; price rises: *Economic Trends,* November 1977, p. 42.

66–67   redistribution of income from the workers: Bernard D. Nos-

siter, "The Phantom of 'Anglocommunism,' " *The Nation,*
March 12, 1977, p. 299.

67 composition of NUM executive board: estimate by NUM
official.

68 money supply increases: *Economic Trends,* February 1978, p.
50, table for M3; oil price rise: from British Petroleum, the
price of crude oil was $2.70 per barrel in early October 1973,
$10.84 on January 1, 1974.

68 Heath's wage limit and miners' pay: Lord Diamond, *Royal
Commissions,* Report No. 5, Appendix A: Summary of National Incomes Policies from January 1970 to July 1977; *Historical Abstract of Labour Statistics, Labour Statistics Yearbook* for
1969–74; *National Coal Board Annual Report and Statistical Tables*
for 1970–74.

69 Whitelaw proposal: from Whitelaw; February 1974 general
election result: *The Times Guide to the House of Commons for October 1974,* p. 283, and *for 1970,* p. 246.

70 a change of view concerning left-wing unions: "The Social
Contract Lives On," *The Economist,* July 30, 1977.

70–71 the new list of left-wingers: "The TUC Power Balance," *The
Economist,* September 10, 1977.

71 comparative strike records: "Industrial Disputes: International Comparisons," *Department of Employment Gazette,* December 1975, p. 1276.

72 concentration of strikes: "Distribution and Concentration of
Industrial Stoppages in Great Britain," *Department of Employment Gazette,* November 1976, pp. 1220–1224; post-1974 UK
strike record: press release of the International Labour Office,
Geneva, November 21, 1977.

73 after tax incomes: Lord Diamond, *Royal Commission,* Report
No. 1, p. 36.

Chapter III: Leisure over Goods

75 incomes in Queen's reign: *Economic Trends* Annual Supple-
ment, 1977, p. 37; social indicators: *Social Trends,* Central
Statistical Office, No. 7, July 1976, p. 152; *The Economist,*
June 4, 1977; *Department of Education and Science: Statistics of
Education, Vol. 2, School Leavers.*

75–76 G. C. Fiegehen, P. S. Lansley, and A. D. Smith, *Poverty and
Progress in Britain 1953–73* (Cambridge: University Press,
1977), pp. 27, 29, 111.

76   London's winter sunshine: from the CSO, new matter 5; oaks: "Cleaner Air Brings Oaks Back to London Parks," *The Times,* March 6, 1978.

76-77 Thames pollution: "The River That Came Clean," *Horizon,* BBC, September 2, 1977.

77   the arts: from the Arts Council; holidays: from the CSO; cars per household and emission of sulfur dioxide: *The Economist,* June 4, 1977; stagnant output and real incomes, 1974-77: *Economic Trends,* February 1978, p. 10.

78   OECD study by outside experts: *Council Towards Full Employment and Price Stability,* published in mimeograph for the Organization for Economic Cooperation and Development, Paris, June 1977, pp. 107-140; comparative unemployment and inflation: *OECD Economic Outlook* 22, December 1977, pp. 28, 54; real incomes and output, 1971-74: output, *Economic Trends,* February 1978, p. 6; incomes, *Economic Trends* Annual Supplement, 1977, p. 39.

79   economic improvement for Britain: *OECD Economic Outlook,* December 1977, pp. 99-101, 121; 1975 oil import bill: from U.K. Treasury; "Britain's North Sea Oil: Signs Point to a Gusher," Washington *Post,* November 22, 1976; self-sufficient exporter of oil: *OECD Economic Surveys:* United Kingdom, March 1977, p. 34; Treasury study: *Economic Progress Report,* U.K. Treasury, July 1976, pp. 1-3.

79-80 foreign debts: *Economic Progress Report,* U.K. Treasury, May 1977, pp. 1, 2.

80   1980-85 oil earnings projection: from U.K. Treasury; perennial balance of payments deficit: *OECD Economic Surveys,* United Kingdom, March 1977, p. 36. (White Paper March 21, 1978, *The Challenge of North Sea Oil,* p. 7, reduces balance of payments gain to £8-9 billion a year in the mid-1980s, reflecting the oil companies' lower strategic targets); 1976 sterling crisis: Anthony Harris, "Sterling: New Role Means New Problems," *Financial Times,* January 12, 1977.

81   import sector of cost of living: *Economic Trends,* January 1978, pp. 6, 46.

82   National Institute of Economic and Social Research: D. T. Jones, "Output, Employment and Labour Productivity in Europe since 1955," *National Institute Economic Review,* August 1976, p. 84; exchange rates: Robin Marris, "Is Britain an Awful Warning," *New Republic,* September 17, 1977, p. 24.

83-84 growth rates: *National Institute Economic Review,* February 1978, p. 36; Edward F. Denison, *Why Growth Rates Differ*

(Washington, D.C.: The Brookings Institution, 1967).

84 economies of scale: p. 312; contraction of farmer and self-employed groups: pp. 202, 337, 341; factors contributing to rise in national income: pp. 307, 309, 315.

85 drop in agricultural employment: p. 206; continuation of slow British growth rate: pp. 293, 294.

85 gross fixed domestic capital formation as a percent of GNP: from table supplied by National Institute of Economic and Social Research.

87 comparative capital-output ratios: Confederation of British Industries, *The Road to Recovery,* October 1976, p. 25.

88 British Leyland: "Leyland: An Executive Speaks His Mind," *The Observer,* October 30, 1977.

89 management perquisites: for example, Paul Ferris, "Everybody Has Fringe Benefits," *The Observer,* November 28, 1976.

89 destinations of 'best' graduates: Robert Dunsmore and David Lethbridge, "Shun Business," *The Director,* August 1975, p. 147.

89-90 Foreign Office recruitment: Central Policy Review Staff, *Review of Overseas Representation* (London: HMSO, 1977), p. xiii; "Excellence Is Bad," *The Economist,* August 6, 1977.

90 "150 Faces for the Future," *Time,* July 15, 1974; university graduates: *Annual Report of the Appointments Board for the Year 1976,* Cambridge University, February 24, 1977, Table 3; *Appointments Committee Report for 1975-6, University of Oxford,* pp. 13, 14.

91 course vacancies: Michael Crick, "Glittering Prizes," *New Statesman,* November 5, 1976; also from U.K. Department of Education and Science; background of top executives: "Science Greats?" *The Economist,* December 31, 1977.

93 Leslie Hannah and J. A. Kay, *Concentration in Modern Industry* (London: Macmillan, 1977), p. 1; S. J. Prais, *The Evolution of Giant Firms in Britain* (Cambridge: University Press, 1976), pp. 4, 141, 159, 161; EEC Commission, *Sixth Report on Competition Policy,* Brussels-Luxembourg, April 1977, p. 162; "Different pictures, same story," *The Economist,* December 3, 1977.

94 Marshall, in Prais, *Evolution of Giant Firms,* pp. 21, 22; Hicks, in Hannah and Kay, *Concentration in Modern Industry,* p. 20; Hannah and Kay, *Concentration in Modern Industry,* pp. 36-39.

94-95 Ibid., p. 40.

95 Robert Bacon and Walter Eltis, "The Age of U.S. and U.K. Machinery," NEDO Monograph 3, September 1974.

96   Central Policy Review Staff, *The Future of the British Car Indus-*
        try (London: HMSO, 1975), pp. v, 80, xi, xii, 87.
96–97   *National Institute Economic Review,* August 1976, p. 74.
97   effect of three-day week: industrial production, *Monthly Digest*
        of Statistics, CSO, October 1977, p. 168.
98–99   "Britain at Work," *The Economist,* January 1, 1977.
101   night shift at Solihull: "Rover Output Checked by Sex 'Haz-
        ard,' " *Daily Telegraph,* September 9, 1977; C. F. Pratten,
        "Labour Productivity Differentials within International
        Companies," Occasional Papers 50, Department of Applied
        Economics (Cambridge: University Press, 1976), p. 53.
101–102 Ralf Dahrendorf, "Not by Bread Alone," *Financial Times,* De-
        cember 30, 1976.
103   German nonfiction: "Best-selling Angst," *The Economist,* July
        30, 1977.
103–104 symphony orchestras: *The Economist,* August 20, 1977.
104–105 tourists: *Annual Report of the British Tourist Authority* (for the
        year ended March 31, 1977); "Cashing In on the Golden
        Horde," *The Economist,* September 3, 1977, p. 90.
105   Fred Hirsch, *Social Limits to Growth* (London: Routledge and
        Kegan Paul, 1977), pp. 27–31; job satisfaction: *Social Trends,*
        No. 7 (London: CSO, HMSO, 1976), p. 105.

Chapter IV: One into Nine Makes Zero

107–108 Heath speech to Commons, *Hansard,* vol. 823, October 28,
        1971, col. 2202.
109   Tom Nairn, *The Break-up of Britain* (London: New Left Books,
        1977), p. 57; Enoch Powell speech to Commons, *Hansard,* vol.
        889, April 9, 1975, col. 1300; Central Policy Review Staff,
        Review of Overseas Representation, p. ix.
110   initial attempts to join the EEC: useful accounts in Miriam
        Camps, *Britain and the European Community, 1955–1963* (Lon-
        don: Oxford University Press, 1964); Uwe Kitzinger, *Diplo-*
        macy and Persuasion (London: Thames and Hudson, 1973).
111–114 speeches in the House of Commons during the 1971 EEC de-
        bate: *Hansard,* vol. 823, Heath: October 28, cols. 2202, 2203,
        2211, 2212; Stewart: October 26, col. 1515; Carr: October 25,
        cols. 1364, 1365; Tugendhat: October 27, col. 1834; Sandys:
        October 28, col. 2179; Owen: October 26, col. 1638; Jay: Oc-
        tober 25, col. 1349; Foot: October 25, col. 1261; Powell: Octo-

ber 28, cols. 2187, 2189; Heath's remarks in 1975 EEC debate: *Hansard*, vol. 889, April 9, cols. 1274–86.

114   Western leaders' views of British entry: "Europe applauds entry," *Daily Telegraph*, October 29, 1971.

114–115   signing the treaty: "4 Nations Sign with Commart," Washington *Post*, January 23, 1972.

116   Wilson speech: *Hansard*, vol. 889, April 7, 1975, col. 836.

116–117   renegotiation and referendum: "EEC Summit to Weigh British Role," Washington *Post*, March 9, 1975; "British Win Key EEC Concessions," March 12, 1975; "Britons Seen Backing EEC in Vote Today," June 5, 1975; "Britons Vote on EEC: Polls Predict Approval," June 6, 1975; "British Vote Heavily for Link to EEC," June 7, 1975; *The Times* Diary, March 13, 1975.

118   Michael Foot, "Putting Parliament at Stake," *The Times*, May 23, 1975; high inflation and rising unemployment: Research Group of the Labour Common Market Safeguards Committee, *The Common Market: The Cost of Membership*, p. 3.

118–119   Callaghan speech: *Hansard*, vol. 889, April 9, 1975, cols. 1359, 1360.

119   Callaghan's 1971 opposition to the EEC: *Hansard*, vol. 823, October 28, col. 2200.

120   opinion polls in 1971: *Diplomacy and Persuasion*, pp. 352–70; referendum result: *Britannica Book of the Year 1975*, Encyclopaedia Britannica, 1976, p. 682; views of Peter Shore: Ian Aitken, "How Peter Shore Learned to Live with Europe," *The Guardian*, September 5, 1977.

122   truck limits: *The Economist*, March 25, 1978.

123   percent employed in farming: from EEC Information Office.

124   reform of CAP: "Can Gundelach Move Those Mountains?" *The Economist*, September 17, 1977.

124–125   John Vaizey, "The FO Stumbling Block," *The Spectator*, March 12, 1974; *The History of British Steel* (London: Weidenfeld and Nicholson, 1974), pp. 71, 81, 82.

125   EEC steel production: "Steel's Shambles," *The Economist*, October 15, 1977; "A Protectionist Christmas Parcel," *The Economist*, December 24, 1977. "Brussels Fixes Minimum Import Prices on 140 Steel Products," *The Times*, December 30, 1977; EEC shipbuilding: "Docked," *The Economist*, October 22, 1977; William Drozdiak, "EEC Shifts to Protectionism to Fight Unemployment Rise," *International Herald Tribune*, October 6, 1977.

125–126   EEC oil policy: Louis Turner and James Bedore, "Saudi and

Iranian Petrochemicals and Oil Refining: Trade Warfare in the 1980s?" *International Affairs,* October 1977, pp. 583–586.

128–129   Vaizey, "The FO Stumbling Block," pp. 256, 257.

129   pro-Market camp: speech by Tom Boardman during 1971 EEC debate, *Hansard,* vol. 823, October 27, cols. 2009–11.

129–130   Williamson and Layton studies quoted by John Pinder, "The Cost of Pulling Out," *New Europe,* Winter 1973–74, p. 9.

130   world boom in commodity prices: Simon Harris and Tim Josling, "A Preliminary look at the UK Food Industry and the C.A.P.," paper delivered at Agra Europe Conference, April 20, 1977, pp. 7–17; *Britannica Book of the Year 1974,* Encyclopaedia Britannica, 1975, pp. 268, 269.

132   *The Effects on the United Kingdom of Membership of the European Communities,* February 1975, ch. 3, p. 3; *The British People: Their Voice in Europe,* Saxon House, 1977, pp. ix, x, 108, 109, 141.

133   Arab oil embargo: *Effects on the United Kingdom,* ch. 3, pp. 88–90; "Energy Crisis Is Bringing Out Double-Talk in British Policy," Washington *Post,* January 10, 1974.

134   Owen interview: "Wanted: A Bolder Britain," *Sunday Times,* September 18, 1977; reaction to Sadat peace initiative: "L'initiative egyptienne a provoque un incident au sein de l'Europe des Neuf" and "M. Barre: La France ne veut pas participer a une escouade qui marche au pas," *Le Monde,* November 22, 1977.

135   U.S. relations: *The Effects on the United Kingdom,* ch. 1, p. 11; Kissinger intervention over IMF loan: "Britain to Miss Its Envoy from Texas," Washington *Post,* March 15, 1977.

136   Helsinki Conference: "It's Usually Dull and Secret, but It Works," *The Economist,* January 29, 1977; *The Effects on the United Kingdom,* ch. 1, p. 12; William Wallace, "A Common European Foreign Policy: Mirage or Reality?" *New Europe,* Spring 1977, pp. 21–33.

137   Eastern bloc trade: *The Effects on the United Kingdom,* ch. 4, p. 16; "Behind the Reserve," *The Economist,* March 16, 1974.

138–140   opposition to the entry of Mediterranean nations: "New Democracies Edge Close to Door of Common Market," Washington *Post,* June 25, 1977.

139–140 fn   Eurocrat salaries: William Drozidiak, "Brussels 'Eurocrats' Reap Lavish, Tax-Free Incomes," Washington *Post,* November 25, 1977.

140   conclusion to European Parliament's report: *The Effects on the*

United Kingdom, ch. 1, p. 8; Jenkins' speeches: Brighton, October 3, 1971; Manchester, May 10, 1975, Norwich, June 3, 1975.

140–141   EEC trade: *Common Market,* pp. 6, 7; Peter Shore, *Europe: The Way Back,* Fabian Trust 425, October 1973, p. 5.

142   invisibles improved the deficit: *Economic Trends,* January 1978, p. 46; *United Kingdom Balance of Payments 1966–76,* CSO, 1977, p. 9.

142–143   levy on manufactured imports: from U.K. Department of Trade. Continental investment: *Common Market,* p. 10; UK subsidies: EEC Commission, *Sixth Report on Competition Policy,* Brussels-Luxembourg, April 1977, pp. 111–114.

144–145   Harris and Josling, "Preliminary Look at the UK Food Industry," pp. 5, 6, 34, 14; *The Economist,* September 28, 1974; *Economic Policy Review,* March 1978, "The Direct Costs to Britain of Belonging to the EEC," Richard Bacon, Wynne Godley and Alistair McFarquhar.

146   the Labour Safeguards Committee: *Common Market,* p. 11.

146–147   opinion polls: David Watt, "Common Market Returns to Centre Stage," *Financial Times,* May 27, 1977; EEC poll in *Euro-Barometer* No. 7, Directorate-General for Information, Commission of the European Communities, July 4, 1977, p. 3.

148   Commission president and annual economic summits: *European Community,* no. 4, May 1977, p. 3.

149   salaries of Strasbourg delegates: Malcolm Rutherford, "A Well Paid House of Europe," *Financial Times,* November 25, 1977; "The Lure of Europay," *The Economist,* June 10, 1977.

Chapter V: Wound in Ulster

152   1961 Census: Richard Rose, *Governing without Consensus* (London: Faber & Faber, 1971), p. 248; August 1969: Rose, *Governing without Consensus,* pp. 143, 144; Geoffrey Bell, *The Protestants of Ulster* (London: Pluto Press, 1976), p. 121; Michael Farrell, *Northern Ireland: The Orange State* (London: Pluto Press, 1976), pp. 259, 260, 262; Report of the Tribunal of Inquiry under Mr. Justice Scarman, "Violence and Civil Disturbances in Northern Ireland in 1969," April 1972, vol. 1 (cmnd. 566, HMSO, Belfast), pp. 67–77, 116–27; killings, woundings and population movements: from Northern Ireland Office.

153 "spongers": Robert Fisk, *The Point of No Return* (London: Andre Deutsch, 1975), pp. 199, 205, 253.

154 Prevention of Terrorism Act: *Public General Acts and Measures* (London: HMSO, 1976), ch. 8.

155–156 Lord Craigavon: Conor Cruise O'Brien, *States of Ireland* (New York: Pantheon Books, 1972), p. 13.

156 the Catholics' lot: Report of the Commission under the Chairmanship of Lord Cameron, "Disturbances in Northern Ireland," September 1969 (cmnd. 532, HMSO, Belfast), pp. 12, 13; internment: Farrell, *Northern Ireland: The Orange State*, p. 281; Richard Rose, *Northern Ireland: Time of Choice* (Washington, D.C.: American Enterprise Institute for Public Policy Research, April 1976), pp. 24, 28.

157 extracting information: *Home Office Report of the Enquiry into Allegations against the Security Forces of Physical Brutality in Northern Ireland Arising out of Events on the 9th August, 1971,* under the chairmanship of Sir Edmund Compton, November 1971 (cmnd. 4823, HMSO, London), pp. 11, 13, 15, 16, 23; Maudling's rebuke: *Report from the Select Committee on Conduct of Members,* Session 1976–77, HMSO, London, July 13, 1977, p. xviii; remarks of Maudling: introduction to the Compton Report, p. vi.

157–158 the European verdict: *European Commission of Human Rights, Ireland against the United Kingdom of Great Britain and Northern Ireland,* January 25, 1976, pp. 402, 473, 463.

158 action by Heath in March 1972: *European Commission of Human Rights,* pp. 389, 390; police surgeons in Ulster: "Ulster Police Doctors Meet to Discuss Allegations of RUC Brutality during Interrogations," *The Times,* October 7, 1977; government compensation: *European Commission of Human Rights,* p. 461; systematic beating: *Report of an Amnesty International Mission to Northern Ireland,* Amnesty International, June 1978.

159 1969 riots: Scarman Report, p. 15.

159–160 "Bloody Sunday": *Report of the Tribunal Appointed to Inquire into the Events on Sunday, 30th January 1972, Which Led to Loss of Life in Connection with the Procession in Londonderry on That Day by the Rt. Hon. Lord Widgery,* April 1972, pp. 32, 33, 38.

160 O'Brien, *States of Ireland,* p. 277.

161 guerrilla wars: Frank Kitson, *Low Intensity Operations* (London: Faber & Faber, 1971), pp. 7, 8; the Army's defense of internment: "British General in Ulster Rebuked for Political Talk," Washington *Post,* April 15, 1975.

161–162   Rees' rebuke: *Hansard,* vol. 890, April 14, 1975, cols. 28–30.

162–164   Curragh mutiny: Robert Kee, *The Green Flag: A History of Irish Nationalism* (London: Weidenfeld and Nicolson, 1972), pp. 471–490.

164–165   Kitson, *Low Intensity Operations,* pp. 3, 24, 25, 71, 93, 192; General Sir Michael Carver, p. x; "Civilian Supremacy and the Military," Washington *Post,* July 23, 1972.

166   army and firemen's strike: "Firemen Dig In," *Sunday Times,* November 27, 1977; Fisk, *Point of No Return,* pp. 152, 13, 87.

167   Andrew Sefton: "August 18th — Five Years On," *Monday World,* Summer 1974, pp. 6, 7.

168   Andrew Wilson, "Sir Harold Accuses MI5 Mafia," "Wilson, MI5 and the Rumour Machine," *The Observer,* August 28, 1977.

169   Protestant settlement: O'Brien, *States of Ireland,* pp. 34, 35; Rose, *Governing without Consensus,* pp. 58, 59, 78, 79.

170   Derry Protestants' march: Farrell, *Northern Ireland: The Orange State,* p. 259; 1916 Rebellion and independence: Kee, *The Green Flag,* pp. 548–731.

171   privileged position of the Roman Catholic Church in the Irish Constitution: O'Brien, *States of Ireland,* pp. 120, 121, 123.

173   gerrymandering: Cameron Report, pp. 57, 59; Farrell, *Northern Ireland: The Orange State,* pp. 84–86; disenfranchisement: Cameron Report, p. 62; Rose, *Governing without Consensus,* p. 441.

173–174   housing: Cameron Report, p. 61; *Sunday Times* Insight Team, *Ulster* (London: Penguin Books, 1972), pp. 36, 37.

174–175   public sector jobs: Farrell, *Northern Ireland: The Orange State,* p. 87; Cameron Report, pp. 60, 63; Fisk, *Point of No Return,* p. 98; police force: Fair Employment Agency for Northern Ireland, "An Industrial and Occupational Profile of the Two Sections of the Population in Northern Ireland," January 12, 1978, p. 13.

175   abolition of the B Specials: Fisk, *Point of No Return,* p. 21; unemployment in Northern Ireland: Fair Employment Agency, "Industrial and Occupational Profile," p. 5.

175–176   private sector jobs: Rose, *Governing without Consensus,* p. 297; Farrell, *Northern Ireland: The Orange State,* p. 91; Fisk, *Point of No Return,* pp. 26, 59.

176   Bell, *Protestants of Ulster,* p. 28.

178   IRA in 1969: O'Brien, *States of Ireland,* pp. 205–208; Farrell, *Northern Ireland: The Orange State,* pp. 269, 270; Provos aping

Marxist phrases: "Hopelessness, Despair Pervade Bloody Ulster," Washington *Post,* March 28, 1977.

176   political general strike: Rose, *Northern Ireland: Time of Choice,* p. 48.

179–180   power-sharing regime: Fisk, *Point of No Return,* pp. 42–49.

180–181   Paisley, Craig and West: Bell, *Protestants of Ulster,* p. 139.

181   pickets: "Ulster Paralyzed by Protestant Strike," Washington *Post,* May 21, 1974; RUC man: "Ulster Stoppage Continues with Few Options Apparent," Washington *Post,* May 24, 1974.

182   Jim Smyth: "Army Put on Alert in Ulster," Washington *Post,* May 20, 1974.

183   Rose, *Governing without Consensus,* p. 285; O'Brien, *States of Ireland,* pp. 12, 13; O'Brien has written that the Ulster problem is "defined not by class, but by religion and religion-linked politics," *The Observer,* October 30, 1977; income figures: Rose, *Governing without Consensus,* p. 289.

183–184   Fair Employment Agency, "An Industrial and Occupational Profile," pp. 5, 7, 12, 13.

185   Paisley's strike call: "King Billy's Head," *The Economist,* May 7; "Ian Paisley Keeps Losing, but the Battle Has Still to Be Won," May 14; "An Opportunity," May 21, 1977; Rose, *Northern Ireland: Time of Choice,* p. 139.

186 fn   level of violence: "Decrease in Violence but More Army Casualties in Ulster," *The Times,* December 20, 1977; Callaghan visit: "Prime Minister in 5-Hour Surprise Visit to Ulster," *The Times,* December 22, 1977.

187   Connolly's neglect of Belfast: O'Brien, *States of Ireland,* pp. 91–92; illegal drinking clubs: Washington *Post,* March 28, 1977; Christopher Walker, "How Organized Crime Buys Arms and Pays 'Social Security' to Ulster Gunmen," *The Times,* November 29, 1977.

188   McGuinness: "5 Ulster Mothers Take on IRA Gunmen," Washington *Post,* June 3, 1972.

189–190   Fogel: "In Ulster, Hate Wins Again over Reason," Washington *Post,* February 3, 1973.

191   President Carter: statement urging peace in Northern Ireland, August 31, 1977; withdrawal: Washington *Post,* March 28, 1977.

192   Roy Mason: speech at Stormont, September 13, 1977, reported in "Between Dublin and London," *The Economist,* September 17, 1977.

192–193   O'Brien, *States of Ireland,* pp. 298–301.

Chapter VI: Disorder at Home

194–195   Central Policy Review Staff: reported in "Think Tank's Race
          Warning," *The Guardian,* October 24, 1977.
    195   stick and carrot in immigration: David J. Smith, *Racial Dis-
          advantage in Britain: The P.E.P. Report* (London: Penguin
          Books, 1977), p. 24; Dilip Hiro, *Black British, White British*
          (London: Penguin Books, 1973), p. 6.
    196   recruiting immigrants: "Race — A Question of Numbers,"
          BBC, September 12, 1977; spoken English: Smith, *Racial Dis-
          advantage in Britain,* pp. 55, 322; Notting Hill riot: Hiro, *Black
          British, White British,* p. 37.
    197   Kenyan Asians: Hiro, *Black British, White British,* pp. 210,
          211; immigration level since 1971: Joe Rogaly, "Political Re-
          sponse to the National Front," *Financial Times,* November 15,
          1977; "Race — A Question of Numbers," BBC; Smith, *Racial
          Disadvantage in Britain,* p. 26; total coloured citizens in 1977:
          Social Trends, Number 8, CSO, 1977, p. 68; plight of coloured
          citizens: Smith, *Racial Disadvantage in Britain,* p. 13.
    198   coloured unemployment: Smith, *Racial Disadvantage in Britain,*
          pp. 68–71; income: pp. 83–87; housing: pp. 243, 251, 210,
          230–233; mortgages: "Racial Discrimination on Mortgages
          Alleged," *The Times,* November 29, 1977; shiftwork: Smith,
          Racial Disadvantage in Britain, p. 80; discrimination in hiring:
          pp. 105–117.
    199   U.S. comparisons: *U.S. Bureau of the Census Population Reports,*
          pp. 60–105; white attitudes: *Report of the Race Relations Board
          January 1975–June 1976,* Home Office, HMSO, London, No-
          vember 29, 1976, p. 21; race relations laws: Smith, *Racial Dis-
          advantage in Britain,* pp. 152, 317, 318; *Home Office News Release*
          concerning the 1976 Race Relations Act, November 23, 1976,
          p. 4; "Britain Moves to Strengthen Laws against Discrimina-
          tion," Washington *Post,* September 12, 1975.
199–200   Dr. David Pitt: "Race Discrimination in Britain Widespread,
          Study Finds," Washington *Post,* November 11, 1974.
    200   immigrant satisfaction: Smith, *Racial Disadvantage in Britain,*
          pp. 128, 183, 239.
    201   unemployment among coloured youths: *Social Trends,* no. 8,
          1977, p. 17; *Department of Employment Gazette,* October 1977, p.
          1115; Bengalis attacked: *The Daily Telegraph,* June 12, 1978.
201–202   immigrant militancy: editorial, *Race Today,* April/May 1977,
          p. 51; "Police Initiative Fails to Halt Wave of Racial Vio-

lence against Asians," *The Times,* December 23, 1977; "The Bangladeshis' Brick Lane Summer," *Time Out,* September 30–October 6, 1977, p. 6; Reuters report, June 25, 1977; "London's 'Little India' Boils," Washington *Post,* June 21, 1976; Washington *Post,* November 11, 1974.

203   Dobson: Transcript of a speech given at the Dorchester Hotel, London, to a group of London businessmen, September 27, 1977; segregation plans: *Housing of Bengalis in the London Borough of Tower Hamlets,* Report by Director of Housing, May 23, 1978; Union membership: Smith, *Racial Disadvantage in Britain,* p. 191.

203–204 National Front organization: Martin Walker, *The National Front* (London: Fontana, 1977), p. 67; "Racist Group Puts on a Show of Strength in North London," Washington *Post,* April 24, 1977; Sally Beauman, "What Lies Behind the Front?" *Sunday Telegraph Magazine,* October 2, 1977, p. 17.

204   "degeneracy of British stock": from NF meeting attended by author in North London, April 23, 1977; National Front voters: "Why the National Front Went Marching," *The Economist,* August 20, 1977; Walker, *National Front,* pp. 140, 142, 198, 203, 217.

205   Enoch Powell: Andrew Roth, *Enoch Powell* (London: Mac-Donald, 1970); Paul Foot review of Enoch Powell biography, *New Statesman,* September 9, 1977; 1968 Birmingham speech: Enoch Powell, *Freedom and Reality* (London: Elliot Right Way Books, 1969), pp. 282, 289.

206   Powell in 1977: "A Question of Numbers," BBC.

206–207 National Front tactics, leftist attacks: Washington *Post,* April 24, 1977; "Riots Divide Bobbies from Their Chiefs," Washington *Post,* August 19, 1977; Will Ellsworth Jones and Michael Jones, "How the Left-Wingers Win New Recruits for National Front," *Sunday Times,* August 21, 1977.

207   Birmingham by-election: "Extremists from Left and Right Soundly Defeated in British Vote," Washington *Post,* August 20, 1977; Labour party–TUC attack: "TUC joins Labour in new attack on Front," *Sunday Times,* December 11, 1977; "Labour–TUC attack on National Front," *The Times,* December 12, 1977; new matter Thatcher appeal: Granada Television, "World in Action," January 30, 1978; MP's response: *First Report from the Select Committee on Race Relations and Immigration,* Session 1977–78, vol. 1 March 13, 1978, pp. lvi–lix; Whitelaw speech: Leicester, April 7, 1978.

209   Lord Justice Scarman: *Report on the Red Lion Square Disorders of*

15 June 1974 (cmnd. 5919, HMSO, London), February 1975, p. 39.

209–210   soccer supporters: "Give a Dog a Bad Name, and . . .," *The Economist,* April 16, 1977; Paul Harrison, "Soccer's Tribal Wars," *New Society,* September 5, 1974, pp. 602–604; Elaine Potter, "Cool Approach to Violence," *Sunday Times,* March 19, 1972; Trevor Bailey, "Spurs Crowd in Contrast with Well-Behaved Swiss," *Financial Times,* October 18, 1977; "For an Unlimited Season, in Chelsea," *The Economist,* August 6, 1977; *Panorama,* BBC, November 14, 1977; "BBC Programme an Incitement to Violence, Minister Says," *The Times,* November 18, 1977.

211   "BBC Chief Rebukes Howell Attack on 'Panorama,' " *Daily Telegraph,* November 25, 1977; Brynmor John, *Hansard,* vol. 928, cols. 1747, 1750, March 25, 1977.

212   George Orwell, *The Road to Wigan Pier* (London: Penguin Books, 1937), p. 62.

Chapter VII: A Model of Sorts

213   Dilip Hiro, *Black British, White British* (London: Penguin Books, 1973), pp. 286, 287, 288.

215   Freedom of Information Act: Roy Jenkins, Granada Lecture, March 10, 1975; Fraser: Statement by the Special Committee of the Stock Exchange on Scottish and Universal Investments Ltd., November 30, 1976; Ogilvy: *Department of Trade, Lonrho Limited, Investigation Under Section 165 (b),* Report by Allan Heyman and Sir William Slimmings (London, HMSO, 1976), pp. 24, 63, 145, 147, 160, 180, 283, 599.

216–217   contempt: Philip Knightley, "The Story Nine Judges Banned," *Sunday Times,* July 31, 1977; "A Courtroom Conflict over the Thalidomide Tragedy," Washington *Post,* November 21, 1972; "Thalidomide Firm Boosts Victims' Aid," January 6, 1973; "The British Press," July 25, 1973; Harold Evans, "Could Davis Get a Fair Trial?" *Sunday Times,* September 25, 1977.

217–218   Official Secrets Act: *Public General Acts and Measures* (London, HMSO, 1911), ch. 28; Washington *Post,* February 24, 1976; "Leaks and Official Secrets," July 2, 1976; "16 Concordes: Last of the Flock?" September 23, 1977; Peter Hennessy, "Anti-Secrecy Bill to Be Drafted by Labour," *The Times,* September 26, 1977.

219   libel laws, Walker's insider dealings: Charles Raw, *Slater Walker: An Investigation of a Financial Phenomenon* (London: Andre Deutsch, 1977), pp. 129–137, 270–272; D-Notice: James Michael, "The Politics of Secrecy/The Secrecy of Politics," *Social Audit*, Spring 1973, p. 61; methods from Rear Admiral Farnhilll of the Defence, Press and Broadcasting Committee.

220   Andrew Shonfield, "The Pragmatic Illusion," *Encounter*, June 1967, p. 11; Civil Service recruitment: *Eleventh Report from the Expenditure Committee, 1976–77, Vol. 1, report on the Civil Service*, London, HMSO, July 25, 1977, pp. xviii–xx.

221   *The Times:* John Evelyn Wrench, *Geoffrey Dawson and Our Times* (London: Hutchinson, 1955), pp. 360–363, 380, 381.

222   abuse of criminal defendants: Marcel Berlins, "Improper Action by Some Barristers on Plea Changes Alleged," *The Times*, May 16, 1977, p. 4; "Study Claims British Judicial System Is Systematically Unfair to Defendants," *Washington Post*, September 28, 1977; "Limits of Plea Bargaining," *The Times*, September 24, 1977.

222–223 nuclear materials: Roger Berthoud, "Nuclear Nations' Anxiety over U.S. Policy Continues," *The Times*, September 22, 1977, p. 9.

223   Cambridge professor: Peter Hennessy, "Fourth Man in Inquiry on Philby, Burgess and Maclean," p. 1: "The 'Much Loved Cambridge Don' in the Philby Affair," p. 16, *The Times*, June 15, 1977; *Times* apology: *The Times*, June 29, 1977; "Sheikh Ali Ahmed": M. Brown and M. Corina, "Bernhard Links with London Financier," *The Times*, March 26, 1976, pp. 1, 17; "West German President among Mr. Ahmed's Friends," *The Times*, March 27, 1976, pp. 1, 19; "Former White House Aide Tells of Ahmed Link," *The Times*, March 29, 1976, p. 17; "Mystery of $125,000 Paid Over to Mr. Ahmed," *The Times*, April 14, 1976, pp. 1, 23; "Businessman Claims Huge Loss in Abortive Ahmed Deal," *The Times*, April 15, 1976, p. 17.

224 fn CIA probe of British unions: C. Walker, "CIA Men in Britain Checking on Subversion," *The Times*, January 18, 1974, pp. 1, 2; Miles Copeland letter to *The Times*, January 22, 1974; Louis Heren, "Increase in CIA Activity in Britain Denied by United States Embassy," *The Times*, January 19, 1974; "A CIA Non-Caper inside British Labor," *Washington Post*, January 23, 1974; "Britain's Spies: Meddling Through," *Washington Post*, December 22, 1975; Louis Heren, "This

Dangerous Game That Could Put a Gun at the Head of British Reporters Abroad," *The Times,* January 14, 1976.

224–226 Parliament: Michael, "The Politics of Secrecy/The Secrecy of Politics," pp. 56–58; *Eighth Report from the Committee of Public Accounts, 1976–77,* HMSO, London, July 26, 1977, pp. 264–281.

227 William Rees-Mogg, "One Dutch Man Hour = Two British Man Hours," *The Times,* September 28, 1977.

228–229 doctrine of comparative advantage: David Ricardo, *On the Principles of Political Economy and Taxation,* ed. R. M. Hartwell (London: Penguin Books, 1971), pp. 152–167.

229 Kalmar plant: "Fighting Factory Blues," Washington *Post,* September 5, 1976.

230 engine plant for Wales: Stephen Aris, "The Battle for Henry's Ear," *Sunday Times,* October 9, 1977; Viewdata: "Viewdata needs more chips," *The Economist,* October 8, 1977; "Post Office Will Spend £100m on Viewdata," *Financial Times,* March 1, 1978.

231–232 Lord Cowdray: Nicholas Bannister, "The Shy Man Who Really Is Something in the City," *The Guardian,* August 12, 1977; Steve Lawrence, "Taking a Look at the Richest Man in Britain," *Morning Star,* April 28, 1969; Michael Gillard, "The Power Men: Britain's Richest, and His Banker," *Daily Express,* October 14, 1968; Desmond Young, *Member for Mexico* (London: Cassell, 1966), a biography of the First Lord Cowdray; The Pearson Group, a prospectus, pp. 2, 3, 5, 9; S. Pearson and Son Limited: Report and Accounts 1976, pp. 3, 6, 14; Pearson Longman Limited: Report and Accounts 1976, pp. 5, 6, 7; "Lord Cowdray Leaving Helm of Pearson Group," *The Times,* November 25, 1977.

232 university summer schools: Ian Bradley, "Attentive Response to Literature and Culture," *The Times,* August 23, 1977; A. J. P. Taylor, *New Statesman,* August 19, 1977, p. 240.

233 spreading words: Ian Bradley, "Spreading Words Is a Growth Industry," *The Times,* August 23, 1977; Lord Grade ad: for example, *The Times,* September 7, 1977, p. 3; BBC Shakespeare films: "Have Bard, Will Travel," *The Economist,* February 25, 1978.

236 improved medical care: "Health Services in Britain," Central Office of Information Reference Pamphlet 20 (London, HMSO, 1974), p. 3.

Index

Index